How to Develop
and Implement a
Security Master Plan

How to Develop and Implement a Security Master Plan

TIMOTHY D. GILES

CRC Press
Taylor & Francis Group
Boca Raton   London   New York

CRC Press is an imprint of the
Taylor & Francis Group, an **informa** business

Auerbach Publications
Taylor & Francis Group
6000 Broken Sound Parkway NW, Suite 300
Boca Raton, FL 33487-2742

© 2009 by Taylor & Francis Group, LLC
Auerbach is an imprint of Taylor & Francis Group, an Informa business

No claim to original U.S. Government works
Printed in the United States of America on acid-free paper
10 9 8 7 6 5 4 3 2 1

International Standard Book Number-13: 978-1-4200-8625-6 (Hardcover)

Visit the Taylor & Francis Web site at
http://www.taylorandfrancis.com

and the Auerbach Web site at
http://www.auerbach-publications.com

This book is dedicated to my wife, Linda, who has encouraged me to undertake this task and supported me through this process as well as my children, Amy and Kelly, who have cheered me on to complete this work. It is also dedicated to the many security professionals that I have worked with over the years as a tribute to their unselfishness in sharing their knowledge and skills with me. I hope my sharing of this information will repay them in some small way.

CONTENTS

CONTENTS

AUTHOR PAGE

Tim Giles is the president of Risk/Security Management & Consulting. Prior to going into business for himself, Mr. Giles was the managing director of security services for Kroll Associates in Atlanta for 2.5 years. Before that, he served as director of security for North America at IBM where he was the executive responsible for the firm's security operations for all of the United States and Canada until he retired after 31 years of service. Mr. Giles has also worked in IBM's Latin America operations as the director of security for  two years and spent three years living and working in the Asia Pacific Region of IBM's security operations as the area security manager. While in Asia he was responsible for the security planning for IBM during the 1988 Olympics in Seoul, South Korea. In previous careers at IBM, Mr. Giles worked in manufacturing and engineering positions in IBM's semiconductor operations.

Mr. Giles was board certified in security management as a Certified Protection Professional by ASIS International in 1997 and as a Physical Security Professional in 2007. He was selected as the Security Director of the Year in 1997 by *Access Control & Security Systems Integration* magazine.

During his more than 25 years in security, he has worked in all aspects of physical security, information protection, investigation, crisis management, emergency planning and response, disaster contingency planning as well as managing major projects in most of these areas. He has also become very accomplished in utilizing all aspects of security technology. He spent 18 years working in the corporate security arena and has spent the following years working as a security consultant. He is also a licensed private investigator.

Mr. Giles is also an accomplished lecturer; he has conducted sessions in the following areas:

- Workplace violence protection programs
- Emergency planning and response
- Crisis management
- Security master planning
- Protection guidelines for today's business person
- Personal and travel security
- Establishing a global security program

Mr. Giles is an active member of ASIS International; he is the host committee chairman for the 2008 Seminar & Exhibits in Atlanta and is a past chairman of the Greater Atlanta Chapter.

INTRODUCTION

For several years I have conducted an education session at the annual ASIS International Seminar and Exhibits on the subject of "Developing a Security Master Plan." Although the sessions were well received, I have been contacted on a number of occasions asking for more insight into and information on the process of how to implement the Security Master Plan. As a result of these inquiries I decided to write this book on the entire process. You may find as you study these writings that I periodically venture away from the primary topic to expand on my own personal beliefs or philosophies in different areas. I try not to indulge in this practice too frequently; however, I do believe it is important to let you know where I am coming from in certain arenas. I doubt that every reader will agree with me on all of my narratives, but that is what makes the security industry so interesting. I hope you find the book interesting and informative and I wish you success as you pursue this endeavor.

This process varies depending on the size of the business or institution. A multilocation or multifacet business (e.g., manufacturing, research, office complexes, warehouses) or an international business will require more work than a single-site business or institution such as a hospital, for instance. However, even a single-location business or institution will have a variety of environments that will need to be addressed (e.g., emergency room, infant care, psychological center). It is very important to make sure that security is being implemented appropriately for each particular environment. It will also vary based on the way the security organization is structured and staffed. For example, if you have a security force consisting only of contract guards and no internal security professional, then you will need to determine if the contract for security includes all of the needed skills such as investigative, education and awareness, and executive protection. If these skills are not part of the contract then you will need to determine if that is appropriate as a part of your recommendations.

You will need to decide how many and which locations will need to be reviewed in order to properly define the current status of security within the business and to develop your recommendation for changes. This does not mean you must review every location of a multilocation business but you do need to look at all variations of the business. If the business, has its own research and development, manufacturing, retail, sales offices, and warehouses in multiple locations, then you should work with the management team to determine which of these locations should be part of the review. You should look at a minimum of two locations of each type, and if you find a wide divergence of how security is implemented between them, then you should discuss adding additional locations to the review with the client. If you are dealing with an international firm, it is critical that you evaluate the risks in each of the countries. The risks that exist in the United States are not the same as the risks in many other countries; therefore, the security requirements will differ as well. For example, in my opinion, workplace violence is basically a U.S. phenomenon; therefore, it would not be appropriate to implement security programs directed at deterring this issue in other countries where this is not a risk.

SECURITY MASTER PLAN PROCESS

Definition:

A Security Master Plan is a document that delineates the organization's security philosophies, strategies, goals, programs, and processes. It is used to guide the organization's development and direction in these areas in a manner that is consistent with the company's overall business plan. It also provides a detailed outline of the risks and the mitigation plans for them in a way that creates a five-year business plan.

INTENT OF THE MASTER PLAN

It is my intent to show you how to construct a Security Master Plan, which will aid you or your client in gaining "buy in" from the executive management team on the direction of the program and the necessary budget to support it. I think most of us know that in the real world, even though clients have an approved budget for the out years, that does not mean that they will actually get all that money when it comes time for it to be approved and released. However, by having a five-year plan that has been agreed to by the management team, they have a much better chance of getting that money released, and even if they do not get it all in the year that they wanted it, that only means that it slips out to the next year as opposed to being lost completely.

BEGINNING THE PROCESS

I have written this book with the idea that a security consultant is performing the work; however, there will be times when I address items to the "in-house" chief security officer (CSO) or director of security. I will attempt to make it clear when doing so. Of course, this work can also be performed by the in-house security professional in lieu of utilizing a security consultant; however, I will point out many areas where this is a less effective process. When these areas are addressed, I will provide the in-house person with some ideas on how to compensate for that concern, and as a result, I feel that they will still be able to significantly benefit from this work. When you begin this process of developing a Security Master Plan, the first step is to request information from the client. If this is performed by someone internal to the operations, you will still need to compile this information. This information will give you the opportunity to do some preparation prior to being onsite and it will give you some insight into the operation to be reviewed. Once you receive the information, you should analyze it in detail. For example, if they send you two years' worth of internal incident data but no trend analysis, then you should do the trend analysis yourself to see just what the incident data tells you. You should also review the reports for quality and consistency as well. The information I usually request includes the following:

- General background information on the company
- An organizational chart for the management of the facility
- A copy of the post orders
- A copy of the site security manual
- Blueprints of the facilities to be reviewed
- Copies of any security-related procedures or practices, including information protection
- Copies of incident reports for the past two years
- Copies of any incident summary or analysis data
- Copies of any crime statistic data on hand
- A copy of the contract guard contract, if applicable
- A copy of any other security-related contracts, such as confidential destruction
- The current staffing of the security organization by rank
- A listing of any cash operation onsite including how much cash is kept on hand
- A listing of any precious metals stored onsite and their value
- Any unique security-related issues you should be aware of
- The location of any high-security areas onsite and why they are so considered
- Security system information, brand name, and model or level
- Type of lock and key system(s) in use at the facilities

Several different aspects of this process will require you to interview some of the top executives of the company. Although these areas of questions will be defined in each of the appropriate sections, it is important that you combine areas of questions and limit the number of times you need to interview the executives. Preferably you will cover all of the questions in only one interview of each of them, because you will want to avoid giving the impression that you do not value their time.

1

The Business of Security

WHY SHOULD YOU DEVELOP A SECURITY MASTER PLAN?

As a security consultant your responsibility with this process is to utilize the information in this book to help the chief security officer (CSO) or director of security gain executive management support and improve their potential for obtaining the necessary budget funding for their programs. It will instruct you and them in the proper process for building a Security Master Plan and its components, which will document the security strategies of their business or institution both for now and more importantly for the future. The end product of this will enable them to gain the support of the executive management team, and when effectively utilized, it will become their preamble to gaining the necessary budget funds to implement their security program. If the client you are working with does not have an in-house security professional, then it is the consultant's responsibility to accomplish these goals.

An important aspect of this development process is to make sure their security strategies are linked to the strategies of the business so you can ensure they are moving their programs forward in unison with the business. By doing this you will demonstrate to executive management that the security operation is no longer just a business expense but it is an integral part of the business and contributes to the success of the business.

FIGURE 1.1   Executives are often focused on numbers and bottom-line results in addition to a host of other day-to-day issues. As such, they often do not recognize how the security department can bring value to the business as a whole.

It is important to understand that although we security professionals are focused on the many diverse risks that face our businesses and people, the executives who manage that business are not (see Figure 1.1). They have many issues that occupy their time and thoughts on a daily basis. That is not to say that they do not care about these issues; they absolutely do. In fact, I have never met an executive who was not extremely concerned about any issue that might affect the employees or the business. I simply wish to point out that they are not as involved in them as we are. This process is the vehicle that will provide you the opportunity to bring these issues to the management team's attention through a business process and give you the platform for gaining the support the security function needs to effectively manage the risks that confront the business or institution.

Building a Security Master Plan will differ considerably from just conducting a site security assessment because you will not only need to identify the good and bad of the current programs, you will also need to help develop the corrective actions and long-term strategies. This would normally require that the person working on this master plan process have extensive knowledge and experience in all aspects of security programs and technology. However, this book will provide the necessary guidance and information to help compensate for a lack of experience or knowledge and assist you to develop the plan. The process defined in this book is designed to be utilized by an outside professional, a security consultant, as opposed to being performed by someone who works within the current security organization. However, it can also be performed by an internal professional, but in my opinion, you will find that with some areas of the process it will be difficult for an internal person to be completely objective. Areas such as defining the current skills and knowledge of the security organization will be especially difficult for them. Also, although I sometimes implement this process on my own, you have the option of supplementing your skills with others who may be more skilled in certain areas than you are. I find this team approach to be an effective way to achieve the end result.

ENGAGING THE STAKEHOLDERS

It will also be important to put together a group of functional representatives from across the business to provide advice on where they believe there are currently areas that need change or improvements and how they perceive the recommended changes affecting the day-to-day operations of the business. Typically these representatives would be from the following groups: facilities or engineering, human resources, information technology, manufacturing, research and development, and administration, as appropriate to the specific client. If the business has union workers you may want to have a union representative in this group as well. The exact makeup of the group will depend on the business or institution that is being evaluated. This group, referred to as "stakeholders," is the representative of all of the internal and possibly some external organizations that would be affected by changes to the security technology, policies, and practices. By involving this group in the process from the beginning you will gain cross-functional support for implementing the necessary changes that will come out of the process. Of course, you may also encounter some resistance to some of the recommendations for change, but this will give the CSO or director of security or you the opportunity to address these issues early on, and even if they are not fully resolved, you will at least have knowledge of what issues need to be addressed with the executives when it is time to meet with them.

I would add that in the corporate world it is commonplace today for many functions to hire outside consultants to do assessments of their operations and provide an unbiased view of what should be changed or improved. This is almost the standard with some functions such as the finance and the information technology (IT) organizations. It is interesting to note that while there has been some change in recent years, typically the security community does not take advantage of this kind of independent review nearly as much as the other functions. I believe this is a change whose time has come, not just because I am a security consultant myself, but because as a community we need to draw on the skills and knowledge of the experts within our profession more effectively and more consistently than ever before. As someone who has been a security director, I understand how difficult it is to just manage the day-to-day operations of your business and how little time there is to keep abreast of the fast paced changes that engulf our industry. By having a consultant come in to look at the operation with a new set of eyes, you can gain immeasurable insight into what changes you should be focused on.

Although many of today's chief security officers or directors of security have a good insight into the technological changes that affect the security world and have their own ideas as to what direction they believe their business will take relative to these technologies, I have found that only some of them have actually documented this direction in a sound business plan and shared it with their management. For example, many of the CSOs or directors of security that I have dealt with over the years who were utilizing magnetic stripe badges had never talked to their management team about migrating to proximity badges until they were in the process of requesting the monies to implement that change. In today's security world I believe you would not find many organizations that have a documented migration plan to move from proximity badges to utilizing either smart card or biometric (or both) technologies for their badges. Just as you would not find many of them that have a documented plan to implement intelligent closed circuit television (CCTV) software for their camera systems. However, I think if you asked the CSOs or directors of security, you would find that all of them believe they will move in these directions within the next few years. The Security Master Plan process will provide them with the right vehicle to correct this situation.

WHAT SHOULD YOUR SECURITY PHILOSOPHIES BE?

This area is to be reviewed by the security consultant; however, the development of the philosophies should be done by the in-house security organization. If there is no in-house security organization then the consultant should attempt to work with the in-house person who manages the security contract to develop the appropriate philosophies for them to follow. First, I believe that the philosophies of the security organization should reflect the culture of their overall business. Next, they should reflect the leader of the security organization's business beliefs and, to some extent, personal beliefs and character. These philosophies are the basis upon which the security program is built. For example, some of the beliefs that I have personally used include the following:

- "Respect for the individual." This respect should be for each and every individual, including the ones who are believed to be violating your security policies and procedures.
- "Excellent service to the customer." This applies to both internal and external customers and at every level of the security organization.
- "Excellence as a way of life." Every action should always be done to the best of one's ability.
- "Managers and supervisors must lead by example." This is a critical aspect of projecting how all employees should act. "Do as I say, not as I do" will never work.
- "We should always be a good corporate citizen." For the security organization this is reflected in the way you deal with and support the many public organizations you interface with such as law enforcement, fire departments, and rescue services.

Of course, these are only examples of some of the philosophies I have used. This is truly a personal choice for the person who is in charge of the security organization. It is doubtful that you will encounter many CSOs or directors of security who have actually written their philosophies down and shared them with their staff. I firmly believe it is an exercise worth undertaking and that it can be a guide for the entire security organization. In many cases the company will have written philosophies or principles that they publish for all employees. If they do, then I would recommend to the CSOs or directors of security that they expand on those to help the security organization understand how they should be reflected in the day-to-day operation by the security staff, and they should also add some of their own philosophies to them and in support of them. If the organization utilizes contract security officers, it is very important that they are also made aware of the organization's philosophies. It may be necessary that they or the contract manager translate these into statements that reflect how these philosophies actually affect the day-to-day duties of the officers as well. This is usually done through the post orders; however, they may need to be elaborated to get the desired result.

CONTRACT SECURITY RELATIONSHIP

It is exceedingly important for the organization to have a "partner" type of relationship with the contract security force. This can be a delicate situation because the client does not want them to believe they are "employees" of the organization, but they should want them to see themselves as an integral part of the team. This is typically achieved by making sure the chain of command is always used when dealing with the security force. It is also critical that their own management, both onsite and offsite, have discussions with them on occasion about maintaining the right relationship with the "client." It will be very important for you, the consultant, to determine if this relationship is sound and appropriate. A common development in this environment is that you will see one of the lead people of the contract force begin to develop a personal relationship with some of the lead people on the in-house security or other staff. Over time this can manifest itself into problems where they begin acting as if they are an employee of the organization, instead of the contract force. Likewise, the organization begins to treat them more like an employee and even gives them more power in the relationship than they should have. Whenever this situation develops, the only effective way I have found to correct it is for that person to be taken off of that site.

WHAT SHOULD YOUR SECURITY STRATEGIES BE?

Before you begin the process of defining or redefining the security organizations strategies, you must first gain an understanding of the strategies of their business. You do this by interviewing the appropriate executives of the company: the CFO, COO, and so on. You need to know for the next five years:

- What growth do they anticipate?
- Do they expect any product or service changes?
- Is the expansion or reduction limited to the existing facilities or will new ones be added?
- Do they expect any overseas expansions or mergers?
- Are there any major layoffs or outsourcing activities planned?

Some of this information will be considered to be highly confidential, especially any mergers or layoff activity, but you need to understand these directional moves if you are to plan how they will deal with them from a security standpoint. It is not necessary for you to know all of the details; for example, you do not need to know who they plan to merge with or who they plan to outsource work to; however, you will need to know what countries are involved if your client will have any stake or ownership in the relationship. If the person performing this master plan activity is an outside consultant, the executives may prefer to only share this information with the in-house director of security or chief security officer. If there is no in-house staff, the consultant will need to discover as much of this information as possible and may need to sign a confidential disclosure agreement (CDA). (I believe a CDA should always be part of the contract with the consultant.)

The security organization's strategies deal with all aspects of the program from policies and procedures to technology and staffing. Their strategies should be documented so that they reflect where they are now and where they are going. You have probably heard this before, but I believe strongly in the saying, "If you don't know where you are going, you won't like where you are when you arrive!" In order to implement new security strategies, CSOs or directors of security should first address the process of change. This is an area where you, the consultant, can provide advice and counsel, but implementation must be performed by someone in-house. It has been my experience over the years that most people are afraid of change. They would prefer that everything just stay as it is. So the question the CSOs should be asking of themselves is this: "Is change a friend or foe?" The answer to this question is really quite simple: "It's up to them!" Change is a topic that is discussed continuously in the business world. But, as the adage says, "Talk is cheap!" As an example of implementing change I would cite the most dramatic project that I have undertaken in my career. If you have not personally been involved in a major change effort, then perhaps my experience can help you to understand the complexities of this effort. As a part of the reengineering effort in IBM, we reorganized the internal security operation in September 1994. We took the security professionals who were managed site by site by nonsecurity personnel and brought them into one single structure, managed by security professionals. However, this did not in and of itself make change happen. What it did do was to provide the opportunity for constructive, consistent, and rapid change.

Over the next two years we reduced costs by approximately 30 percent, we increased customer satisfaction to 94 percent, and we significantly increased our own security employees' morale. In September 1997, I was awarded the Security Director of the Year recognition by *Access Control &*

System Integration magazine. As people passed on their congratulations to me, I explained that I take credit for one thing primarily, and that is creating the environment where "change" is a "friendly" activity. The accomplishments of our organization are directly attributed to our own people embracing the concept of change and making it happen.

So exactly what did we do to create this environment? Basically, we did three things:

- First, we implemented the use of project teams on as many different aspects of our security business as we could think of. These teams had two goals to accomplish: find the best internal or external practice for the specific area they are looking at and — even more important — increase open communications across the organization.
- Second, we implemented a measurement program to find the defects in our processes. To make this successful, I declared this to be a "no fault" measurement program. The primary "failure" in this program would be if you did not find problems. The secondary failure would be if we did not fix the problem.
- Third, we launched a massive campaign to do national contracts and centralized systems to eliminate as many redundancies and inefficiencies as possible. All of this combined translated into massive change for our people and our strategies in the way we implemented security.

We knew that the only way we could be successful was for our people to see this as something that would be good for them, each and every one of them — personally. To make this happen we first had to convince them that change was absolutely necessary to the survival of IBM and our jobs. You might think this would be obvious to all of us considering our company's financial performance over the early 1990s, but some people have a way of convincing themselves that they are not part of the problem. Therefore, what we had to do was to convince them that change had to happen and we had two choices:

- Deny the need, resist the change, and FAIL, or
- Embrace the need to change and DRIVE that change!

If we, the security professionals, truly and fully accepted this, we had the power to decide our future! If we did not drive change in our organization, someone else would and we would have much less control over the outcome.

FIGURE 1.2 For larger organizations, forming project teams to divide labor and tackle key internal issues is a good way to get employee and management buy-in and come up with practical and creative solutions.

One of the primary tools that we provided to our project teams to do their analysis was the implementation of an internal benchmarking program followed up with a detailed resource and task analysis program (see Figure 1.2). After implementing many of the changes and realizing the benefits of those changes, we then launched an external benchmarking effort. This data demonstrated that we were significantly more cost competitive than any of the other companies we compared with.

As any good business manager can tell you, the best resources of any company are its employees. I personally believe that this group of security professionals is the Best of the Best, but I acknowledge that I might be slightly biased on this point; however, the proof is in the results! It is important to remember that change is not something that you do and it is done. Instead, it is an ongoing process that must be continually driven from senior management down through the organization and by the employees up through the company. This is why it is essential that you create the right environment for change to flourish. A critical part of that environment is your own attitude! Your employees will know very quickly if you are just giving "lip service" to this process or if you are serious. Just as the scenery changes as you travel down a road, your business and even you and your employees must be in a continuum of change. If you are, you will not just succeed, but you will have ongoing success! It is this environment that makes it very important that you have documented, long-term strategies and that you reevaluate those strategies on a regular basis. After all, that is the map you will be using for your trip.

So, what are your clients' strategies? As I said earlier, they should cover all aspects of their programs. It would be very difficult for me to suggest any generic strategies because there are many variations depending on the business they are in. As you develop them, you should utilize the functional team, "the stakeholders" that I spoke about earlier, to assist. Here are some examples of the areas that should be addressed:

- Policies
  - Education and awareness programs.
  - Badge wearing.
  - Clean desk policy.
  - Visitor and contractor controls.
  - Employee involvement and responsibilities.
  - When and how to have armed off-duty police officers onsite.
- Investigations
  - Use of hidden cameras along with determining who should be involved in the decision to use them.
  - Use of a polygraph for interrogations.
  - Whether or not to prosecute employees or others when a crime has been committed (even a minor crime).
- Technology
  - What technologies might be utilized in the future and when, where, and why?

- What is the migration plan for moving to the new technologies?
- What is the anticipated end of life of the current technologies in use?
- Develop a replacement schedule for existing equipment.
- Staffing
  - The use of armed or unarmed security officers documented with the reasoning for the decision.
  - Which positions can or cannot be contracted, regardless of whether they currently are or are not contracted.
  - What style of uniforms should be worn and why?

As you go through the process of helping them in documenting their strategies they will find that they are already following several strategic lines; they just may not have documented all of them before. A good example of this is the use of unarmed security officers. I personally do not like to have armed security people onsite except in rare applications such as a nuclear plant or a top secret installation. Obviously, many CSOs or directors of security feel the same way because the majority of businesses in the United States use unarmed officers. However:

- How many of these security managers or businesses have documented that decision to demonstrate it was a well-conceived strategic decision?
- Was executive management involved in or at least apprised of the reasoning for this decision?
- If a workplace violence shooting were to occur onsite, would they be prepared to defend their decision of unarmed officers in court?

Having these strategies well documented can be invaluable in situations of litigation or even when a decision about an unusual situation has to be made in a timely manner. Their documented strategies should always be their guide.

TECHNOLOGY MIGRATION STRATEGY

I would also like to discuss the issue of "migration strategies" for their changes in technology. If you or they believe they might be moving to a different technology for access control, for example, it is very important that they have investigated the issues around migrating from the current technology to the new one. If the client has a single site or even just two or three sites, the migration can be relatively easy to accomplish; nevertheless, it still requires a detailed plan, which includes having test locations and education for the end users. By the way, I have seen situations where the end users were not properly educated in the use of the new technology and this set back the conversion by several months; the security team spent countless hours struggling to convince the end users that the new technology was the right solution for the business.

However, if the client has a large number of sites, there needs to be a plan that addresses how they will operate during the migration to the new technology. For instance, when we looked at migrating IBM from magnetic stripe access control cards to proximity cards, there was no existing solution that allowed us to have both technologies in use at the same time without actually mounting both types of card readers side by side so employees could gain access regardless of which card they were carrying.

The solution offered by our vendor was to just take out the old technology and put in the new one. That might be a workable solution for someone who has only a few locations, but for a company that has hundreds of locations and employees who need to be able to access multiple sites, that is not an acceptable remedy. To resolve the problem we developed our own approach. We went to several vendors and asked them to develop dual-technology cards and card readers. Of course, they wanted us to fund the development work for these new products, but we convinced them that this was an investment they needed to make not just for us but to assist any large company that needed a solid migration path to the newer proximity technology. Eventually they agreed and the new products began to hit the market.

Although this provided the hardware solution to our dilemma, that was only part of the final solution. Issues such as importing or exporting databases and conversions of data, education of users, determining who needed dual technology cards and who did not, along with numerous other minor issues all had to be researched and resolved prior to the start of the migration. When you are changing technologies for hundreds of thousands of end users and hundreds of locations, you also have to have a detailed timing plan as well. You cannot make that kind of a change in a few weeks.

My message to you and your client is this:

- Do not assume that the vendors have the right plan for migration.
- Do not let yourself be limited by what currently exists, especially if it does not solve your problem.

- Spend some time investigating others who have made the changes that you are considering and learn from their experiences.
- Make sure you budget some additional funds to help educate the end users on how to use the new technology.
- If the current vendor they are using has never migrated a client of their size to the technology they are considering, they should investigate other vendors to find one that has.

One other approach to be considered is to slowly introduce the new technology into their business. If they currently have proximity access control and they want to move to biotechnology, I would recommend introducing biotech into their high-security areas first. They might want to try the different biotech readers to see which they like best, so they might use the palm print reader in one area, the fingerprint or iris scan reader in another, and so on. This will give them the opportunity to gain experience with the new technology and get feedback from the users and management. If and when they decide to implement it on a larger scale, it is no longer something that is brand new to the end users, as they will all have heard about its use and the migration can proceed in a much smoother progression. Additionally, end users typically feel much better about new technologies if they have been able to provide input into the decision.

EQUIPMENT REPLACEMENT SCHEDULES

I will also review the subject of developing a replacement schedule for existing equipment. The best way to run a security operation is to develop a list of every piece of equipment that the security department owns. This list should be detailed to include the following information:

- Name
- Model number
- Serial number
- Date purchased
- Supplier
- Purchase price
- Location installed
- Supplemental information (for example, if it is a camera you should also include the lens specifications here. If it is a radio, how many channels are on it, etc.?)

- Manufacturer's recommended life cycle
- Projected replacement date

With this information you can establish a replacement schedule for the equipment similar to what the facilities engineering department does for the equipment that supports the building. Once you have this piece of documentation, it can be used during the budget cycle to project future expenditures for keeping the equipment and systems in peak operating condition. Another use of this data is with the contract vendor that is maintaining the systems. Instead of the client budgeting for replacing the equipment, they could have the vendor build the replacement schedule into their annual contract for maintaining the systems. Some businesses find that to be a more acceptable approach to this issue.

One other consideration relative to the equipment that is installed is the documentation of the location and wiring specifications. The wiring specifications should include both the communication cables and the power system. Most facilities these days have their drawings on CAD/CAM or other computer software files. These are files that can be accessed by computer that show every aspect of the facility. However, I frequently find that the security systems have not been included in these drawings; they typically only include the base building information that is used by the facilities organization. This leads to numerous problems whenever these systems need to be upgraded or replaced. It also creates havoc with the systems when there are renovations performed at the facility because the contractor performing the renovations would not have knowledge of the security systems. As the consultant for the client you should review a sample of their drawings and determine if they are fully documented. If they are not, that should be part of your recommendations, and getting them documented should be a part of the Security Master Plan action items.

2

Evaluate the Business's Risks

POTENTIAL RISKS TO THE BUSINESS

The list below is not exhaustive or complete, but merely intended as a guide only. Not all of these risks are applicable to every business, and some businesses may have other risks that are not listed here. If the business you are reviewing is an international business, you will have many risks to consider that a domestic business will not. You should be able to tell from this list that you are not just looking to find out the security types of risks, you want to be sure you are aware of all of their risks because there are many times that business risks will have an impact on security operations. The following is a list of risks a given business can potentially face:

- Fraud
- Lack of accurate and timely intelligence
- Corruption
- Economic espionage
- Theft
- Patent and trademark infringement
- Foreign travel
- Gray market and counterfeit products
- Organized crime
- Political instability
- Business disputes and litigation

- Legislative requirements
- Terrorism and sabotage
- Kidnapping
- Extortion
- Unsecured data and communications
- Workplace violence
- Workplace suicide
- Sexual harassment and discrimination claims
- Acts of nature

DEFINING WHAT YOUR RISKS ARE

The purpose of defining risks is so that you can determine the appropriate actions to "manage the risks." For each risk that is identified you will need to assist the client to make a decision to do one of the following:

- Risk assumption. Accepting the potential risk and continuing to operate as is. You should always ask the question, "Who has the authority to accept risks for the company?"
- Risk avoidance. Avoid the risk by eliminating the cause.
- Risk limitation. Implementing increased controls to reduce or limit the risk.

- Risk transference. To transfer the risk through increased insurance or other means.

Many factors need to be considered to arrive at the appropriate risk management alternative. Impact cost is always a primary concern, but you also need to consider factors such as the safety of employees and others onsite; the company's reputation; delivery schedules; manufacturing needs; customer loyalty issues; environmental impacts; and employee morale. To choose the proper method that is appropriate to each risk you will need to collaborate with the client's security and executive management teams so you can review each of the alternatives and arrive at the choice that they feel most comfortable with.

INFORMATION GATHERING

A critical part of defining the risks is the process you use to gather the information. To do this effectively you need to begin by conducting interviews with many of the management team to get their input and insight. You should understand that conducting interviews is an important skill, similar to conducting interrogations. However, with interviews it is important that you not be intimidating, and it is equally important that you not be intimidated. Although I can guide you on the various areas that need to be reviewed through this process, I will not be able to lay out all of the questions to be asked. I can tell you one of the major components of an interview is your ability to listen! Many years ago I was told the following: "God gave you two ears and one mouth for a reason." You should listen twice as much as you talk. While I was in IBM marketing school I was taught this, but it is applicable here as well. It seems that many sales or marketing people tend to be so focused on delivering the presentation that they spent hours preparing that they sometimes do not even hear the client say "I'm sold." Instead of stopping and closing the deal, they keep right on giving their spiel. When conducting your various interviews you need to listen to the answers (or lack thereof) and formulate your next questions from them. It can also be valuable to employ one of the effective interrogation techniques of "not responding." When you get an answer to one of your questions that really is not an answer or not a very complete answer, just sit and look at the person as if you are waiting for him or her to finish. Most people find that uncomfortable and volunteer more information.

Most CEOs, CFOs, and HR directors will be able to give you a reasonably complete list of risks; however, they may not know all of them because some of these risks may not have materialized before. For example:

- When you interview the director of human resources and he or she tells you there are only a few workplace violence cases (or none at all), this should prompt you to ask about the workplace violence prevention program.
- Do they have a program that educates the employees and managers to inform HR and security whenever someone makes a threat or whenever a coworker tells them that their "significant other" is separated from them and they are worried about what he or she will do?
- Is there a program in place to evaluate employees prior to initiating termination to determine if they might have a propensity toward violence, and is the security function involved in this evaluation?
- Do employees report cases of stalking, harassment, or bullying to HR and security?
- Do HR and security have plans to deal with those cases when they do arise?

THE WORKPLACE VIOLENCE RISK AND BEYOND

Because I believe that workplace violence is one of the most widespread potential risks to businesses and institutions in the United States, I feel it is important that I expand on this issue. I will not attempt to completely define what a good workplace prevention program is in this book, but I have included additional information (Appendix A, "Workplace Violence Guidelines") that can give you a good example of what this program should look like. I would like to expand on an issue that is part of the workplace violence prevention program, however. Although I believe more and more professionals have now recognized that domestic violence in the workplace is a major part of this problem, I am not convinced that many people have addressed this concern adequately in their prevention programs. Appendix A lists "Indicators of Dangerousness," which include past behavior, drug and alcohol abuse, access to weapons, anger or resentment, fascination with past events (of violence), deteriorating performance, suicidal tendencies, stress or depression, and mental deterioration (see Figure 2.1). These are all indicators that can be recognized in the work

FIGURE 2.1 Workplace violence incidents can occur as the result of issues in the workplace, but equally from domestic situations that spill over into the workplace.

environment and can be related to domestic violence cases as well. But, in this appendix, you will not see many references to the issue of domestic violence in the workplace, and you will not see any ways to recognize that this problem exists. I personally studied this issue through the 1990s and found that about 50 percent of the cases of harassment, stalking, threats, and violence were domestic issues that occurred on company property. Some of these were the result of relationship entanglements between coworkers but many were simply due to the fact that an estranged significant other had come onto company property because that was the only place he or she could locate the other person.

Unfortunately, many of these cases could not be prevented by the standard workplace violence prevention program such as the one in Appendix A. Addressing this issue of domestic violence on company property is a more complicated area because it gets into the private lives of the employees and others, but it must be dealt with. I have personally been involved in cases of this nature in the past where the level of violence would most certainly have escalated had the company's security organization not interceded on behalf of the victim. For example, in one case an employee came forward and advised her manager that she had left her husband due to domestic problems. She was concerned about walking to her car alone in the dark and she wanted to know if she could get a security escort to her car. The manager contacted security for the escort, but fortunately the security manager interceded and began to ask more questions about the estranged husband. These questions included the following:

- Does he know exactly where your workstation is located?
- Has he made any threats against you?
- Does he have a history of violence against you or others?
- Does he have a police record?
- Does he have access to weapons?
- Is he employed? If so, where?
- Where are you living now? Does he know that location?

As a result of these and other questions we learned that the husband had made threats against her, she was living with her sister, and he knew where that was, although she did not think he knew she was there. He had a police record for assault — a bar fight — and his brother had guns that he could certainly get access to. He had been to her workstation and had picked her up from work on a number of occasions. He lost his job about three months ago and was drinking a lot. The security manager then got a description of the husband and his car, as well as her car. He then sent a security patrol to find her car and look for any suspicious people in the area. The husband was in his car parked and waiting for her to come out. Our security officer asked him to leave and he refused, saying he needed to talk to his wife. Our officer advised him he would have to leave or we would call the police. At that point he left the site. We then advised the employee that it was probably not a good idea for her to be staying somewhere where the husband could find her and suggested that she call a battered women's hot line to see if she could get placed in a shelter, where she would also be able to get other advice and assistance from them as well. She did and was advised to go to a hotel room for the night and they would arrange for her to get into a shelter the next day. Working with her manager, we told her we would pick up the cost of the hotel room for the night and that she should take a few days off until she got everything worked out with the shelter. She was advised to contact her manager before coming back to work and that we would probably move her to another work location for a time until everything was resolved on the home front.

We do not know if the husband had a gun with him that night but he did show up at her sister's house the next night drunk and with a gun. Fortunately, the employee was not there and no one got hurt, but the police were called and he went to jail for a few days. We asked the police to talk to his brother and advise him not to loan his brother any more of his guns. We also had a no-trespass order issued to him to stay off our property and the employee had a protection order issued to keep him away from her. All of this confrontation with the husband finally convinced him to just leave the area, and the last I heard the employee was doing fine.

One of the interesting things in this case was that it was not unusual for a female employee to ask for an escort to her car after dark. When the security manager got the call from the employee's manager he first said OK, then asked the manager to ask the employee if there was any particular reason for the escort. That is when the story began coming to light about the abuse and the threats by the husband. The reason the security manager asked that first question is because we had been conducting training sessions with all of our security people to be alert to the potential of domestic violence cases. We had instructed each of our location security managers to gather information about hot lines and any other support groups in the area so they would have it available whenever it might be needed. This had sensitized the manager to the issue enough so that he thought to ask that first question.

DOMESTIC VIOLENCE IN THE WORKPLACE

In order for a workplace violence prevention program to be reasonably effective, these programs need to address the issue of domestic violence in the workplace. Sensitizing and training the security team is a good start, but employees and managers must also receive the proper training. They need to be informed that when a coworker confides in them about problems at home, a threatening significant other, and so on, those problems need to get relayed to management, HR, and security so the employee can get the right assistance and so the workplace can be kept safe. In our society here in the United States this is not an easy sale to our people. When a friend asks them to keep something "just between us," they do not like to break this confidence. Although that is commendable in most situations, they need to understand that there are times that the person is telling them that because they need and want help; there are times when the protection of our work environment demands that they break the confidence. A good training program will help them to understand and overcome this reluctance to share the information with the right people. These training programs must be conducted under the authority of the HR function in order for them to be effective. When the security organization tries to do this training it can backfire on them, as some people see them as just looking for snitches. To counter domestic violence in the workplace you should, at a minimum, implement the following controls:

- Offer and publicize an employee assistance program
- Move the victim to a new work site, when appropriate
- Establish safety and security measures to keep abusers away from the work site
- Provide additional paid leave for domestic violence victims
- Train managers to recognize and address domestic violence in an effective, helpful, and legal manner
- Train employees to recognize signs of domestic violence and teach them that they need to talk to their manager or HR or security about it
- Give managers and security professionals contact information for organizations to refer employees to for domestic violence

As you conduct reviews of facilities and their security programs, even though you might not be specifically reviewing the workplace violence prevention program in detail, you should always look for opportunities to ask questions about the program and whether or not they have focused on the domestic violence in the workplace aspect of it. You need to also inquire as to how often the program and the training are updated.

Back to my original point, although the management team might believe they do not have workplace violence problems, this could be because they do not have the right program implemented that would let them know they do have a problem. If that is the case, then they are far more susceptible to this problem going out of control before they even see it coming. This situation exists for most of the risks that businesses and institutions are faced with. If there are not good programs in place to obtain the information about the risks, the management team can be oblivious to their existence altogether.

OTHER RISK FACTORS

Although I will go into some of the many common risk factors that I have outlined in the beginning of this chapter, I will not take you through all of them. Some of them such as economic espionage, patent and trademark infringement, and gray market and counterfeit products can be very complex issues; if you encounter these risks with the business you are working with, then I would recommend that you get input from a security professional who has expertise in that area. In Chapter 6, I outline a basic information asset security program that will assist your client protect themselves against some of these risks I just outlined.

Additionally, there are many security-related risk issues that the executive management team may not be aware of. Risks that range from street crimes in the area to terrorism may be on the CSO's or director of security's radar, but not the executive's. This is not uncommon, especially if the security team is doing a good job of prevention. As you conduct interviews of the security team and review data that is gathered from various sources, this should become apparent. You must also be very observant as you conduct your survey of the site and look for areas of risks that may not have been identified by anyone before.

For example, I once did a review of a campus-style site that had active railroad tracks on the site, which means that trains came through the site regularly. The business had taken the precaution of installing lights and gates at the intersection of their road that crossed those tracks onsite; however, no one had ever looked at the condition of the tracks or evaluated what would have happened if they had a train derailment onsite. We had the tracks inspected by an independent inspector and found that they were not maintained as well as they should be. The tracks were also on a curve through the site, which added to the potential of a derailment. When we investigated what cargo traveled on that set of tracks we discovered that tank cars full of chlorine regularly passed through the site. Of course if one of those tanks were ruptured they would release deadly chlorine gas clouds. Prior to this discovery the management at the site assumed that the railroad did what they were supposed to do to ensure the safety of the cargo that passed through the site. After reviewing the reports with the railroad management they agreed to increase their inspections and maintenance of that area, and the site management implemented regular independent inspections to verify that everything was in good condition.

Unfortunately, it is always easier to just review the standard risks that most people associate with their business and ignore the other factors that may surround them. As the consultant, it is critical that you think outside of those parameters and explore all relative factors to ensure your client has a complete risk management portfolio.

RISKS OF FRAUD AND CORRUPTION

These are risks that can be evident in most any business. Typically they are most prevalent in the areas of contract management or purchasing activity, but depending on the type of business you are working with, there may be many other areas of opportunity for fraud or corruption. As the consultant you should ask questions to determine if they have had any known problems in this area of the business. You should determine if they have a centralized purchasing organization or not. I have found many smaller and medium-size businesses do not have this level of control. They may have contracts with certain vendors to provide products at discount prices, but the actual purchasing activity is left up to the individual departments. Often there are numerous other contracts with suppliers or contract service companies that are also arranged for and managed by a department. There is typically no set structure that makes sure someone is double-checking these dealings other than a second signature by a higher level manager, who is frequently very trusting of their team and has little or no time to make sure everything is being handled appropriately. The best way to investigate whether or not there is any fraud in this area of the business is for someone to spend some time questioning the people who lost the bid to see what they have to say about the process. It is interesting how many times, in a fraudulent situation, they will tell you that their competitor "bought" the contract and they will frequently be able to give you details. Therefore, you should inquire as to whether anyone is conducting these types of investigations for the company.

In these situations I typically recommend that there be an internal audit group that establishes some standards for a competitive bidding process and then audits the existing contracts on a periodic basis to ensure that everything has been handled properly. If the business does have a purchasing department that manages all of the contract activity, that should not lead you to believe that there is no corruption or fraud in this area. There have been many cases of this happening within these groups as well. However, when you have a group of purchasing people being managed by a professional purchasing manager who is very familiar with these issues, the potential of it happening in that group is much smaller.

THEFT RISKS

It has been said that employee theft is a major problem within many, if not most, businesses. I do not mean just the small stuff of taking home some office supplies, but there are major thefts that are perpetrated by employees on their own employers on a daily basis. For the sake of this discussion I am considering contractors and other nonregular employees as one and the same. It is interesting to note that frequently when items are missing at work, the first people everyone wants to blame is the cleaning staff or even the security staff, because they regularly have access to areas when no one else is around. In my experience, however, it is more often the regular employee who is the thief.

This situation of employee theft is especially prevalent in the retail industry, but it is not limited to them. The major problem with being able to combat this issue is that employers want to have an open and friendly working environment for their employees. This type of environment promotes a productive work ethic and a high level of good morale with employees. If you have an environment of mistrust and "Big Brother" watching their every move, people just will not want to be in that environment and the company will experience a high level of turnover. Additionally, I believe most people are basically honest, with the caveat "as long as you don't put too much temptation in their path." My personal belief is that the "90–10" rule applies here, meaning that 90 percent of the thefts are perpetrated by 10 percent of the employees. What kinds of assets are being stolen by employees will depend on what is available and how easy it is to steal. I firmly believe in the practice of helping to keep people honest by making it too risky for them not to be. As you probe this area you need to see if the security team is doing a reasonable job of investigating lost assets; are they doing trend analysis of what is being stolen, when, from where, and so on? Does the company have a toll-free fraud line where employees can call in anonymously to report suspected thefts or fraud situations? I usually recommend an additional measure of having periodic checks at exit doors of boxes or other items that people are carrying out. To implement a program of this type requires a process of parcel pass controls, where a manager signs off on a form that identifies what the employee is carrying out, so when they get to the door the security officer can know if it is OK or not. Having a program such as this in place also makes it easier to look for a valuable asset that has been identified as being missing. Here is a simple example of a parcel pass program:

- All XYZ employees, staff, contractors, and visitors are subject to a random search at anytime they are leaving any XYZ facility. Parcels, attaché cases, book bags, and so on may be inspected when exiting the building. This is especially true when leaving after normal first-shift hours. If you are going to be taking an asset out of the building, you must have a written property pass allowing the item to be removed. Department managers will authorize property pass forms. (You should note that in many states you are required to post signage on the outside of your building advising people who are entering that they may be subjected to a search. Personally, I believe it is a good practice to follow whether it is required by law or not.)
- Employees, staff, contractors, and visitors are required to comply with this policy to avoid confusion, inconvenience, and theft of any asset.
- Search and inspection procedure: When asked by security or management to show what is inside your package, parcel, attaché case, or bag, you will be asked to either remove some items or to move the items around so that the inspector can clearly see everything that is inside. They have been instructed not to put their hands inside the container; therefore, you must assist in allowing them complete and unobstructed view of the entire inside area of the container. (I always recommend this search procedure to avoid injury to the inspector and to prevent accusations that the searcher stole something from the item being searched.)

Of course, beside employee theft, there are many variations of external thefts that occur to the different businesses, such as "office creepers," retail thefts, and burglaries. One of the more notable thefts recently has been the removal of copper wire and pipe from utilities and others. In some cases they have even tried to steal live high-voltage electric wire from substations. For the majority of businesses I believe these situations are much less of a risk than internal theft. You will need to determine this as you evaluate the loss reports from the security organization.

OVERSEAS-RELATED RISKS

There are a number of risks that I identified at the beginning of the chapter that are, for a U.S. company, related to doing business in other countries.

But, first of all I want to be sure I do not give you the wrong impression that doing business overseas is always more risky than in the United States, because that is not the case in all countries. We have risks unique to the United States that we do not even think about because we are used to them. For the most part, most countries have risks that are unique to them, which foreign travelers may not understand. Risks such as foreign travel, organized crime, political instability, terrorism and sabotage, kidnapping, extortion, and even workplace suicides are risks that you will encounter in some foreign countries that are different from what you have been used to seeing in the United States. I usually recommend that people start with the U.S. State Department Web site (www.state.gov) for information on specific countries. The information you can get there on travel and health issues in addition to other specific country requirements can be very helpful. You can also contact the "Country Desk Contact" of the State Department to get more specific information. If you travel to another country the first stop I recommend is the local U.S. embassy to meet with the Regional Security Officer to get a briefing from him or her on the current issues that exist. If you are a non-U.S. security person I would expect you can do the same with your country's embassy in most foreign countries. They might have a different name for this position, however.

It is valuable that you understand the unique areas of risks or crimes in the countries that your client is doing business in. For example, in the United States we have a major problem with workplace violence; however, when I worked in Asia I encountered problems with workplace suicides, and in Mexico and some South American countries there were problems with kidnappings. In some countries the government officials will expect a businessperson to provide them with payoffs in order to do business there as a relatively standard practice. Of course, if your client is a publicly traded company, then it is against the law in the United States for them to do this. Therefore, my recommendation to you as the consultant is that you enlist the aid of an overseas expert to assist in the risk evaluation of any country that your client is doing business in.

ACTS OF NATURE

I know that this risk area seems fairly straightforward. But you need to make sure they have identified all of the potential natural risks that could affect them, which sometimes they have not. There are a number of areas of the United States that have fault lines under them, but many of the people and businesses in those areas do not consider that they are in danger of earthquakes, simply because they have not had one in recorded history. When I lived in Vermont, we did not consider ourselves at risk from a hurricane, but we actually got hit by one in the 1980s. Therefore, I believe it is very important that you fully investigate all of the potential natural disasters for the areas that your client has facilities and people to be able to properly advise them on the associated risk management procedures.

INFORMATION SOURCES

Of course there are many sources of information that can be accessed to gain information relative to the particular industry that is applicable. As the analyst, you need to seek out all of these sources and do a thorough job of gathering the intelligence. I have found many times that not all of the internal functions of the business communicate well with the security function. For example, most large companies have internal audit and business intelligence groups. The internal audit group does not want to share information they learn from their audits because it is "confidential" or, like the business intelligence group, they do not share their information with security because they do not see the relevance. Similarly, the security function does not share their knowledge that they have gained from various investigations because of confidentiality. However, when you get together with these groups and share information — both to and from security — everyone gains a better insight into some common areas of concern and sometimes into some major issues that did not appear to be major when all of the information was compartmentalized. Of course there are many aspects of this information that will be too highly confidential to share in detail; however, I believe that if the information is sanitized by removing names and even job-related information, then you can still share what is relevant to ascertain what risks are confronting the business. This sharing works best if it is done only at the higher management levels of each function.

The following are additional sources of information:

- Local crime statistics can be acquired from a *Cap Index Crimecast Report*, which are available for a fee.
- Uniform crime reports from the U.S. Department of Justice for that jurisdiction.

- Internal incident reports.
- Intelligence information from local, state, and federal law enforcement.
- Industry analysis groups.

The following are sources for weather-related information:

- Federal Emergency Management Agency
- The National Weather Service
- U.S. Geological Survey

Although these are U.S. sources, which I am most familiar with, other countries have similar national and local sources as well. There are also some on-line sources that can provide information about past and pending lawsuits and other legal information. Most of these sources, like LexisNexis, charge for the information, but they are an important resource and should not be missed. You should also evaluate the economic conditions in the area as well as the presence of other businesses in the area that might drive crime issues, such as bars and nightclubs. When you talk to the local police, they can point out the problem businesses and areas.

When you are reviewing the internal incident reports it is important that you inquire as to any threats that have been made against any of the executives or the company in general. Frequently, this type of information is not kept in the same location as the day-to-day incident information and may not be volunteered; however, it is a critical piece of risk data. It is also possible that the security organization may not be aware of these threats, especially if it is a completely contracted organization.

HUMAN RESOURCES AND THE SECURITY PLAN

Another source that needs to be probed is the HR department. Reviewing employee complaints can gain you some valuable insight and I have found many situations where HR decides not to share that data with security. Again, this is especially true in an environment where the security department consists of contract management and officers with no internal security professional. Because the security manager works for another company, the HR people may decide the information is too sensitive to share. They may also choose not to share it with you, as the one conducting the assessment. If that is the case, you should attempt to get them to at least provide you with some summary-type information such as the following:

FIGURE 2.2 Information should be shared internally whenever appropriate and possible to better protect the corporate assets.

- If there have been any threats, what type and how many? (see Figure 2.2)
- Whether or not they have had the threats analyzed by an expert to determine their seriousness. (They may not even know that this kind of a resource exists.)

- Has there been any stalking, workplace bullying, or harassment cases, including sexual harassment?
- Have they had a number of discrimination claims?
- Have any employees requested assistance with their personal situation due to domestic violence or other issues?

If you are not successful with that, then I would make a note to discuss this with the appropriate executive in the company. When it is time to put your recommendations together, any lack of information sharing must be addressed in a way that resolves this problem. This might be solved by implementing a special confidentiality agreement signed by the contract security manager or even someone higher up in the contract company. Other ways to resolve it could be to recommend that the client hire their own in-house security professional or contact you, as their consultant, when needed or some other solution. Whatever is decided, it must result in this information being provided to a security professional that has the knowledge and skills to evaluate the information and take the appropriate action.

REACTING TO A DEFINED RISK

I would like to add a word of caution here. There have been situations where some security managers have overreacted to some risk situations, causing their company to expend excessive resources to compensate and mitigate the perceived risk. I believe many executives are cautious about this issue, which sometimes makes it more difficult to get them to pay the proper attention to the appropriate risks. You need to be sure that whatever risks you identify, and subsequently bring forward to management, have sound reasoning behind them. You also need to understand that it makes little sense to spend more money on risk mitigation than what might be lost if the risk were realized.

Therefore, you need to quantify the potential cost impact of the risk whenever possible. That is not always easy to accomplish, so for a situation such as "impact on the company's reputation," where you would not be able to put a dollar amount on it, you should at least talk to some of the different company executives and see if they can put a cost figure to it, as you conduct your various interviews. If this were a business or institution that had some reliance on donations or contributions, then I would suggest that a major impact on their reputation could impact those donations by as much as 50 percent over the next few years. Of course, depending on what risk was actually realized, it could be less or even more.

One other area of concern, as it relates to risk assessment and mitigation programs, that you need to be aware of is the fact that there are times when executive management overreacts to the latest problems that are being focused on in the press and the media, or even a situation that occurs within the company itself. For example, while at IBM we had two cases of workplace violence that occurred in the 1980s that resulted in some deaths. Some executives were the type of people who personally attended those funerals and took it as their personal mission to ensure that it would not happen again. During this same timeframe we were also found to be the target of a terrorist group that called themselves the United Freedom Front, and when one of the safe houses was raided we discovered that they had performed surveillance on a number of our facilities, looking to determine the best targets. The corporate security organization worked on putting together improved security measures and worked with the HR department to put together a workplace violence prevention program. (A note of interest here is that no one talked about workplace violence in those days.) One of the items that came to the forefront was the installation of a security gatehouse at every site. Of course, to be effective the gatehouse needed to have a level of bullet resistance so the officer in the booth did not just become another one of the victims of a workplace violence shooting. This item was one of the executives' ideas because they had been to another company's site that had that kind of setup and felt it would be a good addendum to the program that corporate security had put together. Although that was not wrong, it was somewhat of an overreaction to do this at every site, everywhere. But if that is what the executives want, that is what you do. As you conduct your assessments and determine that some protection programs are basically more than is necessary to counter the risk they are intended to mitigate, you may want to probe what drove the decision to implement that level of protection before deciding to just write it up as being excessive. If it was one of the top executives' ideas, then you may want to comprise your recommendation with some diplomacy thrown in.

PLACING A VALUE ON THE IMPACT OF RISK

There are two primary approaches to placing a value on the impact of an identified risk or risks: the quantitative and the qualitative approaches. In order to use the quantitative method you need to have good numerical data. Although this is preferable, it is frequently not the situation because many of the risks cannot be boiled down to a number. However, with the qualitative method you develop an estimate of the impact or potential loss. This is the method most frequently used by most security professionals. In order for you to do an effective job of putting together a good qualitative estimate you will first need to become knowledgeable about the operation of the client so you can take into account all aspects of the risk impact.

The next aspect of this process is to identify the people and assets that may be at risk and to establish their value to the business. Assets can vary from tangible assets, such as products or raw materials that are part of the manufacturing process, to information assets such as research and development ideas to intangible assets such as the reputation of the client's business or institution. It is important that you also ask about these assets as you conduct your interviews with all of the various management teams. The area of information assets is one area that has probably been underaddressed more than any other area by many companies in the United States. My assessment is that fewer than 5 percent of security professionals have an in-depth knowledge of these protection programs. Most of the Fortune 500 companies have good information asset protection programs; however, once you move to smaller companies you typically find that they have not invested in these kinds of programs, or in many cases they have not even invested in having a professional security person on staff. I will spend more time discussing what this program should be in another area of this book, but for now it is important that you identify if the client has any information assets, and specifically what they are and what the impact to the business would be if they were lost or compromised. Of course the employees of the client are one of the most important assets they have and should also be considered as you develop this process.

Whenever an asset is identified you should attempt to place a "loss" value on the risk as well. This value must consider all aspects of the loss. For example, if a raw material that goes into manufacturing a product were stolen, you not only lose the value of the material but the impact to the company in terms of lost manufacturing time and meeting shipping schedules, and possibly an impact to the company's reputation. Therefore, as you ask about value you may need to ask some leading questions to get the interviewee to think about the intrinsic value of the asset. For example, in the case of a workplace violence act onsite, consider the far-reaching ramifications of just one incident:

- Loss of productivity. An estimated decrease of 80 percent during the first week after an incident is typical among the employees in the affected area.
- Workplace disruptions. Business can be seriously disrupted by investigations carried out by police, insurance companies, and state and federal occupational safety authorities.
- Employee turnover. Typically, there is a dramatic increase in resignations and drop in morale after an incident.
- Litigation and legal costs. Damages can be ruinous.
- Other costs. Funerals, psychological counseling, the effect on customers, and other less obvious costs.

If you feel you need more information on the risk assessment process I would recommend that you refer to ASIS International's Guideline on General Security Risk Assessment, which you can access online at their Web site, www.asisonline.org.

Another important program that goes hand in hand with the workplace violence prevention program is an executive protection program. Again, it is not the objective of this book to define these types of programs, but I have included an outline of a good basic executive protection program in Appendix B, "Executive and Employee Protection," for your use. What you will find in this appendix does not go into the detail of bodyguards, armored vehicles, countersurveillance teams, or other aspects that might be needed for someone who receives threats on a regular basis or who may be traveling to a country where other risks may be prevalent.

3

Conducting a Site Security Assessment — Part I

ASSESSING ASPECTS OF SECURITY ADMINISTRATION

The following list is intended as a guide to the various areas that need to be reviewed to conduct a complete assessment of security administration.

Security Administration

- Organization and policies
- Procedures and post orders
- Personnel selection and staffing and background checks
- Education and awareness
- Contract management

Each aspect of this assessment is equally important to providing the client with a complete picture of the operation. You should understand that the assessment process is intended to document the current status of the security program for the client. This means that you need to record the good and bad aspects of the existing conditions. Do not just focus on what is wrong. This will be important as you begin to define the Security Master Plan later in this process. It is also important to make sure your assessment is a collection of facts only, no opinions. When you complete the work involved in gathering the detailed information and begin to develop your recommendations, you might want to add some of your opinions into the process. However, if you begin doing that as you gather data, you will have difficulty at the end of the process and your report will be slanted with your opinions.

Appendix C, "Security Assessment Document," is intended as a guide to be used by a knowledgeable security professional. Everything in it is certainly not applicable to all locations or companies; it also does not cover everything you may need to look at for every site or business. You will need to collect your data by many methods: document reviews, onsite observations, questionnaires, onsite and offsite interviews, knowledge tests, and performance tests. As mentioned earlier, you have the option of supplementing your skills with others who may be more skilled in certain areas than you are. This team approach can be an effective way to achieve the best end result.

In security administration you will need to assess how well the security organization is managed:

- You will need to evaluate how they are organized.
- Are the policies and procedures well documented?
- Are they kept up to date, preferably on-line, and communicated to all who need to know?
- For the post orders, is there a document file where each security officer signs off on each change that is made to the post orders?
- Can security management show where new policies or policy changes have been communicated to all of the concerned parties?

DOCUMENTING POST ORDERS AND PROCEDURES

One problem that frequently surfaces during a review is the fact that the "documented" programs and post orders are not what are actually being performed in the field. When that is the case, it is important to determine whether the documented procedures are wrong or the implementation is wrong, so you can recommend the appropriate corrective action. All of these administrative areas of the business contribute to the overall effectiveness of the security organization and programs; they should not be minimized. If they do not have the proper documentation for the programs and policies, then you can be assured that you will find many problems with the implementation of them. You cannot expect tenants, contractors, employees, or the security officers to implement programs and policies that have not been clearly documented and communicated.

As this relates to post orders, the following is a list of what I consider to be examples of best practices:

POST ORDERS — BEST PRACTICES

- Security management should develop a comprehensive set of post orders, which will become part of the onsite security manual.
- Security management will develop a comprehensive list of rules of conduct and standard operating procedures.
- All required documentation should be submitted to client management for approval prior to implementation.
- Post orders and rules of conduct will be routinely updated and maintained, the frequency of which will be recorded in written log(s). This should be no more than one year.
- The sections of the post orders will be numbered and produced in a "bullet" format to make them easier to read. Each page should be dated and the document should have a table of contents to make it easier to find a topic in the document. The post orders will include at a minimum, but not be limited to, the following:
  - Uniform requirements.
  - Reporting and communication protocols, including incident report writing procedures and when such reports are required, the filing of false reports.
  - Normal and emergency operating modes and responsibilities (e.g., shift log procedures).
  - Frequency, focus, methodologies, or randomness for conducting building tours, inspections, and audits including the inspection of alarm and call box systems.
  - Training requirements for security personnel.
  - Building evacuation planning, protocols, and procedures.
  - Disaster recovery and crisis management planning and protocols.
  - Emergency response protocols and contact information for all parties.
  - Specialty requirements such as defensive driving or bicycle patrol techniques, as applicable.
  - Public relations and dispute resolution general guidelines and protocols including fraternization with others.

- How logs and reports will be maintained, techniques, protocols, reporting requirements.
- Record-keeping procedures and requirements.
- Instructions for monitoring and administering building security systems.
- Instructions for monitoring and administering building emergency and mechanical systems.
- Loading dock and delivery procedures.
- Parking and traffic management protocols, if applicable.
- Visitor management and identification procedures.
- Contractor and construction protocols.
- Sleeping on the job.
- Handling of confidential, sensitive, or classified information.
- Requirements for staying on post after reporting for duty.
- The procedures for calling in late or calling off.
- Reporting to work under the influence of alcohol or drugs.
- The locking and unlocking of doors with lists of doors involved.
- Areas to be patrolled.
- Minimum staffing requirements.
- Handling bomb threats.
- Handling suspicious packages.
- Handling deliveries.
- Handling elevator problems, especially trapped passengers.
- Handling fire alarms.
- The procedures and policies as they relate to "use of force." It is preferred that officers utilize their training for de-escalation and avoid the use of force except in extreme cases of self-defense. When it is anticipated that force may be required, the local police should be called to the scene to handle the problem.
- The procedures and policies as they relate to the handling and reporting of actual versus suspected criminal activity.
- Unique programs such as a property pass program or a badge or ID program should have an appropriate post order written to cover these programs so that the officers completely understand their roles.
- The procedures for reporting maintenance problems (lights out, water leaks, etc.). Who should be contacted and what form should be used so there is a record the problem was reported.
- Two types of reports are to be maintained by security personnel, supervisors, and account managers:

- Daily operations log; written record of all activities for each shift.
- Incident reports; contents should briefly appear in daily operations log and be fully explained within the incident report.
- Report writing is consistently one of the worst aspects of performance by security officers and is extremely important to the client. General guidelines for report writing include the following:
  - All reports are signed by the person preparing the report — and the person responsible for reviewing the report.
  - The person responsible for reviewing the reports should do so by the end of the shift on which the incident happened.
  - All blank lines or areas of the form include the designation "N/A".
  - Contents of the report are limited to actual observations and actions taken — not inferences or opinions.
  - Text is accurate, brief, concise, and professionally presented.
  - Follows structure of "Who? What? When? Where? How?"
  - Notifications to the proper people should be predetermined and implemented accordingly.
  - Incident reports should be trended periodically to determine patterns of activities.
- All security personnel should be trained on report generation best practices.
- List who should receive copies of shift logs and incident reports and when these copies must be submitted.
- The post orders should also include instructions for the use of the guard watch system, if applicable, as well as complete instructions for properly completing incident and accident report forms.
- I recommend development of an audio visual training program concerning the duties of the security staff in the roles described above, based on the post orders. The training program should include a written test to confirm the officers understand their duties. This training and testing can be conducted every six months to make sure the officers have not forgotten their required scope of work. The completed tests can be kept on file by the management to show that the officers understood their responsibilities.

SECURITY PERSONNEL SELECTION AND STAFFING CONSIDERATIONS

There are different issues to be considered related to personnel selection or staffing, depending on whether the security force is proprietary or contract or a combination of both. With both categories of employees there should have been the following:

- Extensive background checks including verification of Social Security numbers
- Fingerprint checks at both the state and federal level to check their criminal records and to verify that they are who they say they are
- Criminal records checks at the local level for the past seven years in all of the areas they have lived and worked
- Credit checks to determine if they have extensive financial problems
- Civil records checks to see if they are involved in any lawsuits
- Verification of all aspects of the application including a detailed check of any gaps in employment as well as a credit check

One thing that concerns me in this area is the lack of use of the national fingerprint database. On December 8, 2004, Congress passed a measure allowing employers to request FBI criminal background checks on persons applying for or holding positions as private security officers. The measure was part of the National Intelligence Reform Act of 2004, or "9/11 Implementation Bill."

Under the new law employers do not have direct access to the FBI information but will go through state identification agencies that will intercede with the FBI and report back to the employer. Employee rights are protected in that the employer must obtain written approval from the employee to conduct the check, and they must share the information received with the employee. There are criminal penalties for misuse of the information.

The use of this database was delayed until January 2006 when employers in all 50 states were given the ability to request FBI criminal background checks on persons applying for or holding positions as private security officers, thanks to the Department of Justice's recent implementation of the Private Security Officer Employment Authorization Act of 2004.

The Department of Justice interpreted the legislation and expanded on the act's coverage in its implementation rule to enable employers in states without an FBI background check system to obtain these checks from an "alternative" state.

The way it works is a state bureau will first determine whether the applicant or employee has a criminal history at the state level. If a record is found at this level, the agency may retrieve the remainder of their record by accessing the FBI's Interstate Identification Index. The FBI may also receive the fingerprints of individuals who do not have a record at the state level, and the results of the FBI check will be returned to the authorized state agency. The use of this national check allows employers to know that their security personnel are really who they claim to be and are also not hiding a criminal background. Although some, but not all, contract security firms have implemented this process, I believe it is being underutilized by proprietary security organizations. Unfortunately, this process is still not accessible in all states. Before making any findings in this area you need to determine if it is operational in the state you are working in, and if it is not, you should still recommend that the contract company or the client (in the case of proprietary officers) continue to pursue this fingerprint check every few months as a motivation to the state agency to get the process working.

These records will be in the HR department for employees and with the contract company for their employees. Both categories should have had drug testing as well. Implementing a good pre-employment and background screening process has some costs associated with it but the payback far outweighs the costs. Besides making sure they are hiring the best candidates for the jobs, this process will also help to provide a safe work environment and will reduce their legal liabilities. Other advantages of the process include reducing turnover, improving productivity, increasing morale, and simply reducing the legal risks associated with poor hiring practices.

Clients that are hiring proprietary officers need to also focus on making sure they are getting an employee who wants to work for their business and who has the capacity to grow with the business. Of course, education is always an important indicator, but they also need to make sure they have the right personality and attitude. This is typically done by having two or three experienced people interview the candidates; however, there are some very good personality screening programs on the market that can help with this process. Hiring and turnover are costly to employers, so whatever can be done to hire the best people who will also stay for an extended period of time can reduce some of these costs.

EMPLOYEE SELECTION AND
STAFFING CONSIDERATIONS

Although this information is not really part of this section of the book, it seems simpler to discuss it now. I believe the hiring practices that I have outlined for security officers are also appropriate for the client's non-security employees as well. They may want to make some differences depending on the job that the employee will have; for example, for an entry-level employee they may want to check records only from the past five years and not do a credit check. On the other hand, for a high-level employee who has financial responsibilities they may want to expand it to ten years and they should definitely include the credit check. These differences are appropriate in an attempt to manage the costs of hiring, as long as they effectively protect the client, their environment, and their employees. However, any differences in background check policies must be well documented and reviewed by HR and legal to ensure they do not discriminate against anyone.

The aftermath of some of the more extreme workplace violence cases has shown that had the employer done a thorough job of conducting the background screening on the perpetrator, they may not have hired them in the first place. It has also been shown that potential employees of questionable backgrounds learn which employer is not doing a complete background check and gravitate to that employer. This is especially prevalent in the case of drug testing. When an employer does not do drug testing, I suggest that they will ultimately hire a much higher percentage of drug users than their competitors that do require such tests.

As their security consultant, you need to determine if they have good hiring practices or not and make the appropriate recommendation to them to alleviate any shortfalls their process may have.

APPLICATION FORM

One of the more important documents in this process is the client's application form. There are many different laws that need to be satisfied, and many of the questions on the application are there to provide the employer with accurate information that, if falsified, can be used to dismiss an undesirable employee. I do not typically review this document as a part of this process and I am not suggesting that you should either; however, if you or the client would like more detailed information on this matter, I would refer you to ASIS International's "Guideline on Pre-employment Background Screening," which you can find on their Web site, www.asisonline.org.

SECURITY MANUAL DOCUMENTATION

As mentioned earlier, the onsite security manual will be a very useful document and one of the first pieces of information you should review prior to beginning your review. It should be a collection of all of the pertinent documents that affect the security organization. The reason for having this manual is to provide the security team easy access to any and all information that they may require. For it to be most effective it should be broken into sections with labeled tabs so they can access the needed information as quickly as possible in hard copy and it should be accessible on-line as well. It is preferable that this manual always be kept up to date both on-line and in hard copy so the information is available regardless of the circumstances and because it is an extremely valuable resource during emergencies. At a minimum, it should contain the following:

- Post orders
- Security procedures
- Security policies
- Crisis management plan
- Emergency policies
- Safety procedures and policies
- Emergency contact information, names and numbers, as well as backup listings in case a primary contact cannot be reached (if that is not already part of the crisis management plan)
- A complete list of all contract companies and suppliers that may be needed in an emergency with contact numbers and names, including alternate contact information

SECURITY EDUCATION AWARENESS

A very valuable aspect of a security operation is the education and awareness programs for both the security personnel and the people who occupy the facility.

These occupants may be employees, tenants, and contactors; there should be education and awareness programs for each of these categories of security's clients. Additionally, there should be programs that are directed at the management team exclusively, because you should be imparting information to them that is not generally provided to their employees.

You should evaluate the quality and effectiveness of these programs to ensure they are accomplishing their intended goals. For example, if the facility has a requirement that all employees, visitors, and contractors must display their badge at all times, is that actually being done? If not, then is there an education program to cover this? If there is, it is not effective. If there is not, there should be. Another aspect of this particular program is the ownership of the programs by the management team.

There have been numerous situations I have personally encountered where rules such as displaying your badge at all times are in place but not adhered to by the management team themselves. People tend to follow the actions of their leaders more than the policies. If this is the situation, I usually will attempt to convince the management that they need to also follow these policies. They will usually agree, but to reinforce this requirement, I recommend to the management team that if they do not want to follow the policy, then they should do away with it. To have a policy in place that the management team itself does not follow is destructive to the security program as a whole.

The importance of the education and awareness programs stems from the need to have everyone who works at the facility involved in the security program. These education and awareness programs should educate them to the fact that they know much more about their work environment than any of the security officers do. For example, they can recognize a "suspicious package" much easier than others can because they know what looks out of place in their area. Similarly, they would be aware when an "office creeper" enters their area because they have not seen them before. The education and awareness programs need to encourage them to get involved in protecting their area. They should teach them to challenge people and question when things look out of place. In today's environment with increased workplace violence, most employees are more concerned about their own security and safety in the workplace. The education and awareness programs need to teach them about all of the pertinent issues and problems that exist for that particular facility and what they should do to get involved: to be part of the solution. The programs should instruct them in the best methods to use and what not to do, as well. To be effective these programs need to be continually utilized and re-emphasized so as to remind the occupants of their responsibilities.

Even if a company or facility were to triple the number of security officers on duty, this would not be as effective as enlisting the involvement of the people who are already there, in my opinion. The use of posters or signs can be very helpful to this process as well. Besides reminding the employees of the different programs, they also help to make people feel it is OK to be involved. For example, most people do not like confrontation, even on a low level. Therefore, they are hesitant to challenge someone they see who does not have a badge displayed. If there is a poster or even a small sign nearby that says you should display your badge, people can point to that when they challenge the person, and it feels less like a personal confrontation to them.

As important as these programs are, I rarely find a security organization that has invested in them to the degree of hiring someone with the proper skills and educational background to administer the program. Fortunately, there are companies that can provide this service on a contract basis, which can supplement this lack of resource. As the person conducting the assessment, you need to determine not only if they have implemented these programs but whether they cover all of the needed subject matter and whether or not it is being done in a professional manner. There are numerous programs that can and should be used at facilities, but which ones are appropriate for the particular facility being reviewed depends on the environment of that operation. The following are some examples of the subjects that should be covered:

- Drug and alcohol policy
- Weapons policy
- Cameras and photography policy
- Threat policy and workplace violence prevention
- Display of ID badges and challenging those who do not display them
- Awareness of office creepers
- Clean desk policy (protecting confidential or sensitive information)
- Destruction of confidential or sensitive information
- System security issues such as not sharing passwords and not leaving your system logged on when you are away from your desk
- Building entry procedures (tailgating)
- Parking lot or garage safety, availability of security escorts
- Fire safety rules
- Evacuation plans, floor warden program
- Awareness of suspicious packages

FIGURE 3.1 Using campaigns to raise security awareness can serve to educate all employees and dramatically increase the "eyes and ears" on the ground to help protect people, the work environment, and corporate assets.

One additional program that should be a part of the awareness and educational program is in the area of security organization perception and reputation (see Figure 3.1). To explain what I mean by this I need to provide you an example. When I was a first-line manager of proprietary security officers, one of the officers came to me complaining that they did not get any respect from the other employees of the company. He said they thought of them as just being "night watchmen" with no understanding of the training and skills that they possessed. He asked me what I planned to do about this problem, which had bothered most of the officers for years. My reply was, "What are you prepared to do about it?" He looked at me like I was crazy and asked, "What can I do about it?" I told him that that answer was exactly why the other employees thought of him as not having any skills. That answer said he thought he had no power to effect change, and if that is what he thought, then how could he expect others to think better of him? I suggested that he put together a team of security officers and that they develop a short presentation to educate the other employees on the duties and skills of the security team. Once they had it developed and I had approved it, then they could add that presentation to the other awareness and educational presentations that we give so that every time someone from security gave a presentation on any of our subjects, that one would be given as well. Once we implemented the plan it took only a few short months before we began receiving compliments about what a great job the officers did and how many of the employees never understood the complexity of the job. When the officer came back to thank me for my help and support, I told him that whenever he saw a problem or a challenge, although I would always be willing to help, his first thoughts should always be about what he personally could do to correct the situation. He should never feel powerless, and if he did not, he would never be powerless.

CONTRACT MANAGEMENT AND AUDIT

The area of contract management is a very important part of the business management aspect of security and of the review you are conducting to gather information. One common failure I find is that the company's or institution's security contract manager does not always audit the hiring and training records of the contract security company to ensure that they are fulfilling their contractual requirements. In a situation where there is a lawsuit claiming that a security officer was negligent, it is not enough to just have those requirements in the contract for background checks or training, the company will probably need to demonstrate that they were doing the proper job of ensuring that the contract company was meeting these requirements and these audits will be the answer to that issue. There are other contracts that are also very important to the security of the facility, and I will get into the specifics of these contracts later in the book.

For the purpose of this section, you need to determine if there is someone on the security staff, or somewhere else in the company, who is responsible for managing and auditing contracts and whether or not they are effective and diligent in their duties. To determine this you will need to look at the results of the audits they have done; you may need to perform an audit of the records as well if what you see in their audit is not satisfactory. This evaluation should include looking at whether they utilize a competitive bidding process or do they rely on sole source contracts. I sometimes find that when a contract guard company does a very good job of building a good relationship with a client, frequently the client does not bother to do competitive bidding. I believe it is a good business practice to do competitive bids at least every three years because that will give them an up-to-date feel for what is available and it helps to keep the incumbent on their toes. The best way to implement this is to send out a request for proposal (RFP). I have included a sample RFP in Appendix D, where the company name is my company, Risk/Security Management & Consulting. If you have a good RFP package, then when you select the winning bidder, you can just attach their submittal package to the legal contract document with a statement that it is considered to be part of the contract. This makes the entire submittal package a binding requirement of the contract.

Of course there are times when a sole source contract is appropriate and you should not consider them otherwise until you evaluate the conditions of their use. For example, you may want to modify the existing contract in some way but you are not ready to go out to bid at this time, which would certainly justify a sole source. The key here is how long has it been since the particular contract has been put out to bid? If it is more than five years, then I would certainly recommend that it needs to go out for bidding.

4

Conducting a Site Security Assessment — Part 2

ASSESSSING ASPECTS OF PHYSICAL SECURITY

In the physical security area many aspects of the program must be reviewed in great detail. An effective physical security program relies on the proper balance of people, technology, and procedures. If this balance is not achieved the program will be neither effective nor efficient.

Physical Security

- Vehicle access control and parking
- Proper use of signage
- Security processing operations (e.g., visitor and contractor controls)
- Lighting, barriers, doors, and building perimeters
- Mechanical locking systems
- Security officer patrols
- Security officer review
- Crime Prevention Through Environmental Design (CPTED)

Security Staffing

- Monitoring and administering physical protection systems (PPSs)
- Stationary and high-visibility posts
- Emergency response capabilities
- Training

INTEGRATED SECURITY PLANNING

❖ Each element must be fully integrated to have a sound program

❖ All new construction must have Security designed in!

FIGURE 4.1   Integrated security planning.

As you assess this program keep in mind that the three primary objectives of a physical security program, known as the "Security Triangle," (see Figure 4.2) are:

- Detect. Early detection and assessment of the threat
- Delay. Delay the threat by use of barriers and other means
- Respond. Quick response to the threat by a well-trained force

Note: The total time to detect, delay, and respond must be less time than it takes the perpetrators to accomplish their goals. This is typically accomplished by implementing "Protection in Depth" or "Concentric Circles of Protection" concepts. These concepts are basically intended to make the security defenses stronger, which increases the delay factor, with additional alarm system capabilities, to improve the detection capability as you move closer to the high-value assets that need to be protected the most.

It would be difficult to attempt to outline all of the variations of security protection that might exist in the different environments you may encounter, but Appendix E outlines what I believe to be the basic physical security requirements for a low-risk facility in the United States. This document can assist you as you review the facility's current security program. Additionally, it is important that the person conducting the assessment be someone who has extensive knowledge and experience in a large variety of different applications so as to be able to properly judge whether or not the facility being reviewed has implemented the right physical

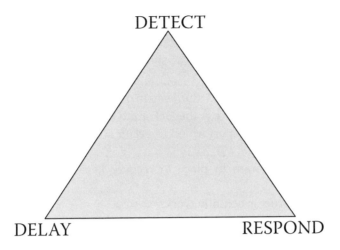

FIGURE 4.2 The Security Triangle of detect, delay, and respond.

security, consistent with the risks that they are attempting to mitigate and the assets they are protecting.

Lacking this knowledge, the next choice is to enlist the assistance of such a person or persons. Again, if you are an in-house security professional and you plan to rely on the aid of someone else who is in-house, you will probably not be able to conduct the best assessment of the operation. You should at least consider hiring a consultant to assist with this aspect of the assessment. If you are working with a tight budget and have to do the work in-house, I would suggest that you develop a list of other companies in the area that you could visit and have them show you how they have implemented security at their facility. This way you gain comparison information and can make reasonable judgments about your own program. The best way to do that is to do an in-depth review of all aspects of your own program first and completely document it. You can then take that documentation with you as you visit the other companies. You should not limit yourself to only visiting similar companies or those within the same industry. I have found that some ideas or concepts that have been applied in a particular industry can be restructured to work very effectively in other industries. New ideas are always good!

You must also be able to determine whether all of the different aspects of the physical security program are being properly maintained and if the necessary procedures are in place to ensure the program remains effective. For example, consider the following questions:

- Are they using a patented key or lock system where key blanks are controlled?
- Have they submastered the system properly? If the locksmith operation is contracted, is the locksmith bonded?
- Are periodic audits performed to verify all blanks are accounted for?
- Is there a program in place to recover keys from terminated employees?
- Does that process actually work?

EXTERIOR SECURITY ASSESSMENT — VEHICLE ACCESS CONTROLS

To begin the assessment of the physical security program start with the exterior perimeter of the facility or facilities and work inward; this is to evaluate the deterrence and detection defenses of the facility. As you move inward toward the more valuable assets, the defenses and the ability to detect intruders should be more effective. Depending on the type of facility you are evaluating and the level of security that is appropriate, you should determine if they have good vehicle access controls first, if applicable. Although some facilities may not need that level of security in their normal day-to-day operation, they may need to have it in a heightened security situation such as a workplace violence threat or an increase in the terrorist alert status. Therefore, as their consultant, you should recommend that certain changes be made that would allow the facility to easily implement increased security measures in those situations. Changes such as adding natural barriers or fences and gates can prepare them for that eventuality. Again, whatever increased security measures are to be recommended should be supported by the risk evaluation results, but I believe it is preferable to spend some monies to prepare the facility to be able to increase security with only a short notice of a pending problem, so they can continue to operate in that environment.

FIGURE 4.3   Parking security can be both a security and a liability issue.

PARKING LOT SECURITY

When you evaluate the parking lots and parking garages you need to understand who uses them, first of all. If they are for employees only, then it is easier to implement a higher level of security. The same access control badge used for the building can be utilized to control access to the employee parking areas (see Figure 4.3). If the facility has a high level of visitors, clients, or customers who use the parking facility, then the parking lot they use must be accessible to the public and therefore a lower level of security must be implemented. It is preferable to separate employee parking from customer parking whenever feasible. Besides allowing for higher security there are also different risks that need to be addressed in the two different applications.

Many crimes occur in both customer and employee parking areas, such as vehicle break-ins, vehicle thefts, robberies, and carjackings. However, many cases of workplace violence primarily take place in employee parking lots. Crimes such as stalking, harassment, bullying, and assault are mostly driven by domestic situations, where an estranged significant other is trying to make contact with a company employee. In my opinion, parking lots and garages should have the following, as a minimum level of security:

- Adequate lighting
- CCTV camera coverage
- Emergency call stations at regular intervals

Whenever possible, access to the area should be restricted to a limited number of access points through the use of fencing or walls. All entrance points, both pedestrian and vehicular, should have good CCTV camera coverage as well. Additionally, it is always advisable to have periodic security patrols of those areas.

PROPER USE OF SIGNAGE

It can be very helpful to make sure the client has posted the property with proper signs in a number of areas. For example, the perimeter of the property should have signs denoting "Private Property — No Trespassing" and "No Weapons Allowed," whenever this is feasible. They may also want to post signs at the vehicle and pedestrian entrances to the property, saying "This Property Is Under CCTV Camera Coverage." I also recommend the posting of all of these same signs at the entrances to parking lots and garages (see Figure 4.4). Additionally, if they have a search policy they should also post signs alerting people that "Your Vehicle and Any Packages or Containers are Subject to Search on This Property." Whatever you and the client decide to use, you should consult the local laws as well as the client's lawyer to determine the appropriate signage and the proper wording for the signs.

FIGURE 4.4 Signage helps inform employees and visitors of standard security policies and procedures.

SECURITY PROCESSING OPERATIONS — VISITOR AND CONTRACTOR CONTROLS

If the facility requires a high level of security, then they will have security processing operations (e.g., visitor and contractor controls at the exterior perimeter of the property). If they are not a high-security facility, then these controls will be at the building perimeter. In either case you need to assess these operations by reviewing the documented procedures and post orders and then the operations themselves. Some key points in this area include the following:

- Are they checking for valid picture and government identification such as a driver's license?
- Are they recording the numbers from the ID? **Note:** Some higher security installations are now utilizing a scanner to scan the picture ID into their system so they have all of that information on file. You can even use the picture from the ID to print it on the visitor or contractor badge if you wish.
- For contractors, are they also checking for a business ID? My preferred method of control for contractors is to have the company send a written list of names of their employees who will be working on the client's property. This list should be in advance of the employee arriving at the site. Additionally, if one of their people arrive at the site and they are not on this list, then there should be at least two contacts with phone numbers that can be called to verify people are who they say they are and that they are authorized to be on the client's site.
- If a sign-in register is being used, are they making sure the name is legible and are they using a single-sheet sign-in as opposed to a sheet where many visitors sign in on the same sheet? **Note**: There have been various problems with having sign-in sheets that allow the person signing in to see who else has signed in before them. For example, the company may be considering changing one of its vendors to another company. Problems can be created if the different companies, including the incumbent, have knowledge of who they are bidding against before the company is ready to begin the formal bid process.

For truck deliveries, is there a list of what deliveries are expected at the site or a contact person who can be called to verify the delivery prior to it pulling into the dock? **Note**: Depending on the layout of the dock area

and the available space, it is preferable that deliveries be checked and verified before they enter the dock area. Even if the facility is considered to be
a low risk for a truck bomb, this is still a prudent process. If they have a
lot of deliveries and limited space, they may not be able to implement this
process but I would look for a way to attempt to do a preclearance before
they reach that area if at all possible.

PROPER USE OF LIGHTING

Evaluating the exterior security measures must be done during both day
and night conditions. You will need to determine if the proper lighting
has been installed and maintained properly. You should take light level
readings at the perimeter, within the area between there and the building,
at the gates, on the roadways, in the parking lots, next to the perimeter
of the building, and at the building entrances. All of these areas require
different levels of light as measured in foot-candles. If you do not know
what they should be I would refer you to the U.S. Department of the Army
(2001) *Physical Security FM 3-19.30 (Excerpted)*. You can get this from ASIS
International's bookstore.

Lighting is considered to be the cheapest security asset you can have. It
provides a high level of deterrence for a very low cost, and it is extremely valuable in allowing security to assess the threat situation. Good lighting is also
a very important factor of the safety program for any facility (see Figure 4.5).

FIGURE 4.5 A truck backing into a warehouse facility.

There are several common situations you may encounter where the lighting is not as it should be. One is where it has been designed by the architect, not as an enhancement to the security and safety of the facility but purely as a way to make the campus look better aesthetically. I do not mean that as a criticism, that is part of their job responsibility, but there are times when the aesthetics need to give way to improved security and safety. I have also encountered situations where the lighting levels have been reduced after-hours in order to save money on electric costs. This is typically a very poor payback for the reduced security and safety that it causes. And another is where the lighting is just not maintained properly, allowing several of the lights to be out, causing dark areas. Maintenance problems can also exist if the trees and shrubs at the facility have not been maintained in a way that continues to provide the maximum benefit of the light. Frequently you will find that trees that were planted as small young trees are allowed to grow larger and eventually block the light, causing areas of darkness. If this cannot be corrected by just trimming the tree there are two alternatives: remove the tree or add more lighting. With shrubs or bushes you will find situations where they not only have become large enough to block the light from some areas but also will provide areas where perpetrators can hide as they await potential victims. You will need to address these situations in your recommendations, as appropriate.

One other area to address as it concerns lighting is the placement of CCTV cameras. You will need to view the exterior cameras in day and night conditions to ensure they are effective in both situations. There are times when cameras are improperly located, where they pick up glare from the lights at night, or where there just is not enough light to be able to get a good picture on the camera. To correct the problem of glare will require relocating the camera or cameras in question. To correct the low lighting levels you can either increase the light or change the camera to one that is designed to work in low light.

BARRIERS, DOORS, AND BUILDING PERIMETERS

You will also need to evaluate the remainder of the exterior area as it pertains to barriers, doors, and building perimeters. Again the variations that can exist here are far too numerous to list. What is essential is that the use or lack of use of these security assets makes sense. If fencing is being used as a human-made barrier, you will need to determine if it meets all of the appropriate standards. It most situations the fence should be seven feet high with an additional foot of height added by using three-strand barbed wire at a 90 degree angle toward the outside of the property. You also need to determine if it is installed and maintained properly with the appropriate lighting at gates and so on. Natural barriers can be extremely effective as well, and in many situations, they are more acceptable than human-made barriers such as fencing. The use of boulders to prevent someone from being able to drive around a gate entrance looks much better than a concrete wall in some settings, for instance. You will need to evaluate their needs and then determine if what is in place accomplishes its goal.

Next you need to review the building perimeter to determine if it has been effectively constructed and maintained to add a high level of delay and deterrence. A rule of thumb is that every door adds weakness to the perimeter. Of course there are other requirements that need to be satisfied such as allowing entrance into the building without creating large lines and to meet fire exit requirements. What you need to determine is whether these needs have been satisfied, or have they been exceeded? A common problem is that too many doors are used to gain entrance into a facility simply for convenience sake. Entrances should be limited to as few as possible and they should be monitored and controlled as much as possible as dictated by the risk evaluation. Every entrance that can be taken out of use will reduce the cost of security and increase the effectiveness of the building perimeter. When you eliminate the use of a door it should then be set up just like an "Emergency Exit Only" door. This means installing alarms on the door along with an exit crash bar and removing the key access from the outside of the door. Of course there are a number of factors to be considered when making these evaluations, such as the number of people who need to enter within a short period of time, the locations of parking lots or garages, and so on.

Whenever possible separate employee entrances from visitor and contractor entrances because different security measures can be utilized at these different entrances such as access control readers for employee entrances.

MECHANICAL LOCKING SYSTEMS — LOCKS AND KEYS

The next area to be evaluated is the use of locks and keys (i.e., mechanical locking systems). Hopefully the facility has implemented the use of an electronic access control system, which can significantly reduce the number of people who will need to have keys to the building perimeter and the internal high-security areas. Regardless, there should be no more than two grand master keys in existence for the facility, but I would prefer that there are none. It would be better for those who need to carry keys to just have submasters. These grand master keys are the keys that can open any lock at the site, assuming that they have implemented one lock system for the entire facility. If they have not done that, you should definitely make that one of your recommendations. Multiple lock and key systems will significantly reduce the security of the facility because of the complexities of tracking all of the different keys. Facilities should always use patented key systems that have special keys that cannot be reproduced or copied at the local key shops. The blank keys and the locks have to be ordered directly from the manufacturer.

Next the facility should be submastered into several different systems that cannot be interchanged. In other words, the submaster key for system A will not open submaster B or C. The number of submasters will depend on the size of the facility. I prefer to see the perimeter of the facility as one submaster system, and as long as they are using an access control system for the employee entrances into the building, I recommend that only two of these submaster keys be produced, one for the facility engineering manager and one for the in-house CSO or director of security. If there is only contracted security at the site, then the second key should go to another high-level, in-house manager. If the facility has that level of control over the perimeter system, then I usually recommend that this submaster series also be used on all of the electronic access control door key overrides. You don't want a situation where people can open doors to high-security areas using their key instead of their badge; this completely undermines the system records, and if the electronic access control system has been installed properly, it will cause alarm conditions. The reasoning for having a key override on an electronic access control door is primarily for situations where there is a malfunction at the door. In years past, these systems used to have a higher level of failure, and the key override would get used on a number of occasions. However, today's access control systems are extremely reliable with very few system problems. There are the occasional individual door problems, but these are also rare. Some people feel they need the key override because of the potential for a power failure; however, any reputable system installed these days has its own internal battery backup that typically provides at least two hours of power for the system.

You will find many situations where different executives of the company will want to have master keys. This should be avoided if at all possible. Whenever one of these keys is lost, all of those locks need to be changed, and that is an expensive project. If a grand master is lost, the entire facility must be completely rekeyed. If during the review you find out that some of the executives have multiple submaster or grand master keys, then you should make a recommendation that the issuance of these keys is out of control. Do not point specifically at the executives but find out what the cost estimates are for rekeying a submaster space or the entire facility when one of these keys gets lost and use that as the risk cost for those unnecessary keys being in existence.

SUBMASTER SYSTEM

To continue with the submastering system, they should have broken up the internal areas along functional or divisional lines. For some large divisions, they may want to divide them into more than one submaster. The value of multiple submasters is that when one of the master keys for that area gets lost, then you have a much smaller area that has to be rekeyed. If you have a very large facility with many different submasters, you can even interchange two areas when one has been compromised and the only cost is the labor cost of the work.

Figure 4-6 shows what I consider a properly structured key system.

The administration of the key system is a critical part of this work effort. The locksmith needs to keep track of who has which keys, if keys are returned when someone leaves the facility, the use of each and every key blank, what the cuts are for each of the keys, where the locks are installed, and which area makes up which submaster series. The locksmith should also audit all of the master and submaster keys on at least an annual basis to ensure none of them have been lost. Most of the better key

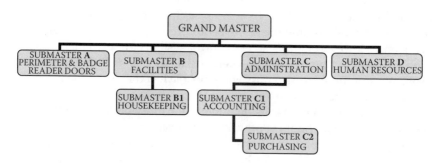

FIGURE 4.6 A properly structured key system.

system manufacturers have software programs that can record all of this data and can produce information for conducting audits.

Also, someone needs to audit the locksmith's operation at least once a year. Typically, I prefer this be done by the security organization. Some of the issues that need to be addressed deal with things such as the destruction of key blanks that were returned when people left the business or when the locksmith damaged a blank while making a key. Every key blank must be accounted for and the auditor of the locksmith must verify the destruction of the blanks. If this process is not followed, there can be no confidence in the integrity of the key system. The remainder of the audit should focus on verifying the results of the locksmith's audit records and results. It is only when you have this independent audit that you and the client can feel reasonably assured that the lock and key system is sound.

There are people who manage to get these master and submaster keys, even when they do not really need them, and then if they lose them, they do not report it because they are too embarrassed. Typically, these are executives in the company, and the locksmith will even have problems at times getting them to comply with his or her audit, which requires them to show that they still have their assigned key or keys. When this situation exists, the in-house CSO or director of security should get involved to resolve the problem one-on-one with the executive who is causing the problem.

One additional point is that the locksmith's shop, which contains all of the key blanks, locks, and key cutting equipment, must be considered a high-security area. It should be alarmed with a door alarm and a motion sensor alarm on the inside and have a camera on the door to view anyone who enters the area. Only the locksmith and one other person, preferably the in-house CSO or director of security, should have a key to this room, which means it needs to be keyed as its own separate master. The room should be constructed with "slab-to-slab" walls as well, meaning that you cannot just lift a drop ceiling tile on the outside of the room and go over the wall to the inside of the room. I do not recommend using a badge reader on this door because that is an expensive tool for such a limited number of people who would use it. There should be a procedure in place where the locksmith radios or calls the Security Control Center (SCC) whenever an entry into the room is made.

KEY ADMINISTRATION

Finally, you need to review the administration of handing out key rings. Typically, on each shift there are key rings that are assigned to security officers, housekeeping personnel, and facilities maintenance personnel. This service is usually provided at the security control center and is handled by having the people physically sign a log as to what key ring they have been assigned. Although this is a workable process you will find it difficult to audit because many of the signatures may be very hard to read. You will find cases where rings were signed out but not signed in, and you may even discover that there is a missing ring that has not been accounted for and steps have not been taken to rectify the situation. When there are 24/7 security posts that utilize the same key ring, the ring is usually passed from one officer to the next without being signed in and out. This is an acceptable practice as long as they radio to the control center to inform them that the ring has been passed and that all keys on the ring are accounted for. This should be logged into the daily log, and the shift supervisor should verify that each officer has the proper key ring at some point during the first half of the shift. This should also be entered into the daily log by the control center officer. I have found numerous situations where there are broken keys on keys rings and no one knows when it actually occurred. There have also been occasions when an officer forgets and takes a key ring home with them. I would always insist that it must be returned immediately upon being discovered that it is missing, regardless of whether the operation could be handled without it for one day or not.

My preferred method of administering the key rings is through the use of a badge-controlled key box. These systems provide for a much higher accountability because each person who is getting a key ring has to provide the SCC operator their badge to open the key box and remove the ring. It can be programmed so certain badges or people can only access certain key rings, thereby limiting some of the mistakes that can be made of giving the wrong ring to an unauthorized person. The system keeps track of all activity and a report can be printed to show exactly who had which rings at which time. You can also use these automated boxes to store submaster or master keys that may be needed in an emergency. The access to the higher level keys can also be restricted to a limited number of preauthorized people. I may be stating the obvious here, but the control of key rings is a critical process because they ultimately allow people access to areas that may contain sensitive or valuable assets. In order to minimize the risks associated with this process you should ensure that the key rings being signed out to the different people only have the keys on them that they absolutely need to have. In order to stress the importance of the key rings I usually recommend to clients that they have the contract companies involved in receiving key rings sign a statement that they understand that if their employee loses a key ring, their company will be responsible for the cost of rekeying the facility as necessary. Because that cost can run into the tens of thousands of dollars, it usually makes them manage this process much more closely.

SECURITY OFFICER PATROLS

You should now move on to reviewing the security officer patrols. In order to evaluate the effectiveness of the patrols you need to understand the objectives first. The history of these patrols is that they were originally begun years ago as a "fire watch." In those days there were few buildings that had smoke and heat sensors or even sprinkler systems. These days that is only a small aspect of the objectives of the patrol. In fact, there are facilities that I have reviewed; where the security officers did not even know that this was part of the job. I believe it still is because there are no sensors that are as good as human sensors. In order to accomplish this objective, the patrol needs to take the officer into those areas of the facility that are most susceptible to fire or other problems as well as through all of the hallways of the facility.

The next objective of the patrols is to conduct a "lock-up" round where the officer is to check that all of the areas that should be locked are locked. This usually includes securing the perimeter doors for after-hours, where facilities are open to the public during the day. It should also be the tour that makes sure that there is no one lingering in the facility after the time that they were supposed to have left. To do a proper job with this objective the officer needs to go into all areas that are accessible to the public and verity that no one is there. This includes all restroom areas.

Another objective, and for many facilities the primary objective, is to act as a deterrent to those who may want to perpetrate some crime or other undesirable action. To be effective in this effort the officers need to conduct tours on a random basis. This means that if you were to observe the facility for seven days, you would not be able to predict when the officer would be at a certain location at a certain time. I find in many cases that while some facilities think they do random tours, there is typically a repeated pattern to their randomness. You always need to go to the same checkpoints; therefore, it can be difficult to completely eliminate a pattern. I usually recommend two changes to make this happen; first they should implement the use of one of the better automated tour systems, which can be set up to generate a different tour at different times on a daily basis. If they use a contract guard company, they can normally get that company to supply the system and most of the time for little or no cost to the client. If they have a proprietary force, the systems are not very expensive to purchase. Next they should implement what I call fast tours. This is where you add one or two additional short tours to each shift. The objective is to make the officer visible to the outside or wherever a potential perpetrator might be observing the facility, at different locations and times, without conducting a complete tour. This can be very effective in confusing any observers as to when and where the officers may be at any particular time. One additional action that should be part of the tours is to notify the SCC whenever they discover a vehicle that is parked near the facility. Even for locations that may be located in a downtown area, this should be done whenever feasible. Naturally you cannot have officers spending inordinate amounts of time calling in vehicles that are legally parked at curbside parking areas, but if they are parked there at 3:00 in the morning when no one should be there, I think that is a valuable piece of information, and if the site is under observation by someone, they will consider this to be a problem to them as well.

All tours should always have a "safety" focus aspect to them. The officers must be trained in areas of safety that are a particular concern to the facility in question in addition to the standard items such as blocked emergency exits, excess trash in areas, reduced hallway space for emergency exit capability, and lights that are not operational. I typically recommend to security operations that it is important for them to not only make note of these types of problems but that they file reports on them as well. This demonstrates the added value they have in making the facility a safer environment for the occupants and in protecting the company from lawsuits due to minor maintenance issues.

SECURITY OFFICER REVIEW

Of course the review of the security officers is one area that must be focused on from several aspects. You need to start with how they are uniformed. Does the uniform match the environment and culture of the company? Do they wear their uniforms properly and are they consistent or are officers allowed to vary the uniform based on personal preferences? Are the officers always professional and project the right image? I personally believe this is more important than some other people think. People tend to act more professional if they are dressed more professional. It is the same principle used in schools that have uniforms. If the facility expects their security officers to interact with the public, their clients, customers, and employees, the officers will do a much better job of this if they are professionally dressed. I also believe that military-style uniforms bring out aggressive behavior in some officers, in my opinion, and therefore I do not recommend their use unless that is the approach that is needed for that particular facility.

The other factor to be evaluated is the training and attitude of the officers themselves. Do they understand why they are doing what they do? I find many times that the security manager has little or no training relative to people management skills. This means that they think they should just tell the officers what to do and they should just do it. If people do not understand the reasoning behind what they are doing, they will typically not do it very well. I am not saying they have to agree with the reasoning, they just need to understand what it is. When an officer asks why they have to do something, telling them, "That's what the client wants" is not a satisfactory response. It is like when a parent tells a child, "Because I said so." Another training aspect is that they need to have some level of countersurveillance training. They need to pay attention to things such as the same person sitting in the same area the last time the officer came through; or the same vehicle being parked at the curb two nights in a row; or when someone approaches them and asks questions that they should not ask such as how many officers are on duty, or even some less obvious questions. The officers need to be trained to pay attention to small details and what they should do when they observe these things. When I conduct reviews I place myself in that kind of a situation of observance just to see if I will get challenged by an officer or even an employee. Occasionally I am pleasantly surprised (but only occasionally).

CRIME PREVENTION THROUGH ENVIRONMENTAL DESIGN

Another aspect of physical security that is important for you to review is the Crime Prevention Through Environmental Design (CPTED) program.

This concept reduces crime by designing the environment around a facility in such a way as to deter someone from committing the crime. It is also intended to make the occupants and visitors to the facility feel safe and secure. The concepts of CPTED can typically be implemented with a minimum of costs. Here are some of the basic strategies to employ when designing or reviewing the implementation of CPTED:

Perimeter

- Provide outside access through no more than two monitored entrances.
- Avoid using materials along the perimeter that might provide hiding places.
- Use plant materials that restrict access such as crown of thorn shrubs, holly bushes, and so on.
- Place pedestrian entrances next to vehicle entrances.
- Control access with fences, gates, and guards.
- Use plantings, paving material, and fences to create formal entrances and to delineate public areas from controlled space.

Site

- Provide outside access to front and back of buildings for security patrols.
- Provide close parking spaces for workers who work late shifts.
- Secure access to areas such as roofs, dumpsters, loading docks, poles, ladders, utility access covers.
- Design driveways and parking areas so they are visible from the building or the guard house.
- Do not create hiding places by having blind pathways or storage yards.
- Make sure the landscaping plants will not block lighting or security cameras as they mature and so they do not provide hiding places, especially along pathways.
- Install highly visible signage but avoid providing information about the building.

Buildings and Parking Garages

- Entrances should be well lit and easily visible to public areas, building occupants, and security patrols.

- Place elevators close to the entrances so the interior of the elevator can be viewed from the entrance.
- Whenever possible, design stairwells to be open so no one can hide in them.
- Have restroom entrances positioned so they are visible to others, not down a secluded hallway.

It's one thing to see if they have done a good job of using the landscaping, lighting, and natural barriers in the way the site is currently set up, but have they also implemented procedures with the facilities organization to ensure that all of these aspects are properly maintained to provide for continuing effectiveness (see Figure 4.7)? Will the trees and shrubs be trimmed on a regular basis to ensure they do not degrade the effectiveness of lighting or the visibility of cameras? It is not enough that the two organizations have discussed and agreed to these issues, it must be documented so if there are personnel changes or budget constraints, this "gentleman's agreement" does not get forgotten. Most facilities utilize contract companies to provide these services so they can include this in the contract, and it can be detailed to the point of identifying the specifications of the height and breadth of the shrubs and trees. It should also be included in the Security Master Plan.

FIGURE 4.7   Notice that both the palm trees and bollards serve as deterrents to driving a vehicle directly up to the entranceway.

SECURITY STAFFING

In the area of staffing there are a number of issues to be addressed. We have already discussed the hiring issues, but we need to ensure that they have the proper mix of skills and training as well. You need to make sure that all security personnel have received the appropriate training and that their training is updated on a regular basis. As mentioned earlier in this book, most security programs rely heavily on the employees of a company being involved in the implementation of security programs. This is usually driven by various security education and awareness programs; however, the security organization does not typically hire someone with the skills to develop and conduct these educational programs. Instead, they rely on their security personnel to develop and conduct these sessions. Of course, they may acquire the education and awareness programs from external professional groups, which would supplement their staffing requirements, but these "canned" programs are not always as effective as a program that is tailor made for their exact environment. Therefore you must evaluate whether all of the proper skills exist, either internally or externally, to perform all the various duties of the security organization in a professional manner.

MONITORING AND ADMINISTERING
PHYSICAL PROTECTION SYSTEMS

The training and experience of the Security Control Center operator is a critical part of both the security systems monitoring and the emergency response capability. The security community has migrated over time to utilizing more and more electronic systems to improve our ability to protect people and property. However, these systems must be operated by people who have been effectively trained in their use, or the system's value to the program is considerably eroded. The days of having someone sitting in a room watching TV screens to see if anything happens in view of the camera system is long gone. These integrated systems require trained operators who can add the human intelligence to whatever event is being reported by the systems. As much as we may wish to, you cannot eliminate the need for human intervention with the systems. I believe the best solution for training these operators is to have them attend a certified course and I usually recommend the Security Industry Association's (SIA's) Central Station Training Program, which is a train-the-trainer program

(Security Industry Association, 635 Slaters Lane, Suite 110, Alexandria, VA 22314; www.siaonline.org). Experienced central station personnel (such as senior operators, supervisors, training coordinators, or even station managers) are trained and certified through SIA in how to set up and conduct in-house operator training using the Central Station Operator Course and its *Student Guide* workbook.

The Central Station Operator Instructor Course is held in classes given by SIA. When individuals complete the Central Station Operator Instructor Course, they receive certificates that have a Central Station Operator Instructor identification numbers and order forms for additional Central Station Operator *Student Guides*. Then, using their Instructor ID number, instructors can order as many Central Station Operator *Student Guides* as needed for in-house training. At the end of the Central Station Operator course, the instructor gives the operator trainee the final exam and sends the completed test to SIA. SIA then issues an operator certificate and sends it to the instructor to give to the newly certified operator.

The Central Station Operator Course contains core material that all operators should know, such as an overview of alarm systems, the role of monitoring centers, and central station equipment. It also covers basic, standardized, good practices for operators in such activities as processing alarm signals through automation systems, calling for verification, and handling natural disasters and other emergencies. In addition to the core material, there are a number of marked sections that may only apply to some central stations or certain types of alarm accounts. There are also marked sections that, in general, apply to all central stations, but are specifically determined by a central station's internal policies and procedures, where the instructor provides supplemental materials.

STATIONARY AND HIGH-VISIBILITY POSTS

These types of posts can be some of the more problematic or beneficial, all depending on how well the officers attend to their duties. To fully evaluate the performance for these posts, you will need to observe them for a period of time, preferably without the knowledge of the officer at the post. When you have officers positioned in a certain area, such as a receptionist post or a loading dock monitor, you will find that there can be a number of problems that can occur. First of all, it can become very boring day after day, which can tend to make the officer get somewhat lackadaisical about their duties. Next, there are frequently problems with employees and others who want to just drop by and chat with the officer for a while. In both of these situations, the officer will not be doing their job very effectively, but there is also another problem, which is a perception problem. When people, especially managers of the company, see officers just standing around chatting with people, then tend to think that this might be a good area for some cost cutting. My message to you is to make sure that the officers are being trained not only in how to do their job, but also in understanding the perceptions they create in situations of this nature and how to avoid those problems. It is very important for them to know how to avoid long, drawn-out, casual conversations without offending the person they are trying to get rid of.

EMERGENCY RESPONSE CAPABILITIES

The same situation exists with the emergency response capability. If the security team does not regularly (at least once a quarter) conduct emergency scenario tests, they will not be ready to respond effectively when it is needed. Of course in order to conduct scenario testing, they must have a detailed emergency response plan in place that addresses all potential emergencies for each facility. For most facilities the following scenarios would be appropriate:

Facilities Service Interruptions

- Major fire
- Major water leak
- Chemical spill or gas leak

Natural Emergencies

- Hurricanes
- Tornados
- Snow storms
- Floods

Civil or Hostile Attack or Violence

- Strikes
- Demonstrations

- Threats: bomb or workplace violence
- Terrorist attack
- Hostage situation

Your client might need to have some other scenario that would be appropriate to their unique situation. At least once a year the client should engage in a scenario test that also includes the local public response agencies: police, fire, and medical. The annual evacuation drill, although very important, does not constitute an emergency scenario test. (see Figure 4.8)

TRAINING

No matter what the investment of electronic systems at a facility, they must have well-trained security officer. That training must be balanced across all aspects of the requirements as well. I have found few locations that I have reviewed have done a thorough job of training their officers in the area of countersurveillance. Although most locations are not the direct target of a terrorist attack, I still believe it is critical that the security officer be trained to recognize when the facility is under observation by someone who intends to use that information to negatively effect their operation.

FIGURE 4.8 It is advisable to test emergency plans and establish relationships with local police, fire, and medical departments before an emergencies occurs.

Of course, this can apply to many other situations as well, in addition to terrorist activity.

To ensure the officers are getting the balanced training they need, I recommend that you utilize the ASIS International "Private Security Officer Selection and Training Guideline." The following information is excerpted from that guideline:

Establishing a requirement that each private security officer pass a written or performance examination(s) to demonstrate that he or she understands the subject matter and is qualified to perform the basic duties of a private security officer. Training should include the following core training topics:

1. Nature and role of private security officers
   a. Security awareness
      i. Private security officers and the criminal justice system
      ii. Information sharing
      iii. Crime and loss prevention
   b. Legal aspects of private security
      i. Evidence and evidence handling
      ii. Use of force and force continuum
      iii. Court testimony
      iv. Incident scene preservation
      v. Equal Employment Opportunity and diversity
      vi. State and local laws
   c. Security officer conduct
      i. Ethics
      ii. Honesty
      iii. Professional image
2. Observation and incident reporting
   a. Observation techniques
   b. Note taking
   c. Report writing
   d. Patrol techniques
3. Principles of communications
   a. Interpersonal skills
   b. Verbal communication skills
   c. Customer service and public relations
4. Principles of access control
   a. Ingress and egress control procedures
   b. Electronic security systems

5. Principles of safeguarding information
   a. Proprietary and confidential
6. Emergency response procedures
   a. Critical incident response (e.g., natural disasters, accidents, human-caused events)
   b. Evacuation processes
7. Life safety awareness
   a. Safety hazards in the workplace and surroundings
   b. Emergency equipment placement
   c. Fire prevention skills
   d. Hazardous materials
   e. Occupational safety and health requirements (e.g., OSHA-related training, blood-borne pathogens, etc.)
8. Job assignment and post orders

Depending upon the requirements and specifications applicable to the assignment, consideration should be given to the following additional training topics, which include, but are not limited to:

9. Employer orientation and policies
   a. Substance abuse
   b. Communications modes (e.g., telephones, pagers, radios, computers)
10. Workplace violence
11. Conflict resolution awareness
12. Traffic control and parking lot security
13. Crowd control
14. Procedures for first aid, cardiopulmonary resuscitation (CPR), and automatic external defibrillators (AEDs)
15. Crisis management
16. Labor relations (strikes, lockouts, etc.)

It is very important that the officers receive this training not only as their initial training, but as an ongoing refresher training program as well. I typically require the contract company to provide at least one hour of ongoing training for officers every month.

5

Conducting a Site Security Assessment — Part 3

ASSESSING THE ELECTRONIC SYSTEMS

The issues to be reviewed for the electronic systems are vast. I believe that some security professionals become overwhelmed when they look at new installations or major upgrades to existing systems. However, if you keep your focus on how you expect the system to function and what will be accomplished by the use of the system, I believe you will see that it is not quite so daunting a task.

Electronic Systems

- Centralized monitoring and dispatch
- Closed circuit television (CCTV) system integration and recording
- Access control system (ACS) and badging
- Alarm sensors and reporting
- Communications: radio, intercom, telephones, pagers
- Technology status: current and future

I have watched the progression of these systems over the years and have personally participated in pushing the system manufacturers to provide better and more fully integrated systems. You will find many older locations have system installations that consist of a camera and recording system, an electronic access control system, an alarm system, and a radio system. In some of these installations these systems might communicate with each other or they might rely completely on the operator to manage each of them independently. In today's world you can buy all of these components from one supplier, and in some cases they are all managed by one computer system, with the exception of the radio system. We are now, finally, approaching real system integration for our industry. I believe there are two main focuses for a physical protection system: It should be event driven and fully integrated.

EVENT DRIVEN

"Event driven" means that when an event happens, it triggers all of the appropriate system activity without the intervention of the operator. For example, when an alarm is triggered, it activates the nearest camera to focus on that area and brings that picture up on a separate monitor in the control center for the operator to view as it is recording the event real-time. Or you might program the activation of a particular card reader at a certain time of day to bring up a picture in the control center, while recording it at the same time, so the operator sees who is accessing the area while also displaying the file picture of the badge that is being used. This kind of system interoperability will make a significant difference in the effectiveness of the systems and the operator monitoring the systems. Without this type of integration, you would be relying on the operator to activate these different functions, and by the time they do, the event has passed and they have missed the opportunity to properly assess what was happening.

The alarms that trigger the activity can be anything from a set of door contact alarms to a motion sensor in the camera system to the use of a badge that is a valid badge but being used on the wrong card reader or at the wrong time of day. Basically, the limitations of a fully integrated system are controlled mostly by our own creativity. Anything that can send an electric signal can be used to activate any or all of the systems that are integrated. One of the issues that will come up as you conduct your review is that you will find planning problems with the design of the system as it relates to full integration. For example, the security control center operators might complain that they constantly get alarms from a specific door, but there is no camera in that area to help them to determine the cause of the problem, and by the time the roving security officer is able to respond to the alarm, whatever caused it has gone.

FULLY INTEGRATED

"Fully integrated" means instead of the old approach, where the systems merely communicated with each other, they are actually all part of the same computer system with all of them working together. The capabilities of a fully integrated system far exceed those of the stand-alone systems that only communicated with each other. This becomes even more important when you look to upgrade your system to include analytical or intelligent software for the CCTV system to provide you with a system that evaluates various behavior and other factors that broaden the system far beyond just recording an event.

I would like to add that I believe this is one of the greatest advancements to the CCTV system since the introduction of digital recording. Intelligent software can more than compensate for many of the operator's errors that we all have experienced over the years. There have been studies that prove that you cannot rely on the operator to see everything that happens in view of the cameras, no matter how diligent the person is to their duty. That problem will be virtually eliminated with this software. You will still need for operators to interpret what is happening in many cases, but the software will make sure they see the issue at hand and deal with it. If you are not fully versed on this application I recommend that you get educated on it prior to beginning your project of developing a Security Master Plan.

One other very critical aspect of these systems is to make sure that they meet all of the requirements of the company's IT organization. You need to remember that many of these systems are stand-alone computers that may be tied into the IT infrastructure and have their own access to the Internet. Some of them are also set up so that the installing company can access the computer remotely to run diagnostics or to perform software and system updates. These external connections can possibly allow unauthorized access to the internal IT network of the company. There are also numerous protocols that the IT organization will expect these systems to meet. The best way of ensuring that they meet all of the IT security requirements is to have someone from the IT group be a part of the team that reviews any installations of computer and network devices. In your review you need to determine if that was the process they used. If it was not, you should ask for that to happen now to make sure the systems are all in compliance. There may also be network performance issues with some of the security equipment that the IT organization should have reviewed and approved.

To accomplish this review you should be focused on the equipment that is installed in the security control center (the monitoring station) and the field units that contain computer capability, initially. The manufacturer of the downstream equipment such as the cameras, the card readers, and the alarm sensors is not as important to the efficiency and effectiveness of the system as long as they meet the appropriate specifications; however, you will need to ensure that they do meet those specifications and that they are installed and maintained properly.

For a multilocation company, you will also need to evaluate if they have properly networked their systems to provide the appropriate level of security in the most efficient manner. It is not uncommon to find a company with multiple locations, each of them having their own stand-alone access control system. This is far less effective from a business management aspect than having a system that is networked for the entire company. You may not want to have one networked system in the case of a multinational company, but it should be reduced to as few systems as possible.

There are many details to be looked at to ensure that the systems have been installed properly and have the correct settings so the information they gather is useful. For example, if they still have tape recording instead of digital, then that is an immediate recommendation. At today's prices for digital recording, which provides a far superior recording than tape, no one should have tapes. If they have digital you need to look at how they have set up the recorders. Industry standards are that they should have a minimum of 30 days of recordings for every camera. Some businesses that require higher levels of security may need to have more than 30 days. If they do require more, it would probably be 90 days' worth of video. You will need to look at how many cameras per recorder they have, how many frames per second they are recording, if they are using a multiplexer to scan through cameras, will they have a usable investigative recording of those cameras when needed, and so on. You need to review who is doing the maintenance of all of the systems. (I find some companies will use their own internal facility maintenance people to save money, which is typically not a good decision.) Do they have regular preventative maintenance (PM) for the systems? Cameras, especially external cameras, need to be cleaned and adjusted periodically. If they are using magnetic stripe readers, they need to be cleaned and adjusted periodically also. (If they do still have magnetic stripe readers, I would recommend that they migrate to proximity readers as soon as possible.) I will go into more depth on the cameras in the next section, but as a part of this review effort, you need to make sure that they are using the right lenses to ensure they get the picture they want at all times of the day and night.

CLOSED CIRCUIT TELEVISION

The closed circuit television (CCTV) system has several functions. First of all it is used in some environments as a deterrent value. When people see that they are being watched on a camera system, they tend to not do things that might get them into trouble. One of the common problems that I have encountered is that the architects do not like for cameras to be highly visible, due to aesthetic reasons. Because of this they will place them in areas that make them hard to see or in some cases even put them behind a wall with only a small hole to view through (see Figures 5.1, 5.2

FIGURE 5.1   You will notice the small black hole in the exterior wall of this building.

FIGURE 5.2   This is a close-up of the camera behind a glass wall in a very large lobby.

FIGURE 5.3   This is a larger view of the same wall as in Figure 5.2. The camera is behind the top right glass pane.

FIGURE 5.4   An example of a fixed camera installation.

and 5.3). In these situations the camera system has no deterrent value (see Figure 5.4), and frequently these "hidden" placements do not provide for the best field of view for the target.

While you are looking at the "target" field of view I recommend that you find out if anyone has actually documented what the target is for each of the cameras. I have rarely found that kind of documentation but I believe it is very important. Admittedly, some targets are quite obvious, such as entrance doors; however, many of them are not. In many of the reviews I have conducted, I have found cameras that were fixed on locations that no one could explain why. The answer was always the same: "That's the way it has always been!" In most of those situations there had been some incident that had occurred at that spot some time in the past, which prompted someone to change the field of view of an existing camera to that spot, and the original field of view was never covered again, even though it was really a more important location. By documenting the reasoning for each camera's positioning and then reviewing that reasoning on an annual basis, you can make sure that situations like this do not get away from you. This can also be a very important document whenever there is a change in management and the new manager wants to understand how the system is being utilized.

The next function of the CCTV system is to provide the control center operator with the capability of conducting an immediate remote assessment of an alarm condition or a particular event. This can only be done effectively if the system has been designed and installed to anticipate all of the potential alarms and other situations that might occur so as to provide the control center with the necessary view of those areas. When the CCTV system is being designed with this in mind, one of the primary considerations will be whether to use fixed cameras or pan/tilt/zoom (PTZ) cameras. Generally a PTZ camera is about three times the cost of a fixed camera to purchase and install. There are also some data storage issues with these cameras, as they will use more of the digital storage space than a fixed camera. My preference is to use fixed cameras in most areas but to have some PTZ cameras installed in large areas where you might need their capability to evaluate a situation or where there might be multiple potential alarm situations that one PTZ could cover as opposed to more than three fixed cameras.

For example, you might have a courtyard that has four or more doors that open into it, and you have the ability to place one PTZ camera in or near the center of the courtyard, where it can cover all of the doors as well as being able to evaluate any situation occurring in the area. This might be more cost-effective as well as providing better evaluation data than having four fixed cameras. Of course, you would not have recorded data on all of the doors at all times, so if these doors are high-use doors it would be a better solution to have the four fixed cameras. But, if they are not frequently used, then you can program the PTZ camera to automatically patrol the courtyard and to immediately focus on any of the doors that are being used. This is normally done by integrating the camera with the door alarms. As a general rule, you would typically use PTZ cameras on exterior applications more than interior, but that isn't the case 100 percent of the time.

My personal requirements are that the following areas and situations should be covered by the CCTV system:

FIGURE 5.5   An example of a PTZ domed camera.

1. All perimeter entrances should be covered at all times to view who is entering the door.
2. For high-security facilities there should be a camera on both sides of the entrance to see who is exiting as well, along with what they are carrying (see Figure 5.5).

FIGURE 5.6 Video monitor showing pictures from surveillance cameras at multiple locations inside and outside the facility.

3. All receptionist positions should have a camera mounted behind them that views who is standing at the desk; it should not be "watching" the receptionist.
4. All lobby areas should have complete camera coverage; the number depends on the size of the lobby (see Figure 5.6).
5. The elevator lobby bays should have camera coverage on the first floor at least and on any floor that is considered a high-security floor or a high-risk area.
6. General hallway areas should be covered at some facilities where there are medium- to high-risk situations.
7. All high-security areas should have a camera on the entrance door(s) to the area. Some of these areas such as the IT server room, the HR entrance, or areas where money is located should also have a camera on the inside of the door.
8. All loading docks should have complete camera coverage.
9. All parking lots and garages should have camera coverage that views the entrance and exits of the facility as well as the driving lanes. If there are help stations or telephones in the garage, they should be covered as well. The entrance and exit cameras should capture the license plate information (see Figure 5.7).

FIGURE 5.7   An example of a fixed camera in a garage.

10. There should be external cameras that cover the outside perimeter of the building(s), which is handled best by PTZ cameras so they can be triggered to focus in on any emergency exit doors that are accessed and can be used to view large areas that would require too many fixed cameras to cover.
11. For high-security facilities there should be camera coverage of the perimeter fence line and the area between that fence line and the building(s).
12. For campus-style facilities, all roadway entrances and exits should be covered.

Again, these are just the basic areas of coverage that I believe should have camera coverage. What would be appropriate to a specific location will depend on the risks that need to be mitigated based on the use of the facility, the layout of the facility, and multiple other factors. The other side of my philosophy is that I do not like to place cameras in areas where there is an expectation of privacy. I believe it is important for the relationship between the security organization and the occupants of the facility that they not have a Big Brother-type of image. These areas would include someone's work space or inside elevators. An example of this is where I require a camera behind the receptionist position; I would make sure that the receptionist's working space is not in the field of view. I normally take the initiative to have the receptionist come to the security monitoring area to see exactly what area is being monitored so he or she is comfortable with that placement. I do not like the use of hidden cameras except in a situation where it is needed as a part of an investigation or in some retail operations. I prefer to get the full value of the deterrent aspect of the cameras. Also, I have learned over the years that frequently when there are hidden cameras in use, most of the people in the facility learn about this very quickly.

Another function of the CCTV system is to be able to utilize the stored data as an investigation tool. The use of digital storage over tape storage has been a great enhancement in this arena. You will get much clearer pictures, and accessing the exact data you need is far simpler with the search capability of the computerized storage. Of course it is critical that as you assess this aspect of the system, you will need to determine that all of the proper settings have been made. One very important part of this function is that the system creates a forensic watermark for use by law enforcement in criminal prosecutions. Many of the newer systems provide this capability, but not all of the users know how to take advantage of it. Therefore, you should find out which of the staff people are responsible for capturing data from the camera system and have them pull some information for you that would be usable in a court of law.

One serious aspect of camera installations is lighting, both human-made and natural. You must ensure they have sufficient lighting, and you must make certain the lighting does not interfere with the cameras. I have seen many installations where the installer did not consider factors such as the sun hitting a window in the afternoon, causing too much glare. Issues such as this can be resolved either by camera placement or by using the proper lens, such as an auto-adjusting iris. In order to determine if problems like this exist in an installation, it is important that you not only review the equipment but that you talk to the operators who work on different shifts. The first-shift operator might not know that this kind of condition exists because it happens on second shift.

The following are some of the installation factors for cameras that should have been addressed by the system integrator:

- Use the proper focal length lens.
- Cameras with fixed iris lenses should be set to the proper f-stop to give full video level. (F-stop or focal stop is the measurement of the aperture settings in a camera lens; the f-stop determines how much light is allowed to enter the lens and pass through the CCD

sensor. It also determines how much is in focus in front of and behind the subject when it is in focus.)

- Focus the lens to give a sharp picture over the entire field of view.
- Aim and adjust cameras and lenses to provide the field of view as needed based on the identification requirements. In other words, do you just want to see that a person is entering a certain door or do you want to be able to recognize who the person is?
- Cameras installed outdoors in a fixed mount that face the rising or setting sun should be aimed below the horizon to prevent the camera from looking directly into the sun.
- Most cameras today are now using Cat 5 or Cat 6 wiring for either a separate network or to connect to the company's network.

ACCESS CONTROL SYSTEMS

The use of electronic access control systems can provide many different services for the security and safety of the facility. These systems have been the primary source of labor reductions for security over the years when they are implemented properly. However, they can lead to a false sense of security when they are not properly utilized and managed. These systems not only provide for control of access, but they have alarm capability as well. When installed correctly, they can tell you if doors are being held open too long, if they are being forced open, if someone with a badge who is not authorized for that door or time of day is trying to access the door, and other situations.

When reviewing these systems you need to start with the administrative controls. Only certain people should have access to the system as the "administrator," because that level can alter all of the settings and access the history records. I normally recommend that this be limited to someone in security management. The security control center operators might only be able to monitor the system, whereas the security manager or supervisors might need higher levels of access to make badges and add new users to the system. Who has what level of access will differ depending on the structure in place at the facility.

The right way to manage a system at a facility that has internal restricted areas controlled by the ACS is to have the manager of that area be the person who authorizes who can access the area and when. I refer to them as "area managers." You might also need to have higher control levels in place for some high-security areas such as the addition of a biometric reader in addition to the badge reader, or you might have a reader in place on both side of the door so people have to badge in and out with the additional use of an "anti-pass-back" control, which means that if you leave the area without badging out, the system will not authorize you to re-enter the area. It also will not let you leave if you entered the area without badging in. This kind of control is becoming the industry standard for most IT areas and some other high-security areas.

One problem that is frequently discovered with these systems is that people who have left the business have not had their access privileges revoked on the system. This is especially bad if it is combined with another problem where departing employees' badges are not collected and returned to security. Both of these issues are procedural problems that must be addressed. One effective way to help ensure this doesn't become a prolonged problem is to periodically send the area managers a list of everyone who is in the system with access to their area. This provides them an opportunity to let security know that there are people on the list who have left the business, so security should remove their access. The review of the ACS should always include a check to see if this process is in place and if these procedural problems persist.

It is also important to understand the philosophy of the ACS that is installed. For example, I personally believe that for most controlled areas, except for high-security areas, any employee who has a need to enter the area from time to time should be given access via their badge. There are those who would restrict access to the area to only those who work in the area. I believe that drives unnecessary work for everyone concerned and creates an unfriendly environment for the employees. I would prefer to give them the access and have the system keep a record of that entry, because the alternative is that people will let them in and typically not bother to make them sign a visitor's log, which means there is no record of entry. This is the difference between "controlling" and "preventing" access. It is vital that the use of the system be cohesive with the culture of the company; otherwise, employees will find ways to circumvent the system and render it less effective. For some businesses, they may want the access to some areas controlled only after-hours. Therefore, the system can be programmed to have the card reader for those areas go to an "open" or "unlocked" position during regular hours and return to a "closed" or "locked" position for after-hours.

You will need to determine if there is an access control system policy in place for the facility or company. The list below provides an overview of what should be contained in this policy, at a minimum.

· ACCESS CONTROL SYSTEM POLICY

Access System Policy — Purpose

- Electronic access controls are new to some employees and contractors; therefore, they need to be educated in the purpose of the system and why it is needed.
- The system will provide a consistent companywide access procedure that everyone adheres to so people and property are secure.
- There must be cross-divisional agreement and support for the policy to ensure its effectiveness.
- Understanding of intent: "Controlling" as well as "preventing" access is important for every user to understand, especially the area managers.
- Provide understanding of system records keeping so all users are aware that the use of their badge produces a record of when and where it was used. This will help to deter employees from letting others use their badge.

Access System Policy — Terms

- Classes of access: Different levels of access that allows a badge to enter through multiple card readers. There are typically five of these levels:
  - Master Access: Allows access to all areas in the facility. The people on this access level might be some executives, the director of security, the manager of engineering, the site security manager, and the security shift supervisors (for emergency access).
  - Submaster Access: Allows access all areas except for the high-security or restricted areas. The people on this list might be the facility engineering and maintenance staff, the security officers, and housekeeping staff.
  - Perimeter: Access into the general building space from the exterior of the building. The people on this list would be all employees and contractors who have badges; they will have access to these card readers. Some contractors might be controlled by time of day or day of the week.
  - Functional Access: Function- or division-controlled space in the interior of the buildings. The people on these lists would be those who work in these areas or have a need to regularly

enter the area as approved by the manager of the area. Some of these areas might have their doors open to the public during certain hours of the day and on certain days.

- High-Security Areas: Require more security due to various risk factors based on what is stored in the area or a risk to business continuity. The people on these lists would be those who work in these areas only.

- Area managers: The individual who is responsible for the security of a particular functional area and decides who gets access and if and when the area's doors are open to the public.

Access System Policy — Requirements

- Display of badge by all employees, contractors, and visitors at all times. Anyone in a secure area who is not displaying their badge should be questioned by any employee who observes them.
- Divisional or functional responsibility for their space, such as when doors are automatically locked or unlocked, who has access to the area and at what times, and so on.
- "High-security" areas: These areas might be finance, IT, HR, classified records storage, or others. These areas will have access limited to only those employees who work in that area; all others will have to sign a visitor log upon entering and leaving the area.
- Access records audits: Area managers are provided a printout every three to six months showing who has access to their area and they sign off or approve that list as being accurate and up to date or indicate any required changes.
- Exiting employees and contractors must return their badges prior to leaving. The responsible manager will collect the badge and forward it to security.

ALARM SENSORS AND REPORTING

In order to have a complete physical protection system you must have the proper alarm system to accompany other parts of the system, such as fences and other barriers, lighting, CCTV, access control, locks, and monitoring station. The objective of a complete protection system is to provide the ability to detect, delay, and respond. The alarm system must be designed to provide detection early enough to allow the responders to reach the perpetrators before they reach their target. Therefore, the proper selection and placement of alarms is a decisive aspect of the total system. Not only must you evaluate if they have provided alarms in all of the appropriate places, but you need to determine if they have utilized the suitable alarm sensor or system for that application.

The use of the correct type of an alarm sensor is very important to ensuring the complete physical protection system operates to its peak ability. There are numerous options for the type of sensor one might use in various applications. Making the right selection of the proper sensor will be determined by many different factors. The list below is not intended to be all-inclusive, but is an example of some of the factors:

- The object or area being protected
- Perimeter or area points of entry
- The terrain of the area in exterior applications
- Temperature variations
- Potential for interference by electrical or electromagnetic sources
- Whether they will be hidden or visible
- Power requirements
- Ease and cost of installation
- The probability they will detect intruders
- Ease and cost of maintenance
- Size of the area to be protected

The following are some of the possible sensor choices:

- Interior sensors
  - Proximity type such as capacitance sensors for cabinets and safes or vibration sensors that use piezoelectric crystals or microphones to detect sound patterns
  - Mono-static microwave, used to detect movement within a predetermined area
  - Passive infrared, which detects changes in thermal energy
  - Dual technology such as the combination of microwave and passive infrared sensors, which reduces nuisance alarms and improves detection
  - Magnetic contacts on doors or windows, which detect them being opened
  - Metallic foil used on windows to detect when the glass is broken (because the foil breaks)

- Glass breakage sensors, which detect the shock of the glass being broken from one or more windows
- Lacing of fine wire to protect walls, doors, or safes when the wire is broken
- Pressure mats used on floors or under objects to detect placement or displacement of weight

- Exterior sensors (It is important that exterior systems be "zoned" to more accurately pinpoint the point of intrusion.)
  - Buried fiber optic cable to detect the pressure of someone walking across the area
  - Buried electromagnetic field cables, which detect when someone breaks the field by walking through it
  - Fence detection sensors, which can be either microphonic vibration sensing coaxial cable or fiber optic cable that senses movement, vibration, pressure, or sound
  - Video motion detection systems, which utilize the CCTV system to detect movement (see Figure 5.8)
  - Intelligent software systems, which use the CCTV system to detect predetermined actions or inaction that is unwanted
  - Active infrared beam sensors to detect an intruder moving through the beamed area
  - Microwave systems, which detect a break in the microwave beam
  - Laser fences, which will detect a break in any of the beams as someone moves through the area

Another type of an alarm that I typically look for and recommend is the use of "panic alarms" in a number of areas. These alarms should be installed at any location that handles cash, and they are typically a small push button mounted under a counter or desk. (In this application they are usually referred to as "hold-up" alarms.) Additionally, I usually have them installed at the main receptionist desk, the HR receptionist desk, the HR director's desk, the room that HR uses for termination interviews, and some of the executives' desks and their assistants' desks. Basically, they should be used in places where you might anticipate the potential for some type of violent action.

One factor that can have a major impact on the alarm system is the use of line supervision. This will provide a trouble signal at the security control center where the alarms are monitored whenever there is a break in the line. This is a code requirement for fire alarm systems; however,

FIGURE 5.8 Modern high-tech fence detection sensors can be used with traditional chain link fencing for added perimeter security.

the security alarm system has no such requirement unless the client has requested it. There are many system integrators that will only install the alarm systems this way; however, some do not. To have this function requires the installation of an end-of-line resistor, which of course will slightly increase the cost of the system.

In order to properly assess the alarm system you should start by asking to see the "alarm assessment procedures." This is the document that provides the detailed operating procedures for the security officers who monitor the system and describes what actions they should take in response to each and every alarm. There should also be procedures that detail what the responding security officer in the field should do and not do for each alarm. You should also ask to see the documentation that they have showing when the alarms have been tested last and the results of that test. If you find that they do not have any of these documents you should recommend that they begin making those documents as soon as possible.

RADIO SYSTEMS

Most locations that have security systems will also have a radio system for communications. This communication capability is critical in emergency situations. A common problem with these systems is that "dead spots" exist. These are areas where the radio transmission is very weak and the person in the field can usually not hear other transmissions or be heard by the base system. These dead spots frequently exist in parking facilities or other areas where the construction consists of concrete and steel. These problems can usually be resolved with the installation of some remote antennas or repeater stations. Usually you can find out if these problems exist just by asking the operators in the security control center or the security patrol officers. However, you should make some field tests of the system as well by having a radio assigned to you and then going to some of the more problematic areas to test it.

There is also another common procedural problem with the use of radios. Radio communications should be very concise and short. One approach to this issue has been the use of "10 codes." That is where you have codes that signify what you are attempting to say; for example, "10-4" means "OK." The problem with 10 codes is that during emergencies and at other times, people get confused and use the wrong code, which only compounds the problem of good communications. I prefer not to use the 10 codes, but to use disciplined communications instead.

Additionally, whenever one individual is talking on the radio, no one else can. This can be a major problem in emergency situations where people get excited and tend to talk too much. Only by the implementation of strict controls over the use of the radio during everyday activity can this be managed in emergencies. Also, if other functions, such as the facilities group, use the same radio channel as security, this will significantly increase the on-air traffic. This is due to the nature of their work, which requires them to talk much more than the security group. The best solution for this is for them to have a separate channel. At many facilities I have found that they already had multiple channels available for their use, but for some reason they elected to have both groups use the same channel. If a separate channel is not available then they will need to work out some very precise disciplines with all of the users of the one channel to ensure that during an emergency, only emergency communications are made and that they are very concise. Again, this will not happen unless it is practiced during emergency drills with all of the users involved.

TECHNOLOGY STATUS — CURRENT AND FUTURE

As you conduct your assessment you need to document the current status of the client's technology. Your primary focus here is to determine if the technology is "state of the art" or if it is due to be upgraded to the next evolution. This can be evident in the types of cameras in use, whether the recording systems are digital or analog, the access control readers such as magnetic stripe instead of proximity, and so on. When you begin to document the five-year plan for the client, you will need to ensure that there is a technology migration plan to move them to the next level. Even if they are state of the art today, if they do not have a migration plan for the next five years, then they will not be where they should be at that time.

You should also check with the system integrator and manufacturers of the primary security systems and equipment to see what their targets are for end of life for those systems. This will give you more insight into the need for replacing the systems out in time.

A good migration plan can help to reduce costs or at least spread the costs out over a longer period of time. For example, if they are currently utilizing proximity readers, I believe they will need to migrate to smart card technology over the next few years. If the client agrees with that strategy, they can implement a plan whereby they begin investing in dual-technology readers that can process either proximity or smart card technologies for all new or replacement reader installations. Additionally, they can have a plan to begin replacing current readers over time with these dual readers with a target of full replacement by a specific point in time. The cost of the dual-technology readers is only slightly higher than the single proximity technology readers, and they will have avoided

95

wasting their money on those older readers. The same process can be put into place for cameras, recorders, radios, and alarms. The best part of the plan is that you maintain flexibility as to the actual conversion date to a new technology because the old one continues to work until you are ready.

6

Conducting a Site Security Assessment — Part 4

ASSESSING INFORMATION PROTECTION

A recent "Trends in Proprietary Information Loss Survey Report," sponsored by PriceWaterhouse Coopers, revealed that the U.S. Chamber of Commerce and the ASIS International Foundation found that both Fortune 1,000 and small to mid-sized businesses were likely to experience proprietary information and intellectual property losses ranging from $53 to $59 billion. These losses involved the following:

- Research and development (49 percent)
- Customer lists and related data (36 percent)
- Financial data (27 percent)

INFORMATION SECURITY PROTECTION PROGRAMS

For information security protection programs it is important to remember that there are more crimes committed against businesses by authorized insiders than by outside penetration of the systems or networks. In the case of industrial espionage, the insider might have been motivated by an outsider, however. Security and IT directors must walk a very thin line between creating an atmosphere of trust for employees and implementing deterrent programs to prevent those same employees from stealing the company jewels. The best approach to this is to ensure that for highly sensitive or very important information, protection programs exist in such a way as to require that two or more people need to access the complete data in order for someone to get all of the information. This means that there would need to be collusion between multiple employees or the system would have to be circumvented in some way, which will usually leave some evidence of the crime.

This chapter provides some detailed program outlines of what I believe are some of the more important information protection programs. I am aware that some security consultants and other in-house security professionals are not as versed in information protection as they are in physical security, and as I promised in the beginning of this book, I will do my best to help supplement your ability to develop a quality Security Master Plan.

Information Protection Programs

- Computer and network system security
- Disaster recovery program
- Awareness training
- Investigation requirements
- Exit interviews for key employees
- Information asset security

COMPUTER AND NETWORK SECURITY OWNERSHIP

You will find that some CSOs and directors of security do not consider these programs to be a part of their responsibilities. I personally disagree with this approach because the security of the company's information assets, in many situations, ensures the future success of the company. If that is the case, how can the owner of the entity's security not be responsible for this aspect? Even if the security organization does not own the program as it relates to computer or network security, it will still need to be included in the master plan to ensure the plan covers all aspects of security. My reasoning for this is simple: If the facilities function is responsible for the lock and key program, you would not exclude that from the plan, and if the IT function has responsibility for this aspect of security, you must include it as well. You might not have the skills to personally test the effectiveness of these programs, but you should determine if they exist and if the IT department has had them tested by an independent review. If they have not, you should recommend that they do that on an at least an annual basis.

In order to ensure that the right protection exists for the company for the protection of these programs, you should include them in the review and make sure they have implemented the following through internal or external resources, at a minimum:

- Design and implementation of system security programs such as system intrusion deterrence, detection, and protection programs; data security systems programs; and Internet and intranet network security programs.

- Development and implementation of a disaster recovery program for the systems that includes storage of backup data at an offsite location and a contract with a company or a duplicate backup site that can quickly get the IT function operational after a disaster. This plan should include yearly tests of the recovery capability. The extent of the plan depends on how dependent the company is on their IT operation to perform their day-to-day business, but I believe it would be rare in today's world for any company not to be very heavily dependent on this resource.

- Information security awareness training for all employees that focuses on computer security requirements and hard copy information protection (clean desk policy). Although this program is usually found in companies with highly sensitive or confidential information, it is becoming more necessary in many other companies due to privacy laws and other requirements that have been introduced over the past few years. Having employees leave data lying around where anyone can see it, or even take it with them, can lead to numerous problems, from legal issues to damage to the company's reputation. The clean desk program is designed to ensure that all employees who handle sensitive or confidential data as well as customer or client information are sensitive to the need to protect that data. This means that they should have a program with requirements such as the following:

  - Clearly identify what information needs to be protected.
  - Identify who should have access to what data.

- Be aware of outsiders in the area who may be able to view the data.
- Secure the information whenever it is not in use.
- Secure all of the information, during breaks and after-hours, in locked cabinets.
- Be sensitive to where the information is printed; if the printer is in a general access area employees should immediately retrieve the printout.
- Identify how hard copy data is to be destroyed whenever it is no longer needed.
- Managers who have employees who handle this type of information should conduct periodic checks, both after-hours and during the day, to ensure the employees are complying with the requirements of the program. They should not rely on the security department to do these checks, especially if they utilize contract security personnel.
- There should be disciplinary requirements for employees who are found on a repeated basis not in compliance with the program, up to and including termination of employment. A program with no enforcement is not an effective program.

To emphasize the issue of awareness training for all employees I would cite an article published on December 6, 2007, by *Computerworld* that stated, "It's one thing to have a companywide information security policy in place. But it's a whole different ballgame to get employees to actually follow the policies, even those that are IT types. A startling number of technology professionals often knowingly ignore security policies or break them because they are unaware of them, according to a survey of more than 890 IT professionals by the Ponemon Institute LLC." It goes on to state that most employees do not understand the rules, or if they do understand them, they will ignore the rules.

SECURITY AND COMPUTER USE
STANDARDS FOR EMPLOYEES

Here is an outline of a basic computer use program that can be used by you, the consultant, to compare with what your client has implemented. If your client does not have a program, you can use this as a good starting point for them to get started.

Scope

This describes the basic computer security measures that must be followed by all XYZ employees; employees of XYZ subsidiaries, contractors, vendors, and others authorized by XYZ management to use XYZ's internal computer systems.

This includes two major sections: The first summarizes the most critical steps employees must take to protect personal workstations and to defend XYZ's systems against harmful code; the second summarizes employee responsibilities for protecting XYZ confidential information, and lists security and appropriate usage requirements in a number of other circumstances that employees are likely to encounter.

Introduction

XYZ's information and computing assets are critical to the company's success and, as a result, must be protected from loss, modification, or destruction. This document describes the basic computer security measures that must be followed by all XYZ employees, employees of XYZ subsidiaries, contractors, vendors, and others authorized by XYZ management to use XYZ's internal computer systems. **Note:** Individuals who operate multiuser systems and applications that support XYZ production business services, local and departmental services, workstations used as kiosks, or workstations made available for general use in classrooms, visitor centers, and customer briefing centers, and those supporting development processes, must also contact the information technology department for additional security control measures required for those systems and services. This document includes two major sections: The first summarizes the most critical steps employees must take to protect personal workstations provided by XYZ and to defend XYZ's system against harmful code; the second summarizes employee responsibilities for protecting XYZ confidential information, and lists security and appropriate usage requirements in a number of other circumstances that employees are likely to encounter.

FIGURE 6.1   Computer security issues are of the utmost importance in the modern business environment.

SECURITY REQUIREMENTS

Security of Your Personal Workstation

Every employee is responsible to help reduce the possibility and consequences of theft of all personal XYZ computing resources and devices and the information they contain. (see Figure 6.1)

The following security controls must be activated on all personal workstations:

- Activate a power-on password and a hard disk password in your PC's BIOS settings.
- Activate a power-on password in your desktop workstation BIOS settings.
- Set a password-protected keyboard and screen lock that is automatically activated by a period of inactivity. The inactivity time interval should be no more than 30 minutes.
- Encrypt local databases (those residing on your workstation) that contain XYZ confidential information, including mail files, archives, and database replicas. For setting power-on and hard disk drive passwords and encryption of local databases, contact the information technology department.

Note: You are not required to periodically change your workstation's power-on, hard disk, and keyboard and screen-lock passwords.

Note: Desktop workstations located in controlled access areas or in offices that are locked when unattended are not required to have power-on and keyboard and screen-lock passwords applied.

When Leaving Your Office or Work Area

If you do not work in an office that can be locked:

- Activate the password-protected keyboard and screen lock when you leave. (Do not leave the workstation exposed for the 30-minute inactivity period required for the automated screen-lock activation.) If your PC cannot otherwise be physically secured (e.g., locked in a desk drawer or filing cabinet, locked in an office, or taken with you), a cable lock must be used to secure the PC to a fixed object.

When Traveling or Working Away from Your Office or Work Area

- Keep PCs in your possession if at all possible.
- When traveling by air, do not put PCs in checked baggage, and be alert to the possibility of theft when going through security checkpoints at airports.
- PCs should not be left for an extended period of time in an unoccupied vehicle.
- If you must leave your PC in an unoccupied vehicle, then consider securing the PC to the body of the vehicle inside the trunk. Information regarding how to best secure PCs in a vehicle can be obtained from your location security department.
- If you must leave the PC in a hotel, lock it in the hotel safe if one is available.
- If a safe is not available and you have a locking cable, use that mechanism.
- If you are traveling with XYZ confidential material recorded on portable media such as paper, diskettes, or CDs, you must protect this media according to the same guidelines listed above for protecting your PC.

Note: If your PC or XYZ confidential information is stolen or lost, you must report the loss to your XYZ location security organization and your manager.

Handheld Devices

Handheld devices (personal digital assistants, RIM BlackBerry, mobile phones with data access, etc.) require physical and logical access controls if XYZ confidential or other business-sensitive data is accessed or stored by the device (see Figure 6.2). The following actions are required:

- Keep handheld devices in your possession if possible.
- Activate a power-on password and a password-controlled time-out or lock-out feature on all handheld devices supporting these security features.
- Remote synchronization via modem to move the XYZ data between the device and your workstation must go through an XYZ-authorized remote access gateway.

Computer Viruses and Other Harmful Codes

- Install and run an XYZ-approved antivirus program on your workstation.
- If you are running the standard client for e-business (C4eb), Norton AntiVirus is the approved program, and it should already be installed on the workstation. If an antivirus program is not installed on your workstation, contact the information technology department.
- If you are using Norton AntiVirus, you must also run Norton AntiVirus Live Update at least weekly to keep your antivirus signature files current. If you discover a virus, contact the information technology department.

Security Firewalls

- Install and run an XYZ-approved personal firewall program on your workstation.
- For additional information about approved firewall programs and processes, contact the information technology department.

FIGURE 6.2 Although they are useful tools, PDAs, thumb drives, and hand-held devices pose increasing threats to information security in the workplace environment.

File Sharing

You may allow other users to access or store files on your network-connected workstation only under the following conditions:

- The software that allows other users to access your files must be provided by XYZ (this is to ensure that it has been adequately checked for security holes and legal and licensing restrictions).

Note: The use of Internet-based peer-to-peer file sharing services, such as Napster or others, on XYZ workstations is prohibited unless explicitly approved by the XYZ CIO security staff.

- You must not allow any form of unauthenticated access to data or programs that are classified XYZ confidential, or to areas of your hard disk that may contain such data or programs.
- If it is necessary to allow access to areas of your hard disk that are also used for other purposes (for instance, to allow remote maintenance or update of components of the operating system), or to XYZ confidential materials, you must select either userid access control or password access control when defining the share options and the access must be granted only to a limited list of people with a need for that access (not, for instance, to anyone who authenticates with an XYZ intranet password).

For advice on how to configure your system to share files securely, contact the information technology department.

Copyright and Intellectual Property

Most information and software (programs, audio, video, data files, etc.) that is available in the public domain (including on the Internet) is subject to copyright or other intellectual property right protection. Ensure the following when obtaining material for use inside XYZ:

- Do not obtain software from such sources for use within XYZ unless express permission to do so is stated by the material owner.
- You must read and understand any software copyright restrictions. If you think that XYZ will not be able to comply with any part of the terms, do not download or use the material.
- Ensure that you comply with any expressed requirements or limitations attached to the use of such software (for example, not to be used for commercial purposes; cannot charge others for use or distribution; subject to a copyright or attribution notice being affixed to each copy; must distribute source code).
- If you are unsure about the meaning of the restrictive language or have questions about it, you should contact an XYZ attorney to review it before downloading or using the material.
- You must obtain assistance and approval from XYZ legal or intellectual property law counsel before incorporating any public domain material into a product or material XYZ intends to distribute externally.

Releasing XYZ Information into the Public Domain

Seek advice from XYZ legal counsel before uploading any XYZ software to the Internet. You must ensure that any XYZ copyright documents clearly indicate XYZ as holder of the copyright.

Protecting XYZ Information

Passwords

The password associated with a computer access userid is the primary means of verifying your identity and subsequently allowing you access to the computer and to XYZ information. For your own protection, and for the protection of XYZ's resources, you must keep your identity verification password secret and not share it with anyone else.

Note: The power-on and hard disk passwords you use to help protect against unauthorized access to your workstation are not identity verification passwords. These passwords are not associated with your identity, but rather, can be managed like door-lock keys or safe combinations. It is not a violation of security policy for you to notify your manager of these passwords.

Note: Recent changes to information protection and data privacy laws in various countries include specific requirements for the selection of secure identity verification passwords, and compliance with these password rules is a legal obligation. The XYZ password rules listed below are consistent with current international requirements.

Identity verification passwords must not be trivial or predictable, and must follow these guidelines:

- They must be at least eight characters in length.
- They must contain a mix of alphabetic and nonalphabetic characters (numbers, punctuation, or special characters) or a mix of at least two types of nonalphabetic characters.
- They must not contain your userid as part of the password. XYZ internal business systems and applications containing XYZ confidential information require you to change your password at least once every three months (90 days). In cases where the system or application does not use technical control measures to force you to change your password, it is your responsibility to comply with the password change requirement. When changing your password, you must select a new password (i.e., do not change the password to one that you used in the past).

Note: If you access computer systems that are not under XYZ control, do not select the same password on external systems that you selected for use on XYZ internal systems.

Calendars

You must ensure that your calendar can be viewed only by authorized individuals such as your department or team members or your administrative assistants.

Protecting XYZ Confidential Information

The primary requirement for protecting XYZ confidential information is that it must be protected from access or viewings except by people who have a business need to know the information. XYZ confidential information must be properly labeled. These protection guidelines should be followed:

- XYZ requires the encryption of XYZ confidential information when it is sent over the Internet, public networks, or wireless devices.
- When you store XYZ confidential information on computer systems (e.g., group Web sites or other shared data repositories), you must use software security controls to manage and limit access to the information. If you do not understand how to correctly set or use the security controls, you should ask for advice or assistance from your provider of service.
- When you store XYZ confidential information on removable computer media, such as diskettes, tapes, compact disks, and handheld storage devices, you must protect the information against theft and unauthorized access. Label the media "XYZ Confidential" and keep them in a locked area or storage device when they are not in use. Never leave them exposed in unattended areas.
- Do not store or process XYZ confidential information on systems that are not controlled by you or XYZ.
- Do not enter XYZ confidential information on Internet Web sites.
- When printing XYZ confidential information you must protect the information against theft and unauthorized viewing. (The term "printer" includes printers, plotters, and any other device used to create hard copy output.) XYZ confidential information may only be printed with the following restrictions:

- In a controlled access area, with access based on "need to know."
- In an attended XYZ printer facility, where the output is given only to its owner.
- On a printer with a capture and release facility that you control.
- On a printer that you are personally attending.
- If none of these options are available at your location, you may use a printer located within an open area in XYZ internal office space, but you must pick up your XYZ confidential printout material within 30 minutes.

Using Telephones or Fax Machines

When discussing XYZ confidential information, confirm that all participants or recipients are authorized before starting any discussion or transmitting any data.

Using Teleconferencing Systems

When chairing an XYZ confidential teleconference, confirm that all participants are authorized to participate before starting any discussion.

XYZ Internal Networks

Follow these guidelines when connected to and using XYZ internal networks, including local area networks:

- Do not misrepresent yourself (i.e., masquerade) as someone else on the network.
- Do not monitor network traffic (i.e., use a "sniffer" or similar device) without first obtaining explicit management approval and permission from the network administrator.
- Do not run security testing tools or programs against any intranet system or server, other than those that you directly control, without first obtaining explicit management approval.
- Do not add any network device that extends the XYZ infrastructure (e.g., devices functioning as switches, bridges, routers, hubs, modems, or wireless access points) for any reason without first obtaining permission from the network administrator.

- Configure workstation wireless network adapters such that the workstation will only connect to the XYZ corporate WLAN infrastructure, or to "safe" wireless networks such as your secure home network.

IMPLEMENTING A CLASSIFICATION SYSTEM

The best way for any entity to protect their information is for them to implement a classification program. As their consultant, you should determine if such a program exists within the company you are working with. If it does, you need to determine its effectiveness; if it does not, you should recommend that they implement such a program. Here is my personal outline of the basics of a good classification program for you to use as a benchmark:

Classification and Control Requirements

This defines the security classification structure for company information. It applies to classification of information in all of its forms including electronic files, databases, electronic mail, programs, and documents. Classification is a method of identifying and ensuring the protection of information through the use of measures that limit access to and prevent loss of company information. Classification is assigned commensurate with the value of the information and provides a basis for legal resource in the event of a loss.

Labeling the information with the proper classification ensures that persons exposed to it will know that it is company proprietary information, that it is classified, and that certain measures must be taken to protect it. Much of a company's information is not classified. The decision to classify particular information must be made by the originator. This decision is based on the specific content and value of such information. It is equally important that originators not overclassify information because doing so degrades the system, confuses recipients, and adds unnecessary costs to the business.

External disclosure to noncompany employees of information that has been classified can only be authorized by management. Internal disclosure to classified information should only be to those employees who have a valid "need to know" the information.

Classification Structure

The following hierarchical classification program is intended to help establish controls commensurate with the value of classified information:

- "XYZ company" Internal Use Only: Identifies information that is not highly sensitive but because of its personnel, technical, or business sensitivity is intended for use only within the company and for purposes related to the company's business endeavors. **Note**: It can be helpful here to give examples of what might be considered an Internal Use Only document. For instance, some companies will classify their internal telephone directory with this classification because they do not want outsiders to have a listing of their employees.
- "XYZ company" Confidential: Identifies information that provides the company with a competitive advantage in the marketplace or information that would be against the company's best interest to have unauthorized disclosure outside of the company. **Note**: You should give examples here of what might be classified with this classification such as customer lists, detailed product specifications, and manufacturing specifications.

Note: This is a two-tiered classification system. Some companies have implemented three-tiered and four-tiered systems to be able to add higher levels of protection for some extremely sensitive data.

Responsibilities

An originator is the creator of information and is responsible for classifying and labeling the information in compliance with this document.

Managers are responsible for ensuring the accuracy of classification decisions for information originating in their organization and must ensure that all employees (originators or recipients of information in their organization) understand the information security classification process, properly label classified information, and apply the appropriate classification controls. Managers are to ensure the return of classified information upon any employee termination or transfer. They must also ensure the appropriate transfer of ownership responsibility for all data sets and files (physical or electronic).

Employees are responsible for adhering to the classification program as set forth in this document.

Controls

Internal Disclosure
XYZ Internal Use Only
- Release to any regular employee. Supplemental or contractor employees can be given this classification if they have a need to know.

XYZ Confidential
- Release to any regular employee with a need to know. Supplemental or contractor employees can be given this classification if they have a need to know and have signed a confidential nondisclosure agreement.

External Disclosure
XYZ Internal Use Only
- Can only be released outside the company with the approval of management.

XYZ Confidential
- Can only be released outside the company with the approval of management and with the use of a confidential nondisclosure agreement.

Safekeeping and Storage
XYZ Internal Use Only
- Must be secured when not in use.
- Prevent unauthorized persons being able to view the information.
- Secure via standard security-approved lock. Workstation access should also be secured when unattended.

XYZ Confidential
- Must be secured when not in use.
- Must prevent unauthorized persons being able to view the information.
- Secure via standard security-approved lock.
- Workstation access should also be secured when unattended.
- For large amounts of or for specially designated confidential information, special bar-lock cabinets or equivalent may be required.

Travel
XYZ Internal Use Only
- Avoid carrying classified information when traveling.
- When possible and if necessary, mail the information ahead of time.

XYZ Confidential
- Avoid carrying classified information when traveling.
- When possible and if necessary, mail the information ahead of time.
- Management approval required.

Note: If traveling internationally you should seek management and legal approval to transport any technical information. The individual transporting the information must be made aware of any specific security problems in the country or countries that they intend to visit.

Reproduction
XYZ Internal Use Only
- Can be reproduced.

XYZ Confidential
- Can only be reproduced with the approval of management.

Destruction
XYZ Internal Use Only
- Must be destroyed using company-approved cross-cut shredder.

XYZ Confidential
- Must be destroyed using company-approved cross-cut shredder.

Identification
XYZ Internal Use Only
- Mark the classification on all pages.
- In electronic environment, at the beginning of the file or data set intended to be read by a person.

XYZ Confidential
- Mark the classification on all pages.
- In electronic environment, at the beginning of the file or data set intended to be read by a person.

INVESTIGATION REQUIREMENTS

Determine investigation requirements for all incidents of computer and telecommunications misuse, thefts, or compromise of proprietary information and incidents of service interruptions.

This should include forensic examination of systems involved. It is important that these investigations be conducted jointly by security and IT. Although IT professionals may be the ones with the knowledge of how to find the needed information in an electronic investigation, the security professional should have the knowledge of what needs to be done to preserve the "chain of evidence" for use in prosecution. For many companies, it is rare that they have to conduct an investigation of fraud or some other type of crime involving their computer systems. If neither the security investigator nor the IT person have had any training in preservation of data from a computer or network investigation, then they should have a contract company that has that expertise on call to assist in these types of investigations.

PROCESSING DEPARTING EMPLOYEES

The client should have a process in place to interview all key employees who are departing the company. This may include the legal department along with management and human resources. The focus areas should be the protection of whatever proprietary information they may have had knowledge of or access to, while working for the company. For many companies, employees sign a nondisclosure agreement when they start working for the company. At a minimum, these interviews would remind the employee of this contractual requirement. Many companies that are involved in research and development activities will go one step further and have the departing employee sign or initial the agreement again as a reminder of this requirement. When the departing employee has a lot of knowledge of sensitive data or company information such as strategic direction, then it is usual to have the company's legal counsel interview the departing employee to make them aware of their requirement to protect that information and the fact that they cannot use that information in their next company. These interviews can be an important factor if it becomes necessary to pursue legal action against a previous employee. In a few cases there will also be concerns about the departing employee going into competition with the current company; this must be considered as well by management and legal counsel and then addressed in writing at the exit interview.

I believe an important process for a company is to make sure they recover certain valuables such as keys, badges, and credit cards when an employee is leaving the company. The best way I have found to make this happen is for the HR department to issue a termination checklist to managers that has to be submitted when the employee is being processed out of the company. See Appendix F, "Sample Termination Checklist," as an example for your client.

INFORMATION ASSET SECURITY

Information asset security is a critical program for providing protection of those assets that, for many companies, provide them the advantage over their competition and are the foundation for their future success. Some years ago, when I was with IBM, the CEO released the following statement to all IBM employees:

"Information is not only IBM's business; it's the source of our growth. Nothing we own is more important to IBM's long-term success than the proprietary information we develop about our products and our business. IBM's future depends on all of us taking personal responsibility for protecting this information."

I believe this is just as accurate today as it was then (and probably even more so). I also believe that this is just as important to many of the smaller companies that have appeared on the horizon since that statement was made. Most of these companies are in business due to the development of only one or two new ideas or technological innovations, and if they were compromised, they would quickly be out of business. In order to have an effective information asset security program, you must start with helping the client's management team identify what these assets are, as I mentioned in the "Risk Assessment" section of this book, Chapter 2.

For your assessment, I will outline some of the basics of an information asset security program, but what I am providing here is not detailed enough for a company that currently has no program at all. If they have nothing, this outline can get them started but they will need to engage a security professional who has this unique knowledge to be sure they are implementing all of the necessary components of a quality program. As with any control program, there are costs associated with them, and a professional can help them to make sure they are implementing the controls in a cost-effective manner.

A number of factors should be considered in determining whether an information asset is valuable enough to require additional security, such as this program. The following are some of these factors:

- Financial: What costs are attached to the asset in development and manufacturing? If the information were compromised, would there be a potential loss of revenue?
- Competitive: How valuable is the asset to the company's competitive advantage? If the information were destroyed, damaged, or disclosed to competitors, what would be the result of this?
- Intangible: Would unauthorized disclosure of the information cause embarrassment to the company or destroy the confidentiality of sensitive files (e.g., personnel files, customer lists, customer ordering information)?

A basic information asset security program should outline for the management team the major responsibilities in order to comply with the program. These are designed to raise their level of awareness, to define the scope of information asset security concerns, and to clarify their responsibilities as managers:

Determine Information Assets

As a manager you are responsible for identifying, evaluating, and selecting the proper level of protection for those information assets within your area of responsibility that are of the greatest importance to the company. Additionally, you must maintain reasonable vigilance in protecting less sensitive areas.

Assign Ownership of Information Assets

In order to protect and control valuable information, some individual must be held accountable for each information asset. That person is the owner, manager, or management representative who will be responsible for ensuring the appropriate controls are specified for the asset.

When you assign ownership, you are responsible for monitoring the owner's compliance with information asset security requirements. You must also ensure that they strike a balance between protection and productivity. The lack of sufficient controls can lead to serious loss or misuse of assets, whereas implementing too many controls can reduce the efficiency and effectiveness of the business.

Approve Use of Information Assets

The manager is responsible for authorizing the use of information assets and monitoring compliance with controls to ensure that assets are used only for management-approved purposes. These assets may be in the form of data, image, voice, or text. They may be within internal systems or hard copy and they may need to be provided to vendors as well.

You must be alert to the fact that an individual's need to know and need to use may change; whenever such need changes, so must the authorization.

Educate Employees on Their Responsibilities

The manager is responsible for the education of employees on the protection of information assets. It is not enough to just tell the employees what their responsibilities are, you need to ensure that they understand their roles and effectively comply with their responsibilities. The key is to motivate employees with a positive attitude toward the information asset security policy and procedures and to involve them in the daily challenge of keeping key information assets secure. After all, protecting these assets is important to protecting their jobs.

Guarantee Effective Use of Controls

All of the company's data, voice, image, and text assets are subject to both physical and procedural controls. In order to comply with the information asset security program, the owner of the asset must determine the controls required to adequately protect the asset. Then, the manager must monitor assigned owners and authorized users to make certain that they have implemented the correct controls and that the controls are effective.

The installation and use of controls and procedures, while giving the appearance of compliance with the program, may not produce the required results. Satisfactory compliance is achieved only when controls are effectively utilized. For example, a controlled access system will not be effective if tailgating is allowed; passwords will not be effective in limiting access if the passwords are shared with others.

In order for the program to be effective, the manager should regularly seek the input of employees as a part of the information asset security awareness campaign to ensure that the controls are reasonable and usable. This will help the manager to determine if the business is best served by the controls that are in place.

Conduct Self-Assessments to Ensure Compliance

Self-assessment is the process of determining if you are in compliance with the information asset security requirements that have been determined for the assets under your management control. You should conduct a complete formal review at least once a year. However, constantly changing business situations will make it necessary to review your compliance status on a more frequent basis. Ensuring the protection of your information assets must be an integral part of the daily operation of the business.

For example: New employees are hired, existing employees leave or transfer to another part of the business, outside vendors are contracted or their contracts end, new equipment is put into the project and old equipment is phased out. All of these situations must drive the manager to examine their effect on the security of the information assets under your control. Achieving compliance requires an ongoing awareness, periodic self-assessment, and careful adjustment of controls whenever events such as these occur or whenever a weakness in your plan is uncovered.

The annual self-assessment should include evaluating all responsibility assignments, monitoring authorized users and owners, reviewing and validating asset controls, identifying exposures and noncompliance situations, making risk assessments for exposures, and evaluating existing compliance plans for risks that were previously identified.

Assess and Accept Risks

Risk assessment is the process used to evaluate and document an identified exposure or noncompliance situation as it pertains to an information asset, in order to decide whether to fix the problem, reduce the exposure, or accept the risk. If the manager decides to fix the problem or to partially fix the problem, he or she should document the plan and it should be passed on to upper management for their knowledge. The plan should include the details of how it will be fixed or reduced and the timeframe for achieving the resolution.

For assets where you reduce, but not eliminate, the exposure and for those assets where you decide to just accept the risk, you should prepare a risk acceptance document to be forwarded to upper management for their approval. The document should specify the reasons for the decision and outline which compliance options were considered before coming to that conclusion. It is always prudent to consider the cost of compliance or eliminating a risk, and you should not spend more to accomplish this than the loss or compromise of the asset would incur.

Respond Decisively to Exposures, Misuse, or Loss of Information Assets

It is always possible that assets will be compromised no matter how effectively you implement your asset security controls. Problems may also be discovered through your self-assessment, monitoring, and risk assessment process. Any of these situations must be given the immediate attention of the manager of the asset who is responsible for taking prompt and effective corrective action.

When an exposure, misuse, or loss of an information asset is discovered, it is essential that the situation be reported to upper management and security immediately. The risk assessment process should also be followed to document what actions the manager is taking to deal with the situation. We must be decisive in dealing with any compromise of an information asset.

Assign Custodial Authority and Responsibility

As a manager of the company, you may be the owner of an information asset and may, during the course of business operations, transfer custody of that information. The individual who is given possession will be the custodian and will be responsible for protecting the asset while it is in their custody. The custodian is accountable for your information asset and is responsible for ensuring that all applicable control procedures and processes are followed. If additional controls are warranted during this period, they should be specified to the custodian prior to the transfer of the asset. You must include the authorized custodian in your regular program of monitoring to ensure they meet all compliance requirements while they have custodial responsibility.

SYSTEM MISUSE

One additional item that I'd like to discuss is the misuse of information assets. This is an area of concern I frequently hear about when I conduct reviews since there are times when security is asked to be involved in conducting investigations involving this problem. In my opinion, the prevention of this problem is not a security program. It is a management problem and is usually focused on by the HR and IT departments. In many companies, the security organization is not even involved in the investigations of these issues. The primary problem is that some employees or others who have access to the company's computer and network assets will use them for their own personal use. This is not an employee sending the occasional personal email or anything that minor; this is an employee using company assets to run his or her own company on the side or something else just as extreme. This not only wastes computer and network assets, it's also a misuse of the company's time. Most companies address this issue in a document such as a business conduct guideline or in a policy statement for their employees.

If this is an issue in the company you are working with, advise them to make sure there is a written policy that tells employees this is wrong and then make sure the IT organization runs programs periodically to determine if they have a problem in this area. If a problem is detected, I personally believe the security investigator should always be involved in any type of investigation, even if he or she is just overseeing what is being done by IT, HR and management.

SUMMARY — INFORMATION PROTECTION

There are a number of optional control requirements that may be implemented to provide for the protection of an information asset. I typically recommend to my clients that they start with the development and implementation of a classification system, such as I outlined previously in this chapter. By having such a system they can communicate control requirements simply by placing the classification on the document or electronic file. I usually recommend two classifications, XYZ Confidential and XYZ

Internal Use Only. The Internal Use Only classification label simply communicates that the information cannot be released outside the company without the approval of a manager or whoever the company designates as the control point for that type of information. This might be used on an internal telephone directory that the company doesn't want "headhunters" to have possession of. The Confidential classification would communicate more stringent controls in addition to the fact that it cannot be released outside of the company. If the company utilizes part-time employees or contractors then there may be a control that says they cannot have access to confidential information, or if they do then they have to sign a special nondisclosure agreement. There should also be requirements that specify optional physical storage requirements such as the use of a double-locked file cabinet, or not leaving the information in plain sight when you are away from it. For electronic data they might want to specify encryption requirements, or that the information cannot be placed on a laptop computer. Some companies require even more strict requirements such as the use of "DO NOT COPY" paper for any hard copies of a classified document.

There are numerous controls that may be used, but the primary focus of the program is to ensure that each and every employee who comes in contact with this critical company information is immediately alerted to the importance of protecting the information. The use of the classification should communicate a basic level of controls that are required for all company assets that have that classification; however, an owner of a particular asset may want to have even more discretionary controls put in place for the asset they own. If so, they need to communicate those requirements to everyone who has access to that asset.

Of course a program of this nature will only be effective if all employees are regularly trained on the importance of the program and the necessity of ensuring that only those people who have a legitimate need to know have access to the asset. Many assets can be lost simply by the unintentional disclosure by an employee who doesn't understand the importance of the asset to the company. To prevent this, employees must be reminded often of their value and the need to provide the appropriate protection.

GOVERNMENT REGULATIONS

In addition to advising your client on the protection of their own assets, there are also government requirements for the protection of their client information and other regulations. Each industry has its own set of regulations, and I will not attempt to define all of them. A couple of the more common regulations are the following:

- The Sarbanes-Oxley Act of 2002 (Pub. L. No. 107-204, 116 Stat. 745), also known as the Public Company Accounting Reform and Investor Protection Act of 2002 and commonly called SOX.
- The American Health Insurance Portability and Accountability Act (HIPAA) of 1996 is a set of rules to be followed by doctors, hospitals, and other health care providers. HIPAA took effect on April 14, 2006. HIPAA helps ensure that all medical records, medical billing, and patient accounts meet certain consistent standards with regard to documentation, handling, and privacy. In addition, HIPAA requires that all patients be able access their own medical records, correct errors or omissions, and be informed how personal information is shared or used. Other provisions involve notification of privacy procedures to the patient.

My message to you is that you need to be sure you are aware of all government regulations that are applicable to your client's industry before you begin your assessment work with them.

7

Conducting an Assessment of the Security Organization

This is one area of the review that will be difficult for an inside security professional to conduct impartially. This is especially true if the person conducting the assessment has had limited experience with other security organizations or other industries. Therefore, if you are an in-house security professional conducting the review, I would strongly recommend that you bring in a consultant for this aspect of the review. If that option is not available, then talk to other security professionals that you network with from other companies and see if you can get one or two of them to meet with you to either assist with this aspect of the review or at least to go over the results of your review and challenge your findings. Whatever you can do to get an objective opinion from outside the organization will be helpful and is, I believe, essential.

- Reporting Structure
  - Where does the director of security report? Legal, facilities, administration
  - How is the security group organized? Levels of management, shift supervisors

- Skills
  - Does the director of security have the appropriate skills and contacts? Is the director knowledgeable about prevention programs and security technology? Involved with other directors

of security? Does he or she have contacts with police: local, state, federal?

- Does the security organization have the right skills matrix? People and business management capabilities, technical and systems knowledge, investigative skills, educational skills?

- Staffing
  - Are the security officers proprietary, contract, or both? Are there enough officers or too many? Are the uniformed officers disciplined? Do they project the proper image? Do the uniforms match the environment? Are supervisors experienced?
  - Has management made a decision about "armed" versus "unarmed" security personnel?

REPORTING STRUCTURE

When reviewing the reporting structure, it is important to understand that there is no right answer. It is very dependent on the company's general organization. I have seen situations where CSOs or directors of security report to many different areas of the business. A critical factor is that they must report at a high level in the business, typically no more than two levels below the CEO, but preferably only one level below. If the business has a high volume of investigative activity, I believe it can be very valuable for security to report into the legal function. This provides increased protection of the investigative information when it is prepared for an attorney and the primary client for the investigations is the legal counsel. Of course, the CSO or director of security does not have to report to the company attorney to get that protection; it can be standard practice to label all investigative reports "Prepared for an Attorney" and have them sent to the company attorney as a matter of practice (see Figure 7.1).

Many smaller companies, however, do not have an in-house attorney; their legal work is performed by outside counsel. If this is the case with your client, you should understand that there will be costs involved in having all investigative reports go through the outside attorney, and it may be preferable to send them only the more important reports. In this way, if the company is sued and must process a subpoena that calls for all records associated with the case, the information that was labeled and prepared for the company's attorney can be excluded. This provides a measure of protection for the company.

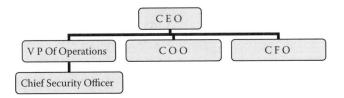

FIGURE 7.1 A typical corporate organizational structure. Here the CSO reports to the VP of Operations. Wherever the CSO reports into, it should be at a high level in the business.

Another consideration deals with the extent of the conflict of alliances. For example, if the security function reports to the facilities engineering function, it is possible and even probable that the person running the organization has far more knowledge of the facilities side of the business than the security side. As a result, this person may tend to give more credence to what the engineering group wants than what the security group needs or wants. This can be difficult to determine, but evidence often lies with the budgeting process. If historical information demonstrates that the security function routinely suffers larger cuts or smaller increases to their budget than facilities, this can demonstrate the problem with having the security function reporting to that organization. However, for obvious political reasons, it will be extremely difficult for someone inside the security organization to make that case as opposed to a consultant.

The same scenario can exist with any organization where security reports to such as legal, administration, or finance. What's Important to determine is whether the security organization is getting the upper management support that it needs. That does not mean that whenever security asks for more money, it gets it. This simply means that security is not singled out by management to make more budget or headcount reductions than any other organization.

THE SECURITY ORGANIZATION'S STRUCTURE

The review of the security organization's own structure is intended to make sure that several issues have been addressed. First, you want to be sure that they are not "top heavy," meaning that they have too many people in management positions. Besides adding extra cost to the business, this also has an effect on how well the organization operates. For example, if a proprietary guard force operates on three shifts, is there a shift supervisor and a shift manager for each shift? If so, that is probably too many managers unless the security force is extremely large. For smaller forces, one manager and five supervisors, which includes one supervisor for each shift during the week and two supervisors for weekend coverage, should be sufficient. A large force might have two managers, one that covers the off shifts and one for day shift.

In addition to the cost issue, the problem with too many managers is that every manager added to the mix also adds deviations in the operation and contributes to inconsistencies in the way the shifts function. This issue is usually referred to as "span of control," which highlights how many people each manager in the company is responsible for. If you feel that the organization has too many or even too few managers, you can discuss the issue with the HR director to get a sense of how many people most managers in the company manage to see if your sense is right or not and if what is happening within the security organization is consistent with the rest of the company.

The other possibility, having too few managers within the security organization, is actually more probable and can also lead to problems. This can cause a higher turnover rate with the guard force because too few managers means insufficient time for them to properly deal with all the personnel issues that arise with security officers, especially when there is a proprietary force. It will also help determine how much time management has to spend on analyzing and managing the organization's business operations. This can be alleviated by having good administrative staff that can be utilized for this type of work report to the manager. Before you decide there are too few managers, gain a complete understanding of how the staff are used to supplement the business work effort. If the client is utilizing a contract security force then there is probably only one site manager assigned to the force. If that is the case, you should determine how much time branch management spends assisting that manager to ensure that all personnel issues needing attention are promptly and appropriately handled.

MIXED SECURITY FORCES

Some companies have both proprietary and contract security officers. In many situations, this is an appropriate solution to ensure that certain tasks are performed properly and that important decisions are made correctly, while also providing the needed security at lower costs. This structure is also, I believe, the best model for most medium to large companies. It is the best model for smaller companies as well, in my opinion; however, they frequently cannot afford the extra expense of a proprietary person on staff. I believe there should always be at least one security professional on duty who is an employee of the company and has the knowledge to properly direct the contract force. In larger companies, I believe there should be at least one proprietary professional security person at each major company location. If the facilities in question operates on more than one shift, I believe there should be an in-house security professional on duty whenever they are in operation. This could mean as many as six proprietary security people on staff at a location, just to oversee the security guard force. I believe in this structure because, in the security business there are always situations that develop that require some immediate decisions to be made, decisions that cannot always wait for a call to someone to see what they want to do. Some of these decisions can have a major effect on the company both reputation-wise and, sometimes, financially. I prefer to have those kinds of situations handled by an in-house experienced security professional who always has the best interest of the company at heart and who would be more aware of how the company wants the situation handled than someone from the contract company. Additionally, it is always a benefit to have a professional in-house security person to monitor the performance of the contract force to be sure you are getting the service you are paying for. Although many people think they know enough about security to perform this monitoring effort without a security professional on staff, you will frequently find that they really do not have the necessary knowledge to understand what is and is not being done well by the contract force.

SEPARATION OF DUTIES

Another primary concern when you have both proprietary and contract security people is to make sure there is the proper separation of duties between the two forces so there is no confusion about who is in-house and who is contract, and no industrial relations issues. My primary concern as it relates to industrial relations issues deals with unionization. If you have a mixed force of proprietary and contract officers where the number of contract officers is a larger percentage of the force, they can vote to unionize the force and that vote, in some situations, would include the proprietary officers, especially if you cannot distinguish between them based on their duties. For example, they may have decided that the security control center operation will be handled by the propriety force, whereas patrols and posts are handled by the contract force. Some companies choose to do this so they do not have to constantly retrain operators due to higher turnover rates that might exist with the contract force, and that is a good separation as it is very clear who has which tasks to perform. But it would not be good if it were done that way on first and second shift but third shift only had contract officers, including operating the control center. I believe the best module is to have an in-house security professional on duty who handles all of the professional security duties. This person would not wear a uniform and they would be responsible for handling various administrative duties such as being the administrator for the access control system, conducting investigations, and dealing with employees or tenants who have some security-related concerns. I have seen a number of variations of mixing proprietary and contract, and they are all workable solutions as long as the separation of duties is made clear.

OTHER ISSUES

Other issues related to hiring practices need to be examined. On several occasions, I have seen, situations where the in-house security organization hires temporary officers to supplement their guard force. This is not a problem initially, but then they migrate to where they use this process as a sort of screening process for hiring permanent employees. This leads to a number of problems, especially if they use this process on a regular basis. The main problem is the industrial relations issue, whereby the temporary force can demonstrate that they are part of the operation due to this hiring practice and they can be included in unionization votes. There are also morale and other issues associated with this practice as it becomes the standard hiring practice.

The use of a temporary security work force is a good solution for handling peak workload issues such as a special event that requires more people than normal. It can be less expensive than having many of the regular officers work overtime to cover the event and avoid problems that occur when people have to work too many hours in a short period of time. My personal preference for dealing with peak workload issues is to use a contract force to cover those situations because the hiring process for temporary security officers is just as expensive as hiring permanent officers. Using a contract force is actually less expensive and less taxing on the management team and HR team. If the client utilizes a contract force primarily and has situations that require extra officers to cover some events, you should check to see if the contract company has extra people that they use to cover those events: people who have had site orientation training for the client's site and who have received the entire basic security officer training.

SECURITY SKILLS

When evaluating the skills matrix of the security organization, you must first gain insight into the workload balance of the group. Workload will normally be distributed between the following disciplines:

- Physical security
- Executive protection
- Information protection
- Crisis management and emergency planning
- Investigation management

You may encounter locations where some of these disciplines are not included or where other tasks, such as the locksmith operation or other duties, are also part of the security function. You may also find that one person has responsibility for multiple disciplines, but whatever the situation you encounter, these responsibilities must be addressed by someone at the facility if the client is to have a complete program. They typically break down like this:

- Physical security will include skills related to the following:
  - Managing the security guard force
  - Managing the electronic systems
  - Incident and emergency response
- Executive protection programs might include the following:
  - Managing the executive(s) drivers and their training
  - Providing armed protection and escort
  - Traveling with the executive(s) for their protection
  - Screening packages
  - Reviewing their home protection status
- The information protection skills will differ widely depending on the type of business but may include the following:

- Auditing the IT organization for administrative and system protocols and their implementation
- Reviewing the IT and other organization disaster recovery plans
- Conducting or managing the clean desk policy (making sure confidential or sensitive information is protected)
- Providing advice to employees on how to classify information
- Overseeing the destruction of confidential information
- Crisis management skills would include the following:
  - Being responsible for updating the emergency plans
  - Conducting periodic scenario tests with the management team
  - Conducting periodic scenario tests with the in-house first responders and with the community's first responders
  - Managing site evacuation drills
- Investigative management would include the following:
  - Managing and conducting investigations
  - Analyzing data on a monthly basis to do trend analysis and provide advice on security strategies to reduce or prevent incidents
  - Interfacing with law enforcement to keep updated on all criminal behavior in the area, terrorist intelligence information, and so on

The skill of contract management also needs to be reviewed. This may fall within each of the disciplines or there may be an administrative person in the organization who has that responsibility.

Additionally, someone will have responsibility for security awareness and education programs for the site populations. This may be one person who handles all of the different programs or someone within each discipline who does the programs for that specific discipline.

It is also important that the security function has good people management skills as well. If there is a contract force, someone in that organization should be charged with the responsibility of managing them. Regardless of whether the security staff is in-house, contract, or a mixture of both, it is always important to get a sense of whether the people are well managed. This affects the morale and the effectiveness of the organization and ultimately it affects the officers' turnover rate.

You also need to determine if the contract company is providing any skills other than the standard security officers and then determine if those skills are adequate. It is fairly common for companies to have the contract force provide extra people to do administrative work and other skills. This is not a problem as long as they do their jobs effectively and have been given the proper training.

Once you have determined which skills are required for this organization, you need to assess if the people doing those jobs have the right skills and if the proper amount of resources have been allocated to the different skills, based on workload. This can be difficult to determine while conducting the assessment, but the best approach is to ascertain if their performance is satisfactory. For example, as it relates to people management skills, I would suggest asking questions about what type of training the supervisory (including shift supervisors) and managerial members of the organization are given on a routine basis and see if any of area of that education applies to people management skills. You should also inquire about employee recognition programs within the organization. This is also the area where I typically look at turnover rates as well. Turnover is usually a consideration relative to contract guard forces, but I believe it can also be a problem with proprietary forces, and if it is, it may be a predictor of bad people management skills and is the ultimate testament to their people management performance. For each of the skill areas, you need to test to see if the incumbent is qualified.

EVALUATING THE SECURITY OFFICERS

I would begin by reviewing the skill level of the security officers. Of course, you should start by evaluating how well they perform the basic responsibilities as a security officer in the areas of conducting patrols, standing posts, and interacting with the site population. But, beyond that you need to understand that the company management, employees, and tenants all make judgments about the security of the facility based on what can sometimes be a 30-second encounter with uniformed security officers. When these people see two or three officers standing off to the side talking to each other, they may evaluate that encounter by observing, "We must have too many security people if they have time to just stand around and chat with each other." When a male security officer is standing at the receptionist desk chatting with the female receptionist, they assume he is just flirting with her and therefore he has too much time on his hands or he is not "doing his job." When an officer's uniform is dirty or does not fit properly, they make a judgment that the security organization is not very professional. Although you may logically understand that none of these situational judgments are valid, you need to be aware that they are, nonetheless, very real and can undermine customer satisfaction including how confident people feel about the security organization, and even impact budget approvals and staffing levels. In the world of security, "perception is reality." As you conduct your review you need to ascertain how the site population perceives the security organization. Does security management cover perception issues in their training courses of the security officers? Do the shift supervisors focus on these types of issues as they observe their people in operation? You then need to review all of the training records to ensure that the officers are receiving the standard training as reviewed earlier.

EVALUATING THE SHIFT SUPERVISORS

Shift supervisors typically provide the day-to-day management of the security officers but are rarely given any training in people management skills. In many operations they are at the site, managing the security force without any on-site supervision from the security manager. As you look at turnover at the site, you should determine if one of the shifts or shift supervisors has a significantly larger number of turnovers than the other shifts. (It is also important to note whether or not the security management has done any analysis of this sort.) You need to review what training these people are given to determine if it is adequate for the job they are asked to do. I have found that there are people who are "natural born leaders," but most are not and they need to be taught the right way to manage people and a business operation. Many times good people get put into the wrong job and then fail because no one teaches them how to do it. It is also true that some people will never make a good supervisor or manager because they just do not interact with people well enough, and unfortunately, some just cannot be taught how to overcome or compensate for the lack of that skill. The role of the shift supervisor is key to the day-to-day performance of the security officer ranks and, therefore, of vital importance to your evaluation of the existing operation.

EVALUATING THE CSO OR DIRECTOR OF SECURITY

Probably the most important function to evaluate, and sometimes the hardest to determine the skill level, is the CSO or director of security. This individual does not need to be an expert in all aspects of the operation, but should have a reasonable level of knowledge of each discipline. This is especially true when it comes to technology. People hired from law enforcement may not have any background in security technology. This does not mean they cannot learn it, but if they may not know how much they do not know and this can be a very real problem for the organization. I have seen situations where an individual is hired based on his reputation from a previous job, but all of the skills needed were not a part of his previous work. If this is the case, you should recommend intense education be provided for this person in as short a time as possible to get him or her ready to properly manage the organization quickly. I have also encountered problems where individuals have been in the job for a very long time. They continue to manage and operate the security organization, "the way they always have done it." Sometimes they resist change, and sometimes they have not kept up with technological changes.

One of the primary skill requirements of this position is the ability to communicate well with the company executives, functional counterparts, the occupants of the facility, and the security organization itself. Additionally, this person needs to be able to develop and maintain good relationships with external law enforcement and other organizations. Some contend that if the individual does not have these skills now, it would take far too long for them to gain those skills without becoming a detriment to the organization in the meantime. I fully support that theory and have seen cases where the security organization's ability to accomplish its mission suffered due to the lack of good communication skills. If the person in command of the security function cannot develop the relationships and the respect of the company executives, a lack of funding and resources for the organization may result.

One aspect that plays a major role in the skills of the CSOs or directors of security is their business knowledge. I do not mean their ability to just manage a budget. While important, that is not business knowledge. The leader of the security organization is not just responsible for protecting the employees, property, and reputation of the business, but also for creating an safe and secure environment that allows the business to flourish. The CSO or director of security cannot do this effectively without being a knowledgeable business person whose knowledge goes beyond just the security industry. I first got into the security business after I had worked for IBM for 12 years. I had worked in manufacturing, administration, marketing, system engineering, computer programming, tooling engineering, and engineering records management. I was asked to take over the first-shift security management job primarily because of my project management skills and my technical knowledge. The facility was expanding and they needed someone to manage the expansion and upgrade of the security technology. As I learned about the security processes, I found it interesting that almost no one in the organization at that location had worked in any other area of IBM except for security. Because of that, I learned that they thought their most important accomplishment was to stop bad things from happening or to catch the bad guys. Although this was not necessarily bad, that thought process sometimes clashed with the overall success of the business.

After a couple of years I was promoted to site security manager'. Once I reached that level I began to make some necessary changes to the organization. First, I would not promote anyone into a security management position unless he or she had experience in some other aspect of the business. Therefore, when my shift supervisors came to me for career guidance on how to get into security management, I advised them to first work in manufacturing or administration for a minimum of one year. Then they would be able to be promoted to a security management job. Next I looked for opportunities to bring new skills into the organization, so I brought someone from HR into a first-level management job as well as others. Although this was not popular at first, eventually the organization began to see how we should operate differently than before by considering what was best for the business, not just what was best for the security organization. My favorite line during those days was, "IBM is not in the security business, it is in the business of selling hardware and software and business solutions to its customers." I would explain that if what we did as an organization did not further that objective, then we were doing something wrong. At a major site like that most people do not get a clear view of the "ultimate" customer because they are too focused on the immediate customers, which were the other IBM functions at the site. However, by having the security people work in those other functions, they began to see beyond their own objectives and focus more on understanding their internal customer's needs. I believe that moved them a step closer to understanding the needs of the corporation as a whole and the "real" customer.

To understand the requirements of the CSO or director of security job more completely I recommend that you review ASIS International's "Chief Security Officer Guideline." You can find it on their Web site, www.asisonline.org. There have been times when I have had to recommend that the person be replaced because I felt that person was just too unqualified for the position. That can be tough, but it is part of the job.

EVALUATING THE OTHER SECURITY POSITIONS

Other positions can be difficult to ascertain if the incumbent is qualified as well. Depending on your client's operation there may be other positions such as first-level managers, administrative support staff, and so on. One of the more key staff positions is the investigator's position, so I will elaborate on how to evaluate that skill. For instance, you cannot make a judgment about the investigator based solely on his or her solved case rate. In fact, there are times when I have made decisions to simply correct a situation that existed in order to stop losses from occurring, knowing full well that by doing so, we probably would not be able to "catch the bad guy." However, it is important that you review the unsolved case file to see exactly what steps the investigator has taken to close them. For example, I once had a case where an influx of used computer parts was hitting the market in a city where one of our major facilities was located. The initial investigation did not uncover the origin of the parts or who was selling them. The company had contacted the local police, who worked with it on the investigation but had not concluded anything of significance. Later, we went through all the open case files at the location and found an interesting anomaly. At this facility a case had been opened that suggested parts were missing from the reclamation area. This was where computers that had been traded in or returned were sent to remove parts that were reusable or needed to be disposed of in a special manner. Some people aren't aware of this, but there are a number of computer parts that are made using precious metals such as gold and platinum. You and I cannot really remove those metals from the parts; it takes a special process, but for the manufacturer it can save them some money by implementing this process. Once we learned of this concern we began working with the assumption that this could be the source of the influx of used parts, so we started with the controls around the reclamation operation. We found the controls to be inadequate. Apparently, no one was overly concerned about the security in this area because it was only used computers that were being stripped.

One of the decisions that has to be made from time to time in investigations of this type is, "Do we need to catch the bad guys or do we need to just stop the problem?" You can spend a lot of time and resources on investigations; sometimes it can be significantly more than the losses you are suffering. We believe this was the situation here so we decided to just fix the problem. We implemented additional business controls and procedural steps to make sure we had adequate accountability for what came into the area and what went out. Then we implemented the use of a controlled access and egress door coupled with a jewelry-level metal detector for all personnel entering and leaving the area. Because several of the people working in this area were part-time employees, we also had them replaced with different employees over time. This resolved the used parts problem as the flow of those parts immediately reduced to normal levels; the concerns over the amount of parts and material out of the area were also addressed. No, we did not catch the bad guys in this case, but we did resolve the problem and the solution probably cost the company less than a full-scale investigation would have.

Performing the proper analysis on open and closed cases can be extremely beneficial in determining changes that may be needed in your physical security strategy or changes to best utilize the officer tours and other procedural changes. It can also provide insight into your investigator's capabilities as well. I have had problems with investigators over the years where they did not want to "waste" their time with the simpler, more mundane cases. They wanted to work the "important" cases. As I explained to them, some cases might seem mundane to them, but not to the victim. And the victim is as much the client as the company is. Also the volumes of cases are typically the simpler ones, and it is important to resolve as many of them as possible. Data analysis can also reveal repeated patterns of activity, which can be a great tool to solve cases, so you must review just how extensively the investigator is using the tools that are available.

The best approach to assessing many of these other positions is to ask the CSO or director of security to provide a synopsis of personnel resumés for each member of the security staff. Then, as you have these individuals review the processes they use and the results they achieve, you can get a reasonable feel for their effectiveness. For those you are unsure of, dig a little deeper into their area. If you find that they are not very effective, you can discuss that with the CSO or director of security to see if he or she agrees with your assessment.

STAFFING LEVELS

Next you need to review staffing to determine if the correct number of resources has been allocated to the different tasks that need to get done. Many times when situations develop within a company that drive an increase in people in one area of the security function; for example, an increase in investigative cases that requires more investigators to resolve the cases within a reasonable length of time. Unfortunately, the organization is not always provided with an increase in headcount to match these situations, and they reallocate resources from other areas of the business. This is an appropriate measure as long as the effectiveness of the other areas is not reduced to an unacceptable level. Again, you need to start with the information you have already gathered about the group's workload balance. As I indicated earlier, workload will normally be distributed between the disciplines of physical security, executive protection, information protection, crisis management, emergency planning, and investigation management. Now that you have reviewed the skills of the people doing these various jobs, you already have insight as to whether a particular area is over- or understaffed. Now you need to determine the degree to which this over- or understaffing condition exists for each discipline in order to formulate your recommendations in this area.

You will need to look at whether the security officers are proprietary, contract, or both. Again, this is an area where there is no right or wrong answer; you just need to determine if a good decision has been made and if it has been documented. If documented as a strategy, are they adhering to that strategy? You need to determine the following:

- Are there enough officers, too many, or too few?
- Are the uniformed officers disciplined?
- Do they project the proper image for the corporate culture?
- Do the uniforms match the environment?
- Are the supervisors experienced?

The evaluation of whether there are enough officers or too many can be complicated. For some locations there are a certain number of fixed posts and a roving officer or two. Their needs are consistent on a daily basis with very little deviation. The typical concern that needs to be addressed at these locations is whether there are enough officers on duty to effectively respond to and contain any potential emergency situation. Some businesses have enlisted the assistance of other employees for these situations, such as the maintenance staff. I see no problem with that approach as long as these people are given the proper training, which includes conducting periodic scenario testing. You will need to verify that that training has been given and is updated on a routine basis.

However, at some locations where varying changes occur on a routine basis, there may be a need to have more officers on duty than you would expect. These locations staff to the number of officers required at the peak time, which means they have extra officers on duty for the other times. When this situation exists and I find it to be appropriate, I examine the tasks given to these extra officers during the excess periods. For example, they can check the security equipment to ensure it is functioning properly, or check fire extinguishers to ensure their inspections are not due. To properly examine the requirements for the number of officers, review the post orders and then compare that information with the environment. If you believe there are too many or too few officers on duty, discuss that with security management to gain an understanding of their reasoning and determine if that makes sense.

Additionally, you need to balance the officer requirements with the technology currently installed. The use of access control, alarm, and CCTV systems will reduce the numbers of required duty officers to some extent. However, some facilities may need to have some access control doors open or unlocked during certain hours due to a high level of visitor traffic and may want an officer posted at those doors during these times. When you find these kinds of anomalies, you need to determine if they make good business and security sense. The most common situation you will encounter is that officer assignments are being done that way because "that's the way we have always done it." One of the major contributions an outsider can make is to look at the current setup and ask the right questions such as, "Why are you doing it that way?" or "Have you considered doing this way?" Just as people get into a "comfort zone," so do businesses and security operations.

ARMED VERSUS UNARMED OFFICERS

This final area of review for this sector can be an emotional subject, to say the least. I can tell you that there is disagreement within the security community on this issue. There are those who feel it is important to have at least some armed officers onsite to counter an armed attacker, such as in a workplace violence case or to counter an armed holdup attempt where money or other valuables are at risk. In most cases, I believe weapons bring problems, not solutions. Having a shoot-out occur on a business property almost guarantees that someone will get hurt or killed, and frequently the victim is an innocent bystander. Furthermore, even if the armed security officer is well trained in this area, the perpetrator may not be.

I will agree there is a need for armed officers in some situations or environments. For example, I believe there is ample justification for armed officers when a valid threat has been made. However, my preference in that situation is that either the police be requested to provide this protection or that off-duty police officers be hired to provide the service. An environment such as a bank or a nuclear power plant certainly justifies having armed officers as well. I do not recognize many normal business environments where I believe it is better to have armed security officers. I believe the best approach is to train the officers in de-escalation techniques and then to have an emergency plan that outlines specific threat situations where armed off-duty police officers are brought in to provide increased security for the site.

What is vital for the sake of this review is that you determine whether this decision has been formally made by the client. Has it been documented along with the reasoning for the decision and has that documentation been reviewed by the company legal counsel and the executives to be sure everyone is in agreement? If it has not, this work must be performed and included as a part of the Security Master Plan to ensure that it is reviewed on a periodic basis by the appropriate people.

8

Determining What Prevention, Crisis Management, and Recovery Programs Exist

As I discussed in Chapter 2 on the risk assessment process, most CEOs, CFOs, and HR directors may not know all of the risks because some of these risks may not have materialized before. This situation exists for a number of the risks that face businesses and institutions. If good programs are not in place to obtain the information about the risks, the management team may be oblivious to their existence. The following list of prevention and recovery programs outlines the kinds of programs that can be very helpful to determine when new risks have developed or existing risks have increased and how to prevent the problems from escalating. When a problem does occur, as some inevitably will, the right recovery program, one that has been well planned and practiced, can get the company back into operation as quickly as possible.

PREVENTION AND RECOVERY PROGRAMS

- Business intelligence
- Crisis management planning
- Corporate reputation crisis planning
- Corporate investigations: fraud, financial, criminal, computer, and network

- Due diligence processes
- Emergency response planning and testing
- Business continuity and disaster recovery
- Executive protection program
- Internal audit and business controls
  - Monitoring programs
  - Fraud and integrity programs
- Pre-employment screening and drug testing
- Risk assessment process (annually)
- Security systems and procedures
- Terrorism and bioterrorism
- Workplace violence prevention program

BUSINESS INTELLIGENCE INFORMATION

The first item on my list deals with business intelligence. Most medium to large companies will have a dedicated department whose job is to gather information on competitors and to analyze any available information relative to their business. With some smaller companies, this task might be done as a part of the marketing department; some executives will be involved in compiling this type of information, although not necessarily in as formal a structure. The majority of that information is not pertinent to the security organization; however, some information would give light to some of the risks that the business is dealing with. It is important that you find out how your client gathers this information and whether or not anyone reviews the data with the idea of understanding its risk impact.

CRISIS MANAGEMENT PLANNING

This is probably the most important aspect of this chapter because it is normally the direct responsibility of the CSO or director of security, and therefore I will spend more time reviewing and discussing it. It is unfortunate, but you will find many situations where a company has taken the time to develop a crisis management plan and then they just put it on the shelf or in a drawer, never to be seen again. About the only part of the plan that most organizations will test on a regular basis is the evacuation plan. Of course, most jurisdictions require that they be tested on at least an annual basis. Unfortunately, even this aspect of the plan is only tested at

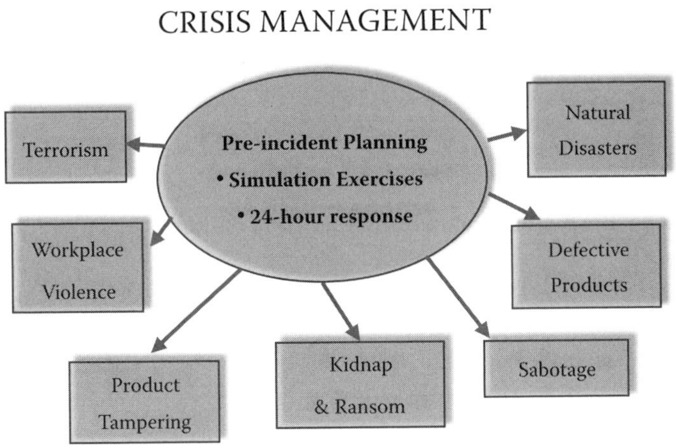

CRISIS MANAGEMENT

FIGURE 8.1   This diagram illustrates some of the types of events that can constitute crisis situations.

a basic level. They are typically tested to satisfy a fire alarm, but no other alternative evacuation needs are tested. For example, in a workplace violence situation you may need to have all of the building evacuated except for one floor or location (if the shooter is in that location). Or in a campus environment you may need for one building to evacuate into an adjoining building. I usually recommend to my clients that they need to develop as many alternative evacuation notices as possible and have them written out ahead of time. The last thing you need is for the person making the announcement to get nervous and say the wrong thing or to just make people panic based on a nervous voice. If at all possible you should even go to the level of having the different announcements pre-recorded and have the system set up so the operator just has to play the right tape or pre-recorded message.

As an example, we once had a problem in one of our buildings in a campus-type setting; the layout of the area in question was three buildings that were side by side and interconnected. (see Figure 8.2)

It was the middle of winter in the Northeast, so we did not want to send the people outside unless we absolutely had to. The problem was in the middle of Building B, and it was decided to evacuate the west side of the building into Building A and the east side into Building C. My immediate concern about the announcement was that it would be too confusing for people to know which way to go. I suggested that we just have

FIGURE 8.2 Evacuation example: three adjacent buildings in a row.

Building B evacuate by the closest building exit and then have our people send them into a safe building from the outside. I had a new boss at the time who was convinced his way was best so he decided to make the announcement himself. (I think he thought I was being too resistive to new ideas.) His announcement was made but he made a slight mistake, he told the occupants of Building C to evacuate to the west and east. We advised him of the error and he immediately made another announcement telling them that the first announcement was wrong, the occupants of Building A should evacuate to the west and east. We advised him of his new mistake and he turned it over to me to handle. At this point I sent every available officer and emergency technician to the building to direct everyone away from the incident. After that incident, my new boss understood my concern about keeping it simple and how a person who makes announcements "off the top of his or her head" can make the problem much worse.

CORPORATE REPUTATION CRISIS PLAN

In some cases you will find a plan that addresses response to issues that can affect the reputation of the company contained within the crisis management plan, along with all potential disasters. However, in most cases it will be maintained by the communications function, if it exists at all, because the response to a reputation crisis will have the primary components of communications to the stockholders and the public. If it is a valid plan, some thought will have been given to possible scenarios that could have caused the problem with responses planned for each. Your primary objective is to find out if the plan exists and to ensure that it is at least referenced within the crisis management plan.

CORPORATE INVESTIGATIONS: FRAUD, FINANCIAL, CRIMINAL, COMPUTER, AND NETWORK

The primary focus here is to make sure that someone within the security organization is comparing the data from the investigations to the documented risks to ensure that any correlation is recognized early and that appropriate plans are developed to counter any degradation in the situation. You need to understand that with crimes in this area of the business, it is important that security and the internal audit group both share information relative to this data and any audit results that indicate problems relative to the financial handling of assets; you should be sure that this is happening on a consistent basis.

DUE DILIGENCE PROCESSES

With most businesses this process is important for them to implement when they are looking to go into business with another entity in some way. It may be as a partner or as a major outsourcing of manufacturing, a merger, or even an outright purchase of another business. Whatever the situation, you must determine if they have a due diligence process in place to protect themselves from a bad financial decision. This is especially important as it relates to doing business in other countries, where information on companies might not be as readily available or as reliable.

EMERGENCY RESPONSE PLANNING AND TESTING

This should be a part of the crisis management plan but in some companies they may not have organized it in that way so I have separated these two aspects. Crisis management/emergency plans and evacuation plans are not effective unless they are tested and updated on a regular basis, at least every six months. Testing must include all people who would be involved during the real emergency. It will not work if you test the plan with the executive's assistants and then when the emergency occurs, the executive steps in to take control. The executive will not understand how the program should work and this will cause even more problems. Tests must utilize different scenarios each time to help the crisis management team understand how fluid the emergency incidents can be and that there are no absolute answers to each and every situation. Therefore, you should review the history of what the client has been doing with testing in the area. If they have done it properly, they will have fully documented results of each test including who was present, what scenario was used, and what lessons were learned from the test. They should have followed this up by making any necessary changes to their plans based on the lessons learned.

The following is a good example of the value of conducting a scenario test from when I worked at the IBM location in Vermont. We had developed many different crisis situation scenarios that might occur at our property. Because we had railroad tracks running through our property, one scenario we developed was a train wreck. One year we invited several of the surrounding town's response agencies to participate in the test of that scenario and learned a number of problems existed, such as the inability to communicate between agencies; the fact that many of them had limited training in dealing with this type of a major incident; a severe lack of gurneys for use in moving the injured; and many more. As a result of that scenario test, we had our woodworking shop build 125 wood backboards with straps; we bought a supply of 125 blankets and about 50 jogging outfits of various sizes. We also began working with the different agencies to investigate solutions to the communications issues that were discovered and we put an amendment in our plans that called for having each jurisdiction dedicate a person with a radio to the on-scene command center during any major multijurisdictional emergency.

Later on that year there was an incident with the derailment of a 13-car Amtrak train, which had 278 people aboard. At that time it was the second worst train wreck in 13 years of operation of that particular run. Five people were killed and 149 injured when, after some torrential rains, a train roadbed, a few hundred yards east of our property, gave way beneath the train early on a Saturday morning.

As you can see in Figure 8.3, the wreck was in an isolated and wooded area. IBM emergency technicians were first on the scene and took command of the rescue operation. Every agency in the area eventually responded to the scene to assist, including the state National Guard. Luckily we had construction equipment on our site that morning so the bulldozers were immediately sent to the area to begin clearing access to the wreck, along with a triage area and a helicopter landing site. The IBM emergency control manager retained command of the rescue operation throughout the entire maneuver, which lasted about 24 hours, until the last of the bodies was recovered. Every backboard that we had had built and every blanket was utilized that day. Because of what we had learned

FIGURE 8.3 Arial photo of derailment of Amtrak Passenger Train No. 60, The Montrealer, on the Central Vermont Railway, near Essex Junction, Vermont, July 7, 1984.

about the communication issues, each time a new responding organization arrived, one of their people was assigned to the command post with a radio to assist in communications. As part of our plan for major emergencies, we called in our cafeteria people to prepare food and drinks for the survivors, and the people with minor injuries were sent to the onsite cafeteria to be treated. I am convinced that if we had not performed that earlier scenario test with all of the surrounding response agencies, the death toll that day would have been much higher.

Train cars were stacked up like cords of wood in the washed-out gully; all five of the people who unfortunately lost their lives that day were in that bottom car. In all that day, 150 IBM people worked on the rescue operation. Some were on duty that day working for security and the emergency control departments; others were volunteer responders with other agencies in the surrounding areas; and others were the cafeteria and medical department employees who were called in to assist. Another important fact is that all of the crisis management team members responded to the crisis management meeting room to assist my team by providing all of the necessary resources to the rescue operation from that location, just as they had practiced in the scenario tests performed over the previous few years. We were even able to watch parts of the operation from our CCTV system, which was fed into the Crisis Management Room from the security control center. There are few situations in life more satisfying than seeing a well-trained team able to save lives because they are well prepared to give their best in the worst of tragedies.

FIGURE 8.4 Some 150 IBM employees from emergency control, security, and other departments assist in rescue operations.

One other aspect of crisis management and disaster response planning deals with the communications aspect of the plan. I think the best way to elaborate on this is to include an article of mine on the subject that appeared in *Security Technology & Design Magazine.*

THE BLAME GAME

When Disasters Happen, Will You Be Ready to Take the Heat?

Disaster planning is a subject that most of us undertake on a routine basis. I suspect that every chief security officer, director of security, and security service provider has a crisis management plan on their shelf ready to use at a moment's notice. I would hope that these plans cover all of the possible contingencies that might occur; they should be well-thought-out plans for how to minimize the impact of the particular event that might be happening, as well as how to recover from that event to get the operation back to normal as soon as possible.

If you do not feel that you have an adequate disaster plan, I recommend that you download a copy of the ASIS Disaster Preparation

Guide (www.asisonline.org), which will give you an excellent checklist to see if you have covered all the aspects of the plan. Additionally, you should review the "Business Continuity Guideline: A Practical Approach for Emergency Preparedness, Crisis Management, and Disaster Recovery," downloadable at www.asisonline.org/guidelines/inprogress_published.htm.

I believe there is an aspect of crisis management that many of us have not considered or planned for. It happens once the situation is already contained; management, politicians, or the media begin to assess the damage and immediately look to point their finger at the person or entity that is at fault for allowing the disaster to happen in the first place, especially if it is a human-made disaster. It seems to me that when a major disaster happens, if it cannot be easily and quickly determined who is to blame, then there seems to be an immediate frenzy to pin the blame somewhere, whether justified or not!

A case in point would be the September 11 attacks. As an aftermath of those horrific events, directors of security lost their jobs, security companies lost work, and even worse, there were individuals and companies that were publicly blamed for allowing the attacks to occur. The most notable of these was Frank Argenbright, Jr., and the company he previously owned, Argenbright Security. That is correct: previously owned. Argenbright had sold his company almost a year before the September 11 attacks, and at the time of the attacks he was no longer involved in its management — yet he was still "fired" on national TV from the position of CEO.

Because Argenbright Security had contracts for many airports around the world, and specifically at Boston's Logan Airport, they were ceremoniously removed from those contracts in very short order.

I wonder how the aftermath of September 11 attacks would have been different if the companies involved had a fully developed plan for dealing with the issue of being blamed for a disaster. Of course most of us have included in our plans that someone in the organization — typically the communications department — is responsible for communicating with employees, clients, and the media following a disaster, but have these professional communicators actually developed the proper plan for this scenario?

We all know that it can be a losing battle when you are put into the position of having to defend yourself when things go wrong, even when it was not a failure on your part. So what if Argenbright Security had had a prepared plan of what to say to the press immediately following such an event? After all, if you are responsible for passenger screening at an airport or multiple airports, you should assume that at some point there will be an incident that occurs that might suggest that your screeners did not do an adequate job. So, before everyone else started pointing fingers and putting them on the defense, what if they released a statement demonstrating that they would immediately begin working with authorities in an attempt to determine if the weapons had been brought on through the screening process or whether they had been placed on the planes in some other way, which would have introduced the concept that they might not have been at fault?

Instead of being in a defensive posture, they would have been in an offensive position, and they might have saved themselves and the other companies that lost that work from being dismissed.

I would recommend that anyone involved in crisis management planning consider taking the process one step farther to determine what potential disasters might occur that either you or your company could be blamed for and predetermine a course of action that addresses how you would respond to such an occurrence. This would be most helpful in dealing with human-made disasters that have an effect on the public, but you might also consider this for emergency situations that are completely internal to your company. You might even want to take this to the level of hiring a professional who is outside of your company to help you draft several versions of release statements relative to your own situation. The same recommendation holds true for your company's statements as well.

I believe the best approach to this issue is to develop several scenarios of what might go wrong — which you probably already have in your crisis management plan — and then get a professional publicist to write some boilerplate statements that could easily be adapted to the exact situation that is being addressed. Yes, I know it just sounds like C.Y.A. thinking, but in the real world if you aren't prepared to cover your A, you'll probably get it kicked!

> If you would like to learn more about emergency planning you should review ASIS International's "Business Continuity Guideline: A Practical Approach for Emergency Preparedness, Crisis Management, and Disaster Recovery," at their Web site, www.asisonline.org.
>
> Also see Appendix G, "Crisis Management Emergency Planning Checklist."

BUSINESS CONTINUITY AND DISASTER RECOVERY

This brings up the subject of business continuity. The reason it's important for the IT function to have a disaster recovery plan is so it can get the business back up and running as quickly as possible. However, I have found that in many businesses this is the only area of the business where a true disaster recovery plan exists. If a business requires office space, office equipment, and so on in order to operate, then it will not be very helpful to get the IT function back up when the employees have no place to work. All businesses should have a disaster recovery plan that identifies the critical operations of the business and defines exactly how these other functions will become operational again, in as short a time as possible. They should define alternate work sites, critical records, mitigation strategies, and testing for the plan including a tabletop exercise and simulation exercises.

EXECUTIVE PROTECTION PROGRAM

In many companies in the United States, this program is not formally implemented, with the exception of some of the much larger corporations. However, I personally believe a formal program should be developed in every company, even if it is just a plan to be implemented when there is a threat situation that develops. With the number of workplace violence cases that have occurred, I think it is ludicrous to stick your head in the sand and think "it won't happen to us." As mentioned before, Appendix B, "Executive and Employee Protection," will provide you with a basic program that outlines a number of areas to focus on. This type of program should be documented for each senior executive, especially those who are the "face of the company" to the outside world. You should also ensure that any threatening letters are given to the security organization for analysis and possibly provided to law enforcement.

INTERNAL AUDIT AND BUSINESS CONTROLS, MONITORING PROGRAMS, AND FRAUD AND INTEGRITY PROGRAMS

These prevention and interdiction programs should exist in almost all companies in some form or another. In a small company it may be performed by one person working within the finance organization; in larger companies it may be two or three departments in the company, usually as a part of the finance organization. Again, your primary focus to determine if these programs exist, if there are communications between these people and the security organization, and if they are a component of the risk analysis program.

PRE-EMPLOYMENT SCREENING AND DRUG TESTING

As was discussed in an earlier chapter this program is a critical aspect of protecting the company by ensuring they are getting the best people with the fewest problems. You should determine if this has been implemented for the hiring of all regular and nonregular employees. It is also important that they have a periodic drug testing program in place, which I find that some companies do not. Just because people were clean when they were hired does not mean they will stay that way.

RISK ASSESSMENT PROCESS (ANNUALLY)

We have already discussed the importance of implementing this program. The point here is that you should verify that clients have an annual process for reassessing their new risks and updating each of their previously identified risks.

SECURITY SYSTEMS AND PROCEDURES

Again we have discussed this aspect of the prevention programs in great detail; however, it would be negligent for me to leave it off the list of these programs.

TERRORISM, BIOTERRORISM, AND THE DHS: THREAT ADVISORY SYSTEM RESPONSE

First you need to determine if your client is a potential target for terrorism. To do this, you should discuss it with the in-house security professional and the local law enforcement agency. Very few businesses would be considered a potential terrorist target, but there are some. Most state Department of Homeland Security (DHS) offices have identified those potential targets and worked on mitigation plans with them. Assuming they are not a target, the next consideration is to determine if they are located within a close proximity to a potential target. Of course this work should all have been done as a part of their risk analysis process and should be available for review, but you should check to be sure they considered the proximity scenario and developed the appropriate response plan. Also, I have referenced bioterrorism here for a very specific reason. The plan that your client has developed may work fine if the weapon of choice is a bomb of some sort; however, the specifics of the plan for a biological attack would need to be quite different. For example, most plans that address a bomb call for evacuating the facility; however, if the weapon is biological, you need to "shelter in place" and make sure that you are not drawing outside air into the facility until you know it is safe to evacuate. This means that many details of the biological plan are considerably different from the conventional attack plan.

When the DHS first introduced the Threat Advisory System, they seemed to frequently change it from **YELLOW** to **ORANGE**, and typically it was done in a way that affected everyone. Although we have not seen the DHS utilizing the Threat Advisory System as much recently, officially that system is still in use. It is important that all companies and facilities have, as a part of their crisis management plan, a plan that addresses how they will respond to an increase in the Threat Advisory System.

There have been concerns in the past about the use of the system by DHS; most security directors have felt that the Threat Advisory System is not specific enough to provide them the information they need to make good decisions as it relates to added security measures. Usually when the threat level is raised from **YELLOW** to **ORANGE** there is very limited information as to what factors went into making the change or even what area of the United States is presumed to be the possible target of the activity. As a result, they feel they are wasting resources when they take action based solely on this system. However, they also feel that it is unwise to just ignore the system because it is very visible to the public. Fortunately, there has been some improvement in data sharing relative to the threat situations recently, which has improved this program somewhat.

In my own opinion, I find the many levels of the system to be very confusing. Since it was introduced, the country has never been below the level of **YELLOW**, yet there are two levels below that, **BLUE** and **GREEN**. Also, we have never been to the highest level of **RED**. I assume we will only go to that level when an actual event has been confirmed or is in progress; however, I really do not know what criteria will be used to make the decision to move to that level.

It should be understood that whatever actions are taken to increase security assumes that a basic security and emergency response program are already in place at your facility. It is important for this program that you develop specific response plans to emergency scenarios that may happen specifically to your facility. Response plans should include but not be limited to the following:

- A bomb threat to your facility
- A bomb in your facility
- That bomb exploding in your facility
- A threat of violence to someone at your facility
- An act of workplace violence in your facility
- All forms of violence or terrorist acts that may occur at your facility or at a nearby facility or even within the community

For each of these situations and any others that may occur, you should all have specific response plans developed. From an operational standpoint, the best approach is to make sure that you have very good communications with local and state authorities, who can alert you that there is a potential event that may occur locally. On the other hand, because your employees and visitors are all aware that the threat level has been raised from **YELLOW** to **ORANGE**, whenever that occurs, it is important that they see visible signs that the security of your facility has been increased in order to better protect them and to help them feel more safe and secure as well. Although this may seem superficial, it is very important for the productivity of your people and your reputation. Therefore, I would recommend the following actions as it relates to the Threat Advisory System response:

- When the level is raised from **YELLOW** to **ORANGE**, without any specific information as to the potential target or geographic area of the country, you should implement the following actions:

1. Advise employees and security staff to be more alert to any suspicious activity or people.
2. Ensure that your security officers are more visible to employees and staff by conducting more frequent patrols and by having more presence at the primary entrances to the facility.
3. Implement more controls over package deliveries by having all of them go to a specific dock, where the delivery person will be checked in and their ID confirmed and recorded before they enter the building.

- When the level is raised from **YELLOW** to **ORANGE,** and there is specific information as to the potential target or geographic area of the country, and the specifics indicate that a facility such as yours or an area of the country such as yours may be the target, you should implement the following actions:
  1. Call a meeting of your crisis management team and advise them of the situation.
  2. Advise employees and security staff to be more alert to any suspicious activity or people.
  3. Ensure that your officers are more visible to employees and staff by conducting more frequent patrols.
  4. Implement more controls over package deliveries by having all of them go to a specific dock, where the delivery person will be checked in and their ID confirmed and recorded and verify that the delivery is expected before they enter the building.
  5. Register all visitors. Provide them with a Visitor badge to be worn at all times while on the premises.
  6. Add additional patrols around the perimeter of the property and post a security officer at all primary entrances.

- When the level is raised from **YELLOW** or **ORANGE** to **RED,** and there is specific information as to the potential target or geographic area of the country, and the specifics indicate that a facility such as yours or an area of the country such as yours may be the target, you should implement the following actions:
  1. Call a meeting of your crisis management team and advise them of the situation.
  2. Advise employees and security staff to be more alert to any suspicious activity or people.
  3. Ensure that your officers are more visible to employees and staff by conducting more frequent patrols.

4. Implement more controls over package deliveries by having all of them go to a specific dock, where the delivery person will be checked in and their ID confirmed and recorded and verify that the delivery is expected before they enter the building.
5. Limit visitors to essential visitors only, wherever possible, and register all visitors. Provide them with a Visitor badge to be worn at all times while on the premises.
6. Add additional foot and vehicle patrols around the perimeter of the property and post a security officer at all primary entrances.
7. Add an additional officer to the security command center (SCC) to monitor cameras and alarms.
8. Evaluate canceling all essential staff travel and any previously approved vacation time for essential staff.

With these increased measures you should also consider placing signs at the main entrances that advise people that the threat level is at **ORANGE** or **RED** and they can expect some additional delays as more stringent security controls have been put in place.

If you would like to learn more about Threat Advisory System response you should review the ASIS International Guideline, "Threat Advisory System Response," at their Web site, www.asisonline.org.

WORKPLACE VIOLENCE PREVENTION PROGRAM

Again we have discussed this aspect of the prevention programs in great detail; however, it would be negligent for me to leave it off of the list of these prevention and recovery programs.

REFERENCES

Giles, T.D. "When Disasters Happen, Who Can We Blame?" *Security Technology & Design Magazine*, June 2008. With permission.
IBM Burlington Closeup Internal Magazine, May–July 1984 (Figure 8.2).

9

Interviewing Executive and Security Management

INTERVIEW EXECUTIVE MANAGEMENT TO UNDERSTAND THEIR CONCERNS AND ISSUES

This is a vital part of the process to ensure executive management involvement and "buy-in" to the process. It is very important that, as the consultant, you interview management at the highest levels of the organization; however, you must interview middle management as well. If you do not have middle management support, the effectiveness of the program will break down, probably during the budget process. If conducted properly, this interview process can be of educational value for management as well. By asking management about their concerns with various issues such as terrorism, workplace violence, theft, sabotage, computer and network penetration, and protecting the reputation of the business, you can effectively raise their awareness level on issues facing the organization. These questions should be formulated in such a way so they do not come across as being an alarmist. For example, you may want to ask the following: "With all of the press that exists today on the subject of terrorism, do you have any concerns for your company in this regard?" As I mentioned earlier, there are a number of areas of concern you need to talk to management about during this process and you will need to determine projected growth for the next five and ten years.

THE APPROACH

The best approach is, after reading the book, you should then go back through it and make notes on the different areas to question management about. Most of these questions will depend on the information that was given to you prior to starting the process; therefore, I cannot really outline this area for you in depth. You should then develop and write down some specific questions that you want to ask the different executives you plan to interview relative to this review.

One area that I always ask about is how the executive feels about the current security program and staff. It is important that you know their thoughts on this as you start the process because it will let you know how much credibility the current CSO or director of security has in the eyes of the executives. (Again, this is another aspect of the process that will most probably not yield the desired effect if performed by an in-house security person.) That will also be a good indicator about how good a job he or she is doing in the area of relationships. This is why, when I am asked by CSOs or directors of security if they can join me for these interviews, I advise them that for it is better if I do it alone so the person will feel comfortable in being completely open with me. I tell them that one of my questions will be about how the executive feels about the current program and staff, as well. I believe in being completely up-front about these matters so when I do get negatives about them, they understand why. I also find that once they know that I will ask about that, they tend to volunteer information about any negative activities that have occurred recently as well.

If you were hired to perform this work by someone in the company other than the CSO or director of security, you will need to focus on issues relative to that. First, the CSO or director of security may not be supportive of your being there; he or she may view this as an invasion of their "turf." You will need to spend time up-front building a working relationship with them to make this process effective. They need to believe that your intention is to work with them and help them in this process. Of course, you also need to be sure you maintain your personal and professional integrity, so do not promise them more than you can give while still maintaining your control. I am not suggesting that they would intentionally undermine the work you are doing, but you need to have them be completely open with you to make this an effective project (see Figure 9.1).

FIGURE 9.1 Openness and candor in the informational interview are the best ways to assess the current security climate and determine what, if any, changes and improvements can and should be made.

This also has an effect on your interviews in that the executives will know who hired you, and if it was not security, they will already be suspicious that the executive who hired you might not be happy with the performance of the in-house security organization. This can taint their responses to questions such as, "How do you think the security group is doing?" Therefore, you will need to be cautious in how you ask those questions and do your best not to damage the security group's reputation or effectiveness. The best way is to convince the CSO or director of security to publicly support the project. He or she can do this by sending a letter to the executives you intend to interview, announcing that you have been hired to work with the organization to build a Security Master Plan and that, as a part of the process, you will be scheduling meetings with each of them to interview them on several different topics. If this is done properly, it can demonstrate that you are working together and possibly eliminate the idea that you are there to "check on the security director's or the security organization's performance."

INTERPRETING THE INTERVIEW ANSWERS

It is important to remember that just because an executive might not have a good feeling about the security program or security staff, this does not necessarily mean that they are doing a bad job overall. It may just be a relationship issue with that particular executive. I have personally encountered many situations over the years in which I had an executive who was negative about security, no matter what kind of performance the organization had. Sometimes, it can be very difficult to turn something like that around because it may be due to an incident that occurred yearsearlier. Regardless, it is always important to know exactly where you stand with those who can affect your program or even your career. If you encounter this situation, it is important that you make the CSO or director of security aware of what you have learned as long as you were not asked to keep it confidential; however, that should typically be the extent of your involvement as the consultant. It is not your responsibility to repair relationship issues because you really will not be there long enough to make that happen. However, if an opportunity to help presents itself , you should not ignore it. Helping the CSO or director of security with a problem such as that can go a long way toward building your own relationship with him or her.

You will need to take notes during the interview so it is important that you ask permission to do so. This will add additional pressure on you to be listening while you are also writing your notes, so I find it works best to write as few words as possible, just enough to remind you of that discussion. If you feel you need to write a lot, you may want to ask them to give you a minute to write that down because you believe it is important for you to focus on. I have had colleagues ask about using a recorder during these interviews. Although I agree that would be much easier than taking notes, I believe most people become self-conscious when they are being recorded, and it inevitably stifles the flow of information and the openness of the session.

THE IMPORTANCE OF LISTENING

As you conduct these interviews, be sure you are in the listening mode so you pick up on issues the executives raise. Remember what I said previously: You have two ears and one mouth for a reason. You should be careful not to be so focused on the question you are going to ask next that you miss an issue of vital concern that has been raised. When they do express concern about a topic, you should probe that subject so that you are very clear on exactly what they are concerned about. For example, the executive might say, "I'm very concerned about the whole terrorism issue." You might interpret this to mean that he or she is concerned that the business could be a target or something along those lines. However, if you ask a simple question such as, "Exactly how does that worry you?" the answer might be something completely different, such as, "I'm concerned that we are wasting resources here on an issue that will never affect us directly." In communications we tend to hear what we think, not what was said, so again it is very important for you to probe these concerns that are expressed until you are sure you are hearing what they have said. To make absolutely sure you are in sync with the executive, once you have finished the interview, say, "If you don't mind, I'd like to summarize our discussion to make sure I am clear about your concerns." Then repeat back to him or her the issues that you have taken notes on in your own words, and ask them, "Have I understood your points correctly? Is there anything else you would like me to focus on during this project?"

It is most effective to have most of the information sent to you ahead of time, as referenced in the Introduction of this book. If so, you can utilize this information to help tailor your questions for the executive interviews. It can also be helpful to get the CSO or director of security's perspective of the people that you will be interviewing. However, you need to be cautious about that to some extent; I have found that when there are issues between them and a particular executive, their input might precondition your thinking and your interview. I have also had situations where security did not want me to interview a particular person because they are "just completely negative about the security program." I usually advise them that this is just the person I need to talk to so we can deal with their issues and move the program forward. It is like the old adage, "Know your enemy." When you have completed your interview with each executive, create the opportunity to come back to them by letting them know that as you conduct the assessment and new issues arise, you might need to ask them a few more questions. This can be very helpful if you learn that information they may have given you turns out to be incorrect. It gives you the opening to go back to them and hopefully correct their erroneous understanding in that area.

WHERE TO START THE PROCESS

I usually begin this process by interviewing as high a level executive as possible. I then work my way down through the chain of command. Of course, you do not need to interview every manager, but it is important that you talk to someone from every function in the company. This way you get different perspectives across the lines. It is essential that you talk to management in those functions that have the most interaction with the security organization such as legal, facilities, IT, finance, HR, manufacturing, and research and development. The in-house security people or the person who hired you can help you determine who they are. As you reach the organization's middle management level, you may encounter more resistance than you have seen at the higher levels. There are a lot of reasons that this occurs, but they are typically not of a personal nature, specifically directed at you. You just happen to be the one in front of them. It is important that you understand that any animosity or lack of cooperation is not personal so you can stay in control of the meeting and accomplish your mission. I have had interviews go bad on occasion, and when they do, I usually just say something like, "Obviously this is a not a good time for you, so if it's all right I'll reschedule the interview for another time." Sometimes that gets them to refocus and continue the session and sometimes I have to come back. You can also try using the "name dropping" technique. If, when you were interviewing one of the higher level executives, they happened to mention a concern that affects the middle manager you are having trouble with, you can say something like, "When I was interviewing Mr. Big, he mentioned that he was concerned about biological terrorism and wanted me to discuss this with you and get your perspective on it." In most cases this will get their attention, but personally, I do not like using this approach except in severe cases where I just cannot get the individual to cooperate any other way.

BEGINNING THE INTERVIEW

As I begin an interview with an interviewee for the first time, I cover several areas. First, I introduce myself and give them some personal background information. I tell them that I am retired from IBM and that I was the director of security for IBM North America at the time I retired. I tell them I spent three years living and working in Asia and two years as the director of security for IBM Latin America. (Understand that I am not trying to brag or build myself up; I am letting them know that I have knowledge of international affairs that I have learned through experience.) I further explain that I have been in the consulting field since 1998, when I retired, and through this experience I have worked with many different companies in many different industries. (I am now establishing that I have experience across many industries outside of the technology industry with IBM. I go as quickly as I can so it does not feel like I am bragging or, more importantly, wasting their time.) Next, I spend a couple of minutes explaining what I'm doing there. I explain that I am working with their company to build a Security Master Plan to ensure that the security business is in sync with the overall business as they move through the next few years and on into the future. I tell them that this process will link specific security plans to specific risks that need to be mitigated for their business, and it will ensure that they are positioned to migrate into future security technologies efficiently and with controlled, possibly reduced cost impacts. In order to implement this plan, I need to gather information about the business, where it is now, where it is headed, and any risk concerns the executives may have relative to the business or even themselves personally.

At the conclusion of that introduction, I ask my first question, which is almost always, "What can you tell me about your concerns?" This open-ended question is intended to solicit whatever is on their mind at that moment concerning their attitude about what I am doing. It may be negative or positive, whichever it is — it is all good. Getting that out on the table is what I want. After I deal with that, then I can move into my prepared questions.

It is important to understand that whatever your background is, you need to present it to the person with the right spin. This means letting them know how your background and knowledge, whatever it is, will benefit their company as you implement the process of developing a security master plan for their business. Which points you stress to one client may differ from what you tell another.

EDUCATING THE EXECUTIVES AND ENSURING THEIR BUY-IN

Your goal in these interviews is not only to gain insight into the company and the executive's concerns, but to also get the executive to think about those security issues that might be pertinent to the business. If you have already learned that they have problems with theft or workplace violence or other issues, make sure you ask them about those problems and get their feedback. You should also ask about other risk issues that may be inactive at the moment, but that they should be aware of. Having those discussions is about educating them on the problems that they might face in the future.

In a discussion about a particular topic, you may be asked questions such as, "How much do you think it will cost to improve our security in this area?" You should not make any off-the-cuff guesses. I usually reply, "I will focus on this issue as I work on developing the Security Master Plan and I will be able to answer that question when I present the results of this work to you." You might also follow that up with a question about what they think the ramifications might be should a situation like this occur at their facility. You can explain to them that you believe that it is important not to recommend spending more to protect against a situation than it might cost if it were to occur. This can help them to see that you are not there just to tell them to spend more money, but that you are looking for cost-effective approaches to mitigating their risks. Just do not forget that this will need to be an item in the final presentation, even if it turns out that it is not a realistic problem for them. I guarantee you that the executive who asked the question will not forget you said you would address it. Having said that, it is important that you do not make too many of these types of promises as you go through this process or it will dilute your final presentation.

INTERVIEW SECURITY MANAGEMENT TO UNDERSTAND THEIR CONCERNS AND ISSUES

Security management should be interviewed and a wide range of topics should be covered. This should be an ongoing process conducted before, during, and after the various reviews and other interviews. The areas of focus should include, but not be limited to, the following:

- Security management interactions with the management team
- Security management interactions with outside agencies
- Their current security philosophies and strategies
- Proprietary or contract security staffing

- Training and education records for the security staff and management
- What contracts they manage
- What contracts they audit, but do not manage
- Security equipment and technology
- Investigation practices and criminal prosecutions
- Incident data and trend analysis
- Physical security standards
- Information protection programs
- Visitor and contractor control processes
- High-security areas
- High-value assets
- Key and lock controls
- Unique security requirements
- Security education and awareness programs
- New employee education
- Other security-related programs: workplace violence prevention, crisis management program, emergency planning and response program

Although you will already have some insight into different aspects of this information based on the requested data outlined in the Introduction, I find it valuable to have the security team go over it with you face to face. This will help you to understand whether some of the information is a plan that sits on the shelf or if it is actively utilized. This part of the review works best if you set up the session so you are meeting with the CSO or director of security one on one, but as you dig into each specific area he or she calls in the person who runs that program to answer the detail questions. From these sessions you will learn about that person's knowledge of the area and the CSO or director of security's knowledge. I would remind you that it is not necessary for the CSOs or directors of security to have in-depth knowledge of every program, but they should understand it well enough to be able to effectively manage the program. You will also learn whether the program is actively pursued, if it is a more in-depth program than what is reflected on paper, and so on. You will hear from the people whether they believe the program is important and if they think they have enough resources to get it done, usually without even asking those specific questions.

Once you have completed this work and moved on to conducting the other aspects of the information gathering process, you should keep someone from the security organization with you at all times (except during the initial interviews with the executives, of course). As much as possible it should be the CSO or director of security, but you will not be able to monopolize all of their time, so when they are not available it should be the individual security person who has responsibility for what you are reviewing. One other point: You will be working at their site for an extended period of time and it would be beneficial if they could furnish you with an office while you are onsite.

10

Review and Evaluate All Security-Related Contracts and the Information Protection Program

The primary concern is to evaluate if the contracts are of good quality. Additionally, you need to determine if good procurement processes have been followed to ensure a competitive bidding process or a valid sole source. You also need to determine if the contracts are being managed effectively: Are the requirements being audited by the security team periodically to ensure they are met, and if not met, what was done about it?

The typical security contracts include the following:

- Contract security personnel
- System maintenance and spare parts
- Destruction of confidential information
- Locksmith and key and lock maintenance

SECURITY BUSINESS CONTRACTS

For many businesses and institutions today, security is performed on a contract basis. Contract guards and contract maintenance typically make up the major part of the security organization's budget. Of course, if the business has proprietary security officers, then their salaries, benefits, and so on will be the bulk of the budget. Therefore, to be an effective manager of the security business, you must be a knowledgeable contracts manager. The first part of effectively managing a contract is to have a good contract in place. I have seen businesses where the contract in place for $1 million worth of contract guard services annually was just a two-page legal document with absolutely no detail in it about the service to be performed other than the annual hours and the bill rate. If you review the RFP document in Appendix D, you will see a very detailed document that can be made part of the contract once it is awarded. This document gives the security manager the right to perform audits for all aspects of the contract that have requirements, including the following areas:

Scope of work
   Performance of work
   Responsibilities of work
   Contractor's personnel
Standards of work
   General standards
   Health and safety
   Management support
Recruitment and hiring process
   Personnel standards
   Personnel screening requirements
   Drug, alcohol, and other contraband policy
   Penalties for violation of policy
Training
   Orientation and initial training
   Ongoing training
   Emergency response training
   Specialized training
Principal posts and post orders
After-hours supervision
Uniforms

CONTRACTUAL RIGHT TO AUDIT

Having the contractual right to perform these audits is only the first step. Next they need to actually do the work. When the audits are performed they should be completely documented, with a letter sent to the contract company outlining the areas that were reviewed and the results that were found. If there are any areas found that are out of compliance, they should be highlighted and a request should be made for an action plan to resolve the issue within a reasonable length of time. Once the action plan has been executed, the company should audit those records again to determine if they are now in compliance. It is important that they keep in mind that all of these records can be subpoenaed in the case of litigation, and therefore the documents should be professional and properly maintained for a period of at least seven years.

I believe the two most important areas to be audited with a guard contract are the areas of background checks and training! These are the two areas that tell you whether you have quality officers working onsite, and also the two areas that will give you the most protection when problems develop that turn into litigation situations. It is important that they understand the difference between "managing the contract" and "managing the contractor." I have seen too many situations where the relationship between the proprietary security management and the contract security management and employees is such that if you had not been told they were contract, you would think they were employees. When you are managing the contract you need to conduct periodic, random audits of the records to ensure that the contractor is meeting all of the requirements of the contract. If there have been verbal modifications to the contract since it began, those modifications need to be documented as an amendment to the contract. For example, the original contract may have required that all officers receive 40 hours of training prior to coming onsite, where they would then begin 24 hours of onsite training. There may have been a situation of heavy turnover, causing management and the contractor to agree that they will only get 24 hours of training before coming onsite, where they will then be given the rest of the training. This might have been an appropriate decision to fix the problem, but if that is going to be a permanent change, the contract should be modified. If it is a temporary change, there should still be a letter between the two parties documenting the temporary change. It is never appropriate to modify a contract verbally without at least having a follow-up letter.

CONTRACT BID PROCESS

The next aspect of good contract management is to periodically go out to bid and see what the competition has to offer. I believe this is not done often enough by most companies. I believe it is important to go out to bid at least every three years. This does not mean you have to actually award the contract to another company, however. When I have done this in the past, I have told each of the bidding companies that I was not set on changing to someone else, I just wanted to see what they had to offer. On the other hand, if a problem arose with the incumbent company in six months or a year, I already knew who the top bidders were and I was able to make a change in a very short period of time. It is also possible that you get a bid from a company that offers you higher quality of service at a competitive price, and you may want to make a change after all. I always include a statement in my contracts that prevents the company from putting noncompete contracts in place so if the new contract company wants to use some of the existing people, they can.

Next evaluate the system maintenance and spare parts contract. These contracts are typically straightforward with specifications for charges during normal hours of operation and after-hours. They usually specify how frequently preventive maintenance (PM) checks will be made as well. They should include a requirement that the supplier keep an ample supply of spare parts on hand to ensure repairs can be performed within a reasonable length of time. I believe those time periods should be detailed to some extent to cover different problems. For example, the client should be OK with a 24-hour turnaround on repairing or replacing a single camera that is malfunctioning, but they will need a much quicker turnaround on a digital video recorder that is not performing. Therefore, the contract should require that the supplier keep loaner equipment on hand to keep the client operating? Likewise with the access control system: Repairs on an incapacitated system are needed very quickly, whereas it might be OK to wait 24 hours for the repair of a single door problem or a single malfunctioning alarm point. For some of these systems, the client may keep some spare parts on hand. If that is the case, you should check to see that the parts are being managed properly and if they are actually needed.

AUDITING SECURITY-RELATED CONTRACTS

The other aspect of contract management deals with contracts that may not be directly managed by the security organization. It is fairly common that the lock and key contract or the confidential destruction contract are managed by the facilities organization. Security management should first review the contracts to make sure they contain the right security and business controls requirements. These contracts should also have a statement that the business has the right to perform unannounced audits at any time to ensure compliance with the requirements. It is my belief that these audits should be performed by a security professional; however, if the security organization does not have the resources to do the work, they should at least make sure the organization that owns the contract does them.

As mentioned earlier, the locksmith should also audit all master and submaster keys on at least an annual basis to ensure none have been lost, so you need to make sure that these audits are being done and that the proper actions are being taken when there are problems. You also need to be sure that all of the key blanks that have been used can be accounted for. For the confidential destruction contract, you need to ensure that the information is secure from the time the employee discards it until the information is rendered completely unreadable. The normal weak link in that process is how the confidential bins are secured at the vendor's site until the information is destroyed. You need to ensure that the client has taken that into account within the contract and that they have audited the vendor's site to ensure compliance.

REVIEWING THE INFORMATION
PROTECTION PROGRAMS

In Chapter 6 of this book I outlined basic components of an information protection program so that you will have the ability to judge if they have a reasonable program in place. You now need to conduct the reviews to see if this program is being implemented as they intended, and to ensure that the program is, in fact, protecting their information assets. The specifics of how to review the effectiveness of their program will depend on exactly what the program is. However, at a minimum you should determine if they have clearly identified what they consider to be their information assets.

For example, do they have personal data such as credit card information that they keep on clients and others, or do they have product development information, and is this data considered sensitive? The first step should always be to determine if they have identified their information assets; the second step is to find out how they communicate the importance of the assets. Have they implemented a classification system or some other formal way of letting employees know what needs to be protected and how?

AFTER-HOURS CHECKS

Next, you should conduct an after-hours check to see if sensitive data is being left out for others to see. If this type of data is behind a secure and alarmed access-controlled door, but it is available for everyone who has legitimate access to the area, that is not sufficient, unless every one of those people is allowed to have access to that data. Are printouts of sensitive or confidential data left after-hours in a central printer room that many people have access to? If they have their own paper shredders, are they sufficient to handle the workload? When they are not, then frequently employees will just discard the material instead of waiting on the shredder. You should look into some of the trash cans in the areas where sensitive data is handled to see if any of it has just been thrown away. One of the best sources of sensitive and confidential information that many private investigators and others have access to, will be the trash bin that sits outside the back door of a company. Again, you need to assess the details of their program and then test to make sure it is effectively implemented and that it truly protects their information assets.

IT INFORMATION PROTECTION

Once you have completed the hard copy data checks, you need to move into the soft copy and electronic arena. In Chapter 6, I outlined a 15-point program, "Security and Computer Use Standards for Employees." The sections of that program are listed below:

1. Security of your personal workstation
2. When leaving your office or work area
3. When traveling or working away from your office or work area

4. Handheld devices
5. Computer viruses and other harmful code
6. Security firewalls
7. File sharing
8. Copyright and intellectual property
9. Releasing XYZ information into the public domain
10. Protecting XYZ information
11. Calendars
12. Protecting XYZ confidential information
13. Using telephones or fax machines
14. Using teleconferencing systems
15. XYZ internal networks

Therefore, your next review is to sit down with the people who are in charge of these programs and have them review with you what they are currently doing. You should first compare the program they have outlined with what I provided you, and see if their program covers all appropriate areas. If it does, then you should conduct a review to see if the employees are actually following the requirements of the program. Most of these areas of review will require you to just ask some employees about the components to see if they are aware of the program and know how to implement it; in some areas you can just observe or test. For example, with item 1 above, you can ask an employee about the password requirements that are outlined in Chapter 6; with item 2, if someone has left his or her computer unattended, you can check to see if it has a screensaver password activated on it or if you can just walk up and start using the computer. So you should just put together one list of areas to ask employees about and one list that you can actually test. You really do not have the time to conduct a test that would actually prove whether the IT programs are being implemented effectively or not, but you can get a sense of it from a small sample; if you feel there is a problem then you can put a recommendation in your findings that the program needs to be reinforced with the employees on a more frequent basis, and compliance should be tested periodically.

DISASTER RECOVERY PROGRAM REVIEW

As outlined in Chapter 6, a disaster recovery program for the systems should include storage of backup data at an offsite location and a contract with a company or a duplicate backup site that can quickly get the IT function operational after a disaster. You will need to sit down with the people who handle this program and have them walk you through what they are doing. Key items to look for would be:

- How frequently is offsite backup data updated and why? For many companies, I think weekly would be sufficient, but the important factor is that they have good reasoning behind the timeframe they use.
- Is the offsite storage facility in business to provide that service? It should not be stored at another office that belongs to the client; it should be a company like Iron Mountain or a similar company that provides secure storage.
- Do they have a contract with a company to provide them computer and network service if their system were destroyed?
- Is that company located in the same geographic area? In other words, is there a potential that the backup could be affected by the same large-scale disaster that shuts them down?
- Have they conducted a live test with that company to make sure they can do what they say? A live test means that the client actually runs their operation from the backup company for a short period to test that all critical operations function properly.
- When was the last test? Were the results documented including lessons learned? Was it less than a year ago?

The extent of the plan is determined by how dependent the company is on its IT operation to perform its day-to-day business, and it should be a balance between how much the client would lose every day its systems were down and how much the backup operation would cost. As with all risk management plans, you should not spend more for protection than what the potential loss would be. By the way, there may be some companies out there that have decided to provide their own backup capability. This is a viable option for some who can afford it, so if your client has implemented this, just ask all the same questions about testing as if it were a system that was in place at a company that provides that service.

INFORMATION SECURITY AWARENESS TRAINING

This is an aspect of the protection program that I frequently find is lacking, and an area in which you can provide real value during your review process. Many IT organizations opt to provide their awareness training via system notices. Unfortunately, most people do not take the time to actually read those notices, so I usually recommend that at least once a year they do face-to-face presentations to be sure everyone understands the requirements and to offer people the opportunity to ask questions about rules that they do not understand. Many companies also have a process where once a year they require employees and other system users to sign a card or electronically sign a statement that they understand the rules and will abide by them. Although this is important in order to discipline people who misuse system assets, it should not be considered as awareness training. Do not misunderstand: I believe this is an important process that every company should have; I just do not think it qualifies as training. Therefore, you should get hard copies of their training materials and ask some of the users of the systems if they understand the various rules. You might find it interesting to include some of the IT people in this sampling as well. After asking them if they understand the rule, you might ask them how they feel the rules affect their day-to-day productivity and if they ever find a need to ignore the rules. I think you will get a few interesting answers. Again, you will not have the time to do a relative sample that is large enough for meaningful data; you are just trying to get a sense of how the program is working. It is important that you stress that information when you are presenting your recommendations to the executives.

INVESTIGATION REQUIREMENTS

As we discussed in Chapter 6, you need to determine the investigation requirements for all incidents of computer and telecommunications misuse, thefts or compromise of proprietary information, and service interruptions. To do this, first see if any of these types of investigations are recorded with the security organization. After you see what they have, then interview the IT director to see what he or she has recorded for these types of investigations. When you compare the two reports, I suspect they will not agree with each other. If the two agree, they are already a step ahead of many companies, because I find that many times the IT group does not report everything that they investigate to the security group. Next, I would suggest a candid discussion with both the IT and security directors to determine if they are in agreement on what investigations they cooperate on and which they do not. This may not be an amicable discussion. Then you need to look at this information and determine if you agree with where their procedures in this regard. I typically do not have a problem with security not being involved in misuse investigations as long as HR is involved, but most any other IT investigation should have a security-trained investigator as the case manager.

Next, find out if they are trained in forensic investigation techniques for computer investigations or if they have a consultant on contract who is. They may believe they do not need that based on the types of incidents they have had so far, but they may not have considered what will happen when they start to investigate what they believe to be a simple misuse case and find that it is actually embezzlement. At that point, it may be too late to start looking for someone to assist them, and if it is not handled properly, they may not be able to pursue criminal prosecution or even civil recourse. It will not cost them anything to have a contract in place with a reputable computer forensic investigator who can be brought in when needed, and it may save them a lot of frustration and lost revenue in the long run.

REVIEW OF EXIT INTERVIEW PROCESS

As I outlined previously, the client should have a process in place to interview all key employees who depart the company. To have an effective process for implementing this, you will need to verify that they have taken the time to actually define what constitutes a key employee to be included in this exit process. It will depend on the type of business, but typically, it is executives of the company and some of the lead engineers or lead manufacturing managers; if it is a software company it would be lead software engineers and so on. A part of the process should be to have these people sign a confidentiality disclosure agreement (CDA) when they join the company, which should include an appropriate time period after they leave when the information is still considered confidential.

Key employees should be interviewed prior to leaving the company, and this may include the legal department along with management and human resources. Focus areas should be the protection of whatever proprietary information they may have had knowledge of or access to while working for the company. At a minimum, these interviews would remind the employee of this contractual requirement. Many companies that are involved in research and development activities go one step farther and have the departing employee sign or initial the CDA again as a reminder. In a few cases there will also be concern about the departing employee going into competition with the current company; this must be considered as well by management and legal counsel and then addressed in writing at the exit interview.

INFORMATION ASSET SECURITY REVIEW

As you know from Chapter 6, information asset security is a critical program for providing protection of those assets that, for many companies, provide them the advantage over its competition and is the foundation for its future success. You should have already determined whether the client has this program in place. If so, you need to see if it has been effectively implemented.

The following are the nine primary aspects of the information asset program that I outlined for you in Chapter 6. However, your client may have their own program that has been implemented, which may be somewhat different. If so, focus your review on whether they are effectively implementing their program or not. If their program does not include aspects of what I have outlined for you, then you should question them about that.

1. Determine information assets
2. Assign ownership of information assets
3. Approve use of information assets
4. Educate employees on their responsibilities
5. Guarantee effective use of controls
6. Conduct self-assessments to ensure compliance
7. Assess and accept risks
8. Respond decisively to exposures, misuse, or loss of information assets
9. Assign custodial authority and responsibility

To conduct this aspect of the review or information gathering process, I would start with the person identified as the primary owner of the program within the company. Have that person explain the program and discuss aspects that he or she may not be addressing. After that interview, I would ask to meet with at least two of the managers who are asset owners and have them explain to you how they ensure compliance with the program. Always ask to see documented proof of what they say they are doing. If you feel reasonably comfortable with what you have learned at this point, you can conclude your review; if not, you could go one step farther and interview employees who are responsible for complying with the program to see if they are clear on their responsibilities and fully understand the program.

11

Constructing the Security Master Plan Document

COMPILING, ORGANIZING, AND EVALUATING THE INFORMATION GATHERED

Once you have completed the information gathering, you need to compile the results: the business's risks, the site security assessment, the security organization assessment, and so on. The compilation work is very important, and it will take some time to complete. I usually find that as I conduct the reviews I can only make brief notes; however, each evening after I have finished working onsite, I sit down and expand my notes to make them as complete as possible. When you are expanding your notes each night, you should also identify any open items that need to be followed up on later. I typically do that work on my laptop and sectionalize the notes as much as possible; doing it that way helps me when I get to this part of the process. Utilizing good organization skills during the entire process will be very valuable to you to make this aspect as simple as you can.

You need to go through all the information and organize it as a rough draft of the Security Master Plan; however, an important aspect of this process is that you need to analyze and evaluate the information as you compile it. One day you may have been reviewing the information protection process and noticed a problem in another area such as locks and keys. You will need to pull that information into the lock and key section.

179

Or you may have been on the dock area looking at physical security and noticed some confidential information in the trash bin that was not shredded. Besides the need to pull that information into the information protection section, I hope you took the time to point this problem out to the in-house security person who was accompanying you on that tour so they could immediately rectify the problem. One mistake I have seen some people make, both in-house and consultants, is that they will save that kind of "look what I found" information to drop as a bomb in their wrap-up presentation, only to have the executive get very upset with them for not mentioning the problem immediately. The executive will feel like you have intentionally allowed them to be exposed, and rightly so.

Therefore, you should review all of the information that you have compiled and make notes as to any conflicting information or any open questions that still need to be resolved. I would be very surprised, by the way, if there were not some open items that needed some closure. When you conduct a review of this magnitude, there almost has to be. Once you have completed data review, you need to resolve any open questions or conflicts before moving on to the next part of the process. This part of the process is truly a test of your organizational and analytical skills, and you may have to review the data several times before you feel sure that you have identified and resolved all of the issues.

DEVELOPING YOUR RECOMMENDATIONS

You should now begin work on developing recommendations relative to the data you have gathered. At this point, you are not going to address the areas of security philosophies, strategies, or goals; these areas will be addressed later in this process. For now, you need to make a complete list of recommendations. You also need to make a list of effectively implemented areas because you want to compliment the organization for those areas. This is an important part of the presentation because you do not want to come across as being completely negative on the existing program. There have been times when I found it difficult to highlight any positives in the existing program, but I can assure you it is valuable that you do so. Of course, you must always be honest and professional in your evaluations, so if you cannot find anything to compliment them on, then so be it.

You next then prioritize your recommendations and separate them into those that need to be brought to executive management's attention and those that just to be passed on to security management. It is important that you not spend any time talking about trivial issues when meeting with executives. I usually just have a one-line entry in the presentation to them stating that I have also given security management a list of minor issues to be addressed. However, you must have that information with you in case you are asked for some. Whenever possible, I attempt to get the CSO or director of security to implement those minor changes prior to my presentation to the executives so I can also say that they have already addressed these items and made changes to those areas. As a consultant, this is another demonstration of the value you bring to this process. Additionally, the more you cooperate with the in-house security team, the more painless the process is for them and the more willing they will be to work with you again. If you are an in-house security person who is implementing this process, you still need to pass on to the executives other minor points of corrections that were learned through this process in addition to the major recommendations so they will understand the full value of the work.

INITIAL DRAFT REVIEW WITH SECURITY MANAGEMENT

Once you have completed your rough draft, review your data and recommendations with the security management team to ensure they understand and agree. I usually start with the CSO or director of security in a one-on-one session. Some recommendations can be quite personal if there are issues with staffing levels or skills. The only recommendation that I would not review with the CSO or director of security would be a recommendation that they, themselves, need to be replaced. That one I would review with his or her manager and see how receptive they were to that recommendation going forward or if they wanted to address it themselves. However, if this manager disagrees and I feel strongly about the need to replace the person, I will still include it in my recommendations to the executives and I will inform him or her of my intent to do so. Barring that kind of an issue, after I complete my review with the CSO or director of security I will then decide if there are any changes that are needed based on that input. You should understand that when you begin this review with the CSO or director of security, this may be the first time you are discussing some of the issues with him or her. The in-house security person who was with you when the issue was discovered may not have understood that problem well enough to explain it adequately. But when you are reviewing it with the CSO or director of security, he or she may be able to explain it to your satisfaction, which might eliminate the problem.

Next, if the CSO or director of security and I feel it is necessary, we may also include other security team members in the review and get their input. I usually have them come in with the two of us, one at a time, to discuss only their specific area of expertise. It is important that you understand the process here; you do not let them tell you what should or should not go into the recommendations. You have to own those recommendations personally and professionally! The reason for the review with them is simply to get their views on the matter to ensure you have not overlooked anything and to be sure they have a clear understanding of what you are recommending and why. Remember, they are the owners of the current conditions that have led to the recommendations in the first place. Some of the recommendations will probably be due to a lack of proper funding of the security budget, and they will certainly support the need for you to recommend increases to that budget. They will make sure you know that they have previously asked for funding in the different areas where you are making those recommendations; however, it is possible that either the CSO or director of security's lack of skill in attaining those funds or the organization's reporting structure have led to that condition.

RECOMMENDATION WITH SOLUTIONS

Some of the problems that have led to these recommendations may be due to a lack of skill or knowledge or simply a lack of focus on that area of concern on the part of the in-house team. These areas will be difficult for the security team to hear, but as the consultant it is important for you to make sure they understand the problems and the solutions to them. As long as your recommendations are sound with a good foundation, most professionals will agree with them and accept that they have made some mistakes. It is important that you couple some explanations with your recommendations whenever possible. Include explanations such as the following:

- "Due to a lack of resources"
- "Due to a lack of funding"
- "Due to a lack of prioritization by the organization"
- "Due to a lack of skill base within the organization"
- "Due to a lack of management support"

However, when you do this you must be sure of what you are claiming; you are not there to make excuses for anyone. You may not have absolute proof, and when you do not, you should state that and add the phrase "in my opinion," but when you are sure this is the reason, it is important that you point it out so the executives understand what needs to be done to correct the problem. For example, although the security team has responsibility for security of the information assets of the company, they may not have anyone on staff who has received any training in this area. Therefore, when you point out that the shortcomings in this program are due to a lack of skill base within the security team, you can also add to the recommendation that they either hire someone with that knowledge, invest in the team by sending some of them to get education in that area, or hire someone to come in temporarily to spend time training some of the security team. Of course, that solution would be projected in the Security Master Plan to be accomplished within the next twelve months of the five-year plan. You should always be prepared to offer reasonable solutions to the problems you discover.

DEVELOPING AND REFINING SECURITY PHILOSOPHIES, STRATEGIES, AND GOALS

What follows next assumes that there is an in-house security professional who works for the client. If the client only has a contract security force, I will address what needs to be done with them at the end of this section. Now that you have the detail recommendations ironed out, you need to start your work with the security team to develop or refine their long-range goals in the areas of security philosophies, strategies, staffing, technology, processes, procedures, and contracts. This is very much an exercise in gaining buy-in from the team. You probably already have your own idea of what these areas should include as a result of your information gathering process, but you need for this team to own them if it is going to be effective. Remember, once this is done you will be gone, if you are a consultant, and they are the ones that need to make it happen year after year. The best approach to this is to have the primary leaders of the team get together to do a brainstorming session, which you will lead. If they already have some of these areas addressed in writing or in practice, you start there and then begin the discussion of how they should change for today and how they should change over time. You need to help them get to where you think they should be by explaining the advantages and disadvantages of the different subjects as they are discussed. However, you should also keep an open mind through this process. None of us have all the answers all of the time, and this process may bring out some thoughts that had not occurred to you previously.

I prefer to do this by getting everyone together in a classroom-type setting so we can write ideas on a board and discuss them. I usually ask one of them to be the "scribe" as a way to get them more involved and hopefully accept more ownership of the process. We divide the board into the different areas of discussion and title each section. Again, the best place to start is with what they already have, so I have them write any already-documented areas on the board first. Then we discuss the areas where they already have implemented things in practice but have not actually documented them, and note those areas on the board. By this time you should have seen their involvement in the process gain some enthusiasm as they see that this is an area where they already have accomplishments. Then you move into the discussions about the areas where you believe they need to expand their long-range goals in the areas of security philosophies, strategies, staffing, technology, processes, procedures, and contracts. Again, you have limited time to get this process concluded so it is important that you not let the discussions just wander. Although you do not want to stifle their thinking, you do want to guide it to some reasonable conclusions within a controlled period of time.

If the client only has a contract security force, you will need to determine the best way to work with them or with the client management that manages the contract. My preference is to work with the client management first to go through the areas that need to be developed and documented. In most cases they will look to you to just recommend what they should implement, and then you and that manager can meet with the contract management team to discuss their implementation of these areas. Of course, if the client is a small company and all they really need is to have a physical security presence, then much of this area may not be needed. I do find situations where that is all the client thinks they needed when I started this process, but by the time I finish they understand they need a lot more. In many of those cases I will recommend that they hire an in-house security manager to manage the programs and the contract force, and they frequently agree with that. If that is what they plan to do, then I will suggest that we table most of the development of this area of focus until that person is on board and then I can come back and work with him or her to finish expanding these areas, because they should have ownership of them.

INVOLVING THE STAKEHOLDERS

Once this process is complete you should now schedule a meeting with the stakeholder group that was established earlier. It can be valuable to review the recommendations and the goals in the areas of security philosophies, strategies, staffing, technology, processes, procedures, and contracts with this group to get their feedback on any concerns or issues or support for the different areas. You need to caution the group that nothing has been finalized yet, so they should not discuss the details outside of the group. However, you should understand that there is always someone who wants to be the first one to tell their boss or someone about things like this, so it is important that you be careful about what you review with them. For example, you should not discuss any personnel-related issues or anything to do with the executive protection program. You should focus on those areas that have some direct effect on them and their organization primarily. These areas will more than likely be the areas of technology changes and procedural changes. It may also involve some areas such as security officer post changes. If you are dealing with a "blended" organization, meaning some in-house and some contract, then you might have a recommendation relative to changing the security contract company. That is also an area that I would not address to this group, as it would certainly get back to the contract company. Just discussing that among the in-house security team might also allow that information to leak out because they will have personal relationships with the contract team. It can be difficult at times to know what can be discussed with others prior to taking it to the executives, but I tend to err on the side of caution because the last thing you want to do is to create a hostile environment situation. People tend to be less open-minded to your ideas when you create problems for them, even when you are right!

DOCUMENTING THE MASTER PLAN

Next you need to document all of this information in the Security Master Plan, working with security management. This will be a very detailed document, and it takes some time to get it into its final form. I usually work on this from my office, as opposed to being onsite, and exchange phone calls and e-mails back and forth with the CSO or director of security as I put the document together. As you construct the document you should remember that the final document will be shared with other functions within the business because some of them have a stake in this as well. One area that I am always concerned about is the topic of executive protection. I do not like for anyone to see the specifics of that plan except for those who truly have a need to know. Therefore, I will usually list that section in the contents, but the only information in the plan is a statement that anyone who needs to know this information should contact the CSO or director of security for details. This plan should be given to only the executives it covers and those that they deem appropriate to see it.

Another area that I do not want to have wide distribution is the area of security personnel changes or potential changes to the contract security company. Again, I would only have a statement in these sections that says that anyone who needs to know this information should contact the CSO or director of security for details. As you go through the development of the plan you will need to identify these sensitive areas that need to be isolated based on the client's structure and what you feel is important to protect.

DEVELOPING THE RECOMMENDATIONS PRESENTATION

Once you have completed the Security Master Plan, the next step is to develop a recommendations presentation that highlights the changes that are necessary for the organization, to present to middle and executive management. Understand that what you present to middle management might not contain everything that will be shown to executive management.

As you continue to put the executive presentation together, you need to make sure that it contains statements that cover all aspects of the master plan. You should make sure you highlight all of the good work that the security team has been doing as well. It is highly probable that there will be a number of your recommendation that the CSO or director of security will inform you that he or she has made before to the executives. When I am told this, I normally ask that they produce those documents that show exactly what they recommended, when they recommended it, and to whom. If they have that information and it truly is the same recommendation, I will make reference to it in the presentation unless the CSO or director of security feels that this may be embarrassing to the executive involved. Remember, most executives are people with big egos, and it would probably be very embarrassing to them for you to tell them they should have listened to their own security team when they told them this was needed to be done. Embarrassing them usually is not the best way to get them to support the recommendations. Having said that, I also believe it is important to give credit where it is due and to let them know that their own internal security team had recommended this previously. You will need to strike the right balance between giving credit and saving face for the executive.

I will give you a short lecture at this point. I have met security professionals who take the position that diplomacy is not a part of their job. Their job is to "tell it like it is!" Well, I believe a security professional's job is to make change happen to provide for improved protection of people, property, and assets. I also believe that if you do not have diplomacy as part of your tools, you will fail more than you succeed. Understanding how to present something to someone in a way where they can get behind it gives you much more advantage than presenting it in a way that embarrasses them. In other words, "Don't bite the hand that feeds you the money!" (see Figure 11.1)

FIGURE 11.1 Presenting recommendations to executive management should be done in such a manner as to garner support and buy-in to effect positive change.

However, this information on what the CSO or director of security has made before to the executives can sometimes be very helpful to support other recommendations. For example, you might want to recommend that the security team be moved out from under the facilities executive and put under some other executive's organization. If there are some examples of them having made recommendation to the existing executive that were turned down and you are making some of the same recommendations, that information can be very useful in demonstrating that the realignment should be made. The CSO or director of security may prefer that you not do this because it may damage the relationship with the existing organization's executive and the move may not happen, even if you are recommending it, but this is a call that you will have to make based on how important you feel it is. If possible, you should attempt to have a discussion of this type with an executive who can make the decision to implement this change, in a one-on-one meeting prior to the formal presentation taking place. That way, even if the change will not be implemented, you have not embarrassed anyone and yet you have planted that seed with the executive who may decide to make the change at some later point in time.

You must remember that the intent of this presentation is primarily to get the executive's approval for those recommendations that need their level of approval. You need to keep the presentation concise and on point. All of the recommendations that you have that the CSO or director of security can make happen should be only briefly referred to in this presentation, but you must have the details of those recommendations at hand in case someone wants more detail. The areas of controversy should be addressed early on to get them resolved within the allotted time for the presentation. When you schedule the meeting with the executives to make this presentation, make sure you ask for enough time to allow for discussions of those items. It may be appropriate to see if you can get some one-on-one time with a different higher level executive to discuss any sensitive recommendations such as the move of the security organization to another executive, as I mentioned before, or the replacement of the CSO or director of security. If he or she agrees with you on those items, you should ask if that can be made to happen prior to the presentation so you can show that change in the master plan. If you get this one-on-one meeting, make sure you have all of the detailed information with you that supports the recommendation so you can get it resolved immediately. Be prepared to leave a copy of that information with the executive so he or she can use it in any follow-on discussions that may be needed with his or her staff. You should also be prepared to leave copies of your presentation and the draft of the Security Master Plan with each of the attendees at the primary presentation meeting, but remember to exclude some of the more sensitive sections from the main body and give them those sections separately in case they want someone on their staff to review the material.

ESTIMATING COST IMPACTS

Cost estimates will be required for those areas that need to be addressed immediately and have costs associated with them, such as adding cameras or migrating to new access control technology. To obtain these estimates you may need to contact some outside sources. If you do, the best approach is to tell them that you are putting together some budget numbers for work that you are attempting to get approval for and may be undertaking in the next year or so and you would like to get some input from them. Most suppliers or integrators can provide you with rough budgetary estimates without too much effort. I believe it is inappropriate to have them do a detailed bid on work that has not been approved at this point. If the client already has a systems integrator working for them, they would be the best source for these estimates because they know the current system configurations, which have a direct impact on the cost estimate. However, you should make it clear to them that these numbers are only so you can gain approval for the system expansions or additions, and once approved, it will probably have to go out for bid. I do not like to mislead a supplier into thinking they have a lock on the future work, just because I am asking them for the estimates. You should also take the timing of the work into account. An estimate today, for work that may not be started for three to five years, will need to be increased by 10 to 15 percent, due to inflation and other increases that may be unforeseeable.

There is another source of information that can be accessed for these estimates, if needed. RSMeans Company provides accurate and up-to-date information for construction projects for North America. Of course, these are only estimates, and typically you would use these if you need to install an entire system, which is typically not the case in most situations. You also need to understand that cost estimates will need to include more than just the cost of the equipment itself; there are labor costs, wiring costs, and other factors.

PROJECT MANAGEMENT SKILLS

One other factor to consider is whether or not the current in-house staff has the skills or the time to manage a major system upgrade, if that is what you are recommending. Project management is a skill that can make a major upgrade go smoothly; if the skills are not there, the client will encounter cost overruns and numerous other problems. Just because someone is knowledgeable of security systems does not mean they have the necessary skills to manage a major project. The primary aspects of project management require that a person have the following traits:

- Well organized
- Process oriented
- Ability to multitask
- Vast follow-up skills
- A logical thought process
- A problem solver
- Analytical ability
- A good budget manager
- Very self-disciplined

The aspects of managing a major project can be overwhelming to someone who has never tackled a project such as this before. Therefore, you should consider recommending that the client hire someone, at least temporarily, to oversee any major system project. Also, if you do not have that skill yourself, then you should ask around to find someone you can recommend for the job. Do not fall into the trap of signing up to do something you do not know how to do.

12

Typical Contents of a Security Master Plan

A number of people have asked me to provide them with a sample Security Master Plan. This presents a problem in that every client's plan is different, and, of course, they are all extremely confidential, so to construct a sample plan would be difficult and possibly mislead you on what your specific plan should look like. Therefore, as the next best thing I have provided you with an outline of the contents of a typical plan and some explanations and rationale of the different sections. As you begin developing the master plan for your client, or yourself, you may find that some of these sections are not applicable and you may need to add some that I have not listed here.

CONTENT LISTING AND ORGANIZATION

- Purpose
- Introduction
- Executive summary
- Areas of focus
  - Security philosophies, strategies, and goals
  - Security organization's reporting and structure
    - Director of security's skills and contacts
    - Security organization's skills matrix

- Security organization's staffing and supplemental staffing
- Contract security staffing
- Armed versus unarmed security personnel
- Security technology plan
  - Security control center
  - Access control system
  - Closed circuit television (CCTV) system
  - Digital recording and intelligent software
  - Radio system
  - Automated guard tour system
  - System maintenance plan
- Physical security standards
  - Exterior
    - Property signage
    - Entrance control points
    - Perimeter fencing, barriers, and gates
    - Crime Prevention Through Environmental Design
    - Lighting
    - CCTV system use
    - Alarms
    - Landscaping
    - Building perimeter
    - Access control system use
  - Visitor and contractor control process
  - Interior security
    - Common areas and interior controls
    - High-security areas
    - CCTV system use
    - Alarms
    - Access control system use
    - Key and lock controls
    - Other locking mechanisms
- Investigations
  - Criminal arrests
  - Law enforcement agencies
- Crisis management plan
  - Emergency planning and response
  - Exterior public agencies
  - Terrorism and bioterrorism
  - Disaster recovery program

- Security awareness program
  - New employee orientation
- Risk assessment program
- Information protection program
  - Information asset security
- Workplace violence prevention program
- Pre-employment screening
- Termination interview room
- Executive protection program
- Unique security requirements

STRUCTURAL FOCUS

Purpose

The "Purpose" section is a simple statement of the intention of the Security Master Plan document and might go something like this:

> The information contained in this document was developed to form a Security Master Plan for (*The Client*). The intent of this master plan is to outline the components of an excellent security program that should be put in place now in order to mitigate the identified risks for (*The Client*) and to provide a safe and secure work environment for their employees, clients, and visitors. Where appropriate, the master plan will also define the future direction of the security program including the supporting technology objectives. The master plan will support proper planning, good coordination, and smooth transitioning, consistent with the overall future direction of (*The Client*).

Introduction

The Introduction defines the objectives of the Security Master Plan along with what might be a major focus area. In this example, the major focus is protecting the client's reputation because this particular client is dependent on receiving donations to stay in business. Therefore this section might look like this:

> The primary objective of this Security Master Plan is to support the safety and security of (*The Client's*) employees, visitors, facilities, and assets. It is also important and prudent to ensure that the reputation of (*The Client*) is protected at all times, as this can be a major factor in the

193

decision process of customers or contributors. To accomplish this goal we have developed this plan as a management tool to delineate our strategies in the area of security both now and in the future. This document will be reviewed and updated on an annual basis to reflect the changes in our environment and in our policies.

Executive Summary

The Executive Summary section is used to highlight the areas of focus and the areas of change that are being implemented. While this is a summary, it is typically a longer section than you might be used to seeing in other documents, because the Security Master Plan is also a very large document. The length of the section will depend on the amount of change that has to be made as a result of your work with this client. You should remember that for some of the executives, this may be the only section of the document that they read, so you might want to repeat some of the previous information. It might look like this:

> The primary objective of this Security Master Plan is to support the safety and security of (*The Client's*) employees, patients, visitors, facilities, and assets. It is important to differentiate between "deter" and "eliminate." No security measures, regardless of how involved or sophisticated, can ensure absolute protection against every possible threat. It is the sole intent of any security program to provide such obstacles and observation methods that the risks to the perpetrator of exposure, failure, or capture are greater than the potential for success in perpetrating the incident.
>
> (*The Client*) will have a well-rounded security program that provides employees and visitors with a high comfort level and will provide for mitigation of identified risks for (*The Client*).
>
> (*The Client*) will have a well-trained, unarmed security force. The use of unarmed security officers in our environment has been determined to be the industry standard and is an effective policy to provide for a secure environment. By having a well-trained, unarmed security force, the employees and visitors will have their comfort level fortified.
> A guard tour system will be used to help confirm that patrol functions are being carried out as expected, especially after-hours. This should reduce potential complaints that the security staff is sometimes not seen and it will provide analytical data on the tours themselves.
>
> The plan calls for all visitors to come under some form of surveillance (electronic or natural), either as they enter the parking deck or the lobbies of (*The Client*). The actions of the lobby attendants and the signage

at the entrances will provide a natural perimeter, making unwanted individuals feel uncomfortable.

The locking of delivery entrances, perimeter doors, stairwell doors, and other doors in the facilities at certain times of the day will help to control the movement of unauthorized individuals. This will be combined with a security awareness programs that teaches employees how to deal with strangers in their work areas.

Access points to the facility will be reduced, increasing general observation of people entering (*The Client*). Adequate lighting will be maintained, increasing the level of user comfort. By reducing access points and providing adequate lighting under basic Crime Prevention Through Environmental Design procedures, unwanted individuals will feel they are under surveillance either by CCTV systems or the visible security staff. They will be more inclined to take their unwanted actions elsewhere. At the same time, (*The Client's*) employees, through their observations and the regular security awareness programs, will feel that the security program in place is more than adequate.

Security practices will include the following:

- Security staff will be well trained in an organized manner and have a thorough understanding of their scope of work. The program should include testing to confirm the officers understand their role. Management should take on this responsibility in developing the post orders and training program so there is no question of the security staff's responsibilities and knowledge. If a contract security firm is engaged or new officers are brought on-board, there will be minimal staff downtime while officers are brought up to speed.
- The security systems will be regularly inspected and maintained by qualified personnel. A program should be developed so there is a limited amount of downtime in the event a part of the security system goes down. For example, an emergency call box in the parking garage with a sign indicating "Out of Order" does not provide a high comfort level. The security staff will regularly inspect these security and safety systems as part of their rounds, and their repair will have an extremely high priority, no longer than a twenty-four-hour period of time.
- The security department will maintain an ongoing relationship with the police department's crime prevention unit and other local directors of security so that the management team at (*The Client*) is kept aware of problems in the neighborhood and solutions available through the city by reports that are initiated by the director of security.

195

- Based on the results of the review and discussions with executive management, a change in the reporting structure has been implemented for the security organization. The organization previously reported into the facilities engineering organization; however, it has been determined that it is more appropriate to have the security organization report into the legal function; therefore, the director of security now reports to the general counsel for (*The Client*).
- There will be an ongoing security awareness program for the various departments' representatives, called "functional security reps," that keeps them informed of potential problems and solutions available. This program will keep the lines of communications open between the security organization and employees and management, helping them to feel they are part of an overall team response to security needs.
- The addition of coverage in some areas that were weak, the use of the various electronic security systems for surveillance, emergency call boxes, and access control systems will help to minimize the number of uniformed security staff members required throughout a twenty-four-hour period and provide excellent investigative information. The continued use and expansion of these systems as (*The Client*) continues to grow will optimize the effectiveness of existing security staff and minimize the need for additional security staff. The projected addition of some technologies such as biometric access control and intelligent software for CCTV surveillance will further enhance the effectiveness of these systems in the near future.

Areas of Focus

You should list the details of the contents of the plan here in this section.

- Security philosophies, strategies, and goals
- Security organization's reporting and structure
  - Director of security's skills and contacts
  - Security organization's skills matrix
  - Security organization's staffing and supplemental staffing
  - Contract security staffing
  - Armed versus unarmed security personnel

After the "Areas of Focus" section you should list each identified section; here you would document these areas and highlight the changes or additions that have been made as a part of your work. If there are any significant changes, they might need to be highlighted in the Executive Summary section as well, such as I did with the change to the security organization's reporting structure. Remember that this document will be disseminated to a number of people within the organization; therefore, you must be cautious about what you put in it as it applies to a specific individual. For example, if you feel that some of the staff or the CSO or director of security need to get additional training or education in certain areas, you might want to just generally list the fact that "Staff members will be obtaining education in the following areas to enhance their career opportunities and further their professional knowledge: security technology and biometrics, IT investigation certifications, security assessment training, etc."

- Risk assessment program
  - Potential impact to the corporate reputation or loss of contributions
  - Potential loss of information assets
  - Potential incidents of violence onsite

As you put together the details of each of these sections, it is vital that you not only document the identified risks but that you also note the details of how the risk will be mitigated. This will become important to the client in later years if there are budget challenges so he or she is capable of easily determining which program improvements are tied to each risk mitigation plan. By the way, it is commonplace for some security program enhancements to be associated with more than one risk mitigation plan. For example, the addition of some exterior cameras can be linked to mitigating risks for both employee safety and asset protection.

- Security technology plan
  - Security control center
  - Access control system
  - Closed circuit television system
  - Digital recording and intelligent software
  - Radio system
  - Automated guard tour system
  - System maintenance plan

Again, you should document the details of what currently exists for each of these sections and highlight any significant changes that have been made and those changes that are planned for the future with an estimate of when and what the costs will be, if any. You continue with this format for every section that you have listed in the contents of the plan. Additionally, where there are policy documents that are important to the plan, such as a policy document on the use of unarmed security officers, you should refer to that document in that section and then attach it as an appendix at the end of the plan.

BUDGETING FOCUS

One of the main objectives of developing a Security Master Plan is to make sure that the business or institution is allotting the proper amount of funding to ensure the success of the security program. As I mentioned in the Introduction section, a Security Master Plan will aid you or your client in gaining buy-in from the executive management team on the direction of the program and outline the necessary budget to support it. The way you do this is by educating the management team to the risks that exist for them and the business or institution so they can clearly understand the need for the expenditures that are required to mitigate these risks. (By the way, I usually stress the point, both verbally and in writing, that risk mitigation is how you manage and reduce risks; it does not eliminate risks.)

Next, you need to structure the plan so the new expenditures are spread out over a five-year period. For example, you may need to significantly upgrade the CCTV system by simply adding additional cameras or by utilizing IP cameras, including the addition of new or more digital recording. You might also want to add the feature of utilizing intelligent software to make the system more productive and to reduce your reliance on the security control center operators. The total purchase and installation costs of the additional cameras, digital recorders, and software might be $500,000. You might need to spend $200,000 in the first year to get a major reduction to the risks that this will mitigate and then spread the other $300,000 over the next four years. However, this is not just a "divide the cost by five" type of an exercise. You need to spend this much money if there are some major holes in the current program that you are attempting to fix. The first year's cost should take a big chunk out of that hole and reduce the risks to a reasonable level. You cannot take two or three years to accomplish that, and the executives would not expect you to recommend doing that.

Perhaps the current setup does not have enough digital recorders to be able to maintain the industry standard of 30 days' worth of recordings, and they may not have enough cameras to provide complete coverage of every entrance around the facility and the high-risk areas. The first year's expenditure should get the digital recording up to where it should be and add enough cameras to cover all of the perimeter entrances. The next two years might add most of the rest of the cameras you need and any additional digital recorders, while you add the intelligent software in the fourth year to make the system much more effective, and in the fifth year you would add the final equipment requirements. Therefore, the costs might spread out like this:

- Year 1 = $200K
- Year 2 = $100K
- Year 3 = $ 75K
- Year 4 = $ 75K
- Year 5 = $ 50K
- Total = $500K

ESTABLISHING AN ROI

The costs referenced above are all considered to be capital expenditures, in most businesses. Meaning they are primarily a one time cost and they are an improvement to the facility itself. You must also address any increases to the expense" budget as well. The expense items are the reoccurring costs such as maintenance or the cost of extra guards. Ideally, when you have major capital expenses you can reduce the number of guards and therefore reduce the expense budget. If you are able to do that then you may be able to get a return on investment (ROI) that would offset the capital costs. Usually, most businesses would like to see an ROI of 2.5 years or less, meaning that the expense savings for 2.5 years would equal the capital expenditures. However, even if you do not achieve that level of savings, if you can show a payback within a longer period of time, that is a better story than no payback at all. I do not mean to imply that having an ROI is absolutely necessary in order to get security expenditures approved. I have seen many projects approved based on the mitigation of risks with no actual ROI. When that is the situation with the client, it becomes even more essential that you do a very good job of making a compelling case that the risks are real. It is also very helpful if you have been able to show the cost avoidance of a situation where the risk is realized. As discussed in the Risk Analysis section earlier in the book, it makes little sense to spend more money on risk mitigation than what might be lost if the risk were realized. Therefore, you need to quantify the potential cost impact of the risks whenever possible, and that cost estimation must have sound reasoning behind it. If you are not familiar with the ROI principles, I would recommend you acquaint yourself with them. For instance, you should never claim an ROI based on the avoidance of cost, only the elimination of current expenditures.

Finally, as I mentioned earlier in the book, even though there is an approved budget for the out years, that does not mean that the client will actually get all of that money when it comes time for it to be approved and released. However, by having a five-year plan that has been agreed to by the management team, they do have a much better chance of getting that money released, and even if they do not get it all in the year that they wanted it, that only means that it slips out to the next year as opposed to being lost completely. Also, the better job that is done associating the annual expenditures to certain risk mitigation, the easier it will be to back pressure any changes to the budget for that year, because you can remind them of the cost impact of that potential risk coming to fruition. For example, in the table above we had listed $200K for Year 2. If a budget challenge happens for that year, the client should have enough risk data to demonstrate that they have to spend $150K in Year 2 to put the business into a reasonable risk posture, and the other $50K worth of work can be moved to Year 3 and added to what is being done that year. Again, the more you can outline specific funding needed to mitigate specific risks, the easier it will be to contain these budget challenge situations.

13

Finalizing the Security Master Plan Process

THE RECOMMENDATIONS PRESENTATION

It is now time to deliver the recommendations presentation, which highlights the changes that are necessary for the organization, to middle and executive management. When making this presentation it is vital that you are well versed in all of the facts that lead to the final recommendations. You do not have to commit all of them to memory, but you must be able to quickly access your reference material to resolve any questions that may come up. You must spend as much time as needed to make sure you are well prepared and confident of your material. A common error made by some of us in the security profession is that we think everyone understands all of the basics of the business. This just is not true, so you have to scrutinize the presentation to determine if it is clear to the nonsecurity people in the audience.

For example, you might be making a recommendation that they plan to implement biometric access readers for their high-security areas within the next year. You should have some examples of those readers to show them and you should explain that the addition of these readers will not necessarily require a change to their basic access control system, although in some cases it might require some additional memory capability to store the additional data associated with the biometrics. This will depend on the current system installed and the type of biometrics you are recommending, which you should have discussed with the equipment vendor to get their assessment. Another situation that might require explanation is the implementation of a security awareness program. You have probably discussed in association with that program that utilizing the eyes and ears of all employees will greatly increase the potential for discovering unwanted activity on the site; you should also explain that this is not something that will cause any reduced productivity for the employees, but in many cases it does result in increased morale because by involving all employees in the program they understand it in more detail and feel safer in the work environment.

WHERE TO BEGIN

It is normally best to start at the middle management level and get their buy in. This is important so they are on board with the recommendations and hopefully in agreement with all of them. However, while is not absolutely necessary that they all agree with every recommendation, you do want to attempt to resolve any major disagreements if at all possible. It is also a valuable exercise to provide you with a dry run before you get in front of the senior executives. If you get lots of questions such as "What does that mean?" or "Why would you want to make that change?" then perhaps you need to rework the presentation before moving on. It is important that you not allow too much time between the presentation to middle management and the senior executives. You do not want them discussing it with your executive audience before you have a chance to present it. I usually try to present it to a group of middle managers one afternoon and already have the executive presentation scheduled for the next morning. This will allow you time that evening to make modifications that came out of the first presentation, but does not give them much time to have discussions about it before the next morning.

Cost estimates need to be addressed for those areas of change that need to be implemented immediately and you should have rough estimates of cost impacts of future changes. You will normally get some discussions on where the budget money will come from, especially in the middle management group. Your answer is simple: That will be decided by the senior executives. Additionally, you will need to make the decision of who you present to and in what order if you are doing more than one presentation to middle management, based on input from the CSO or director of security and based on your own impression of these individuals' level of support as gleaned from your interactions with them during this process. Under no circumstances should you present this to anyone you have not personally interviewed during the process, with the possible exception of a critical manager who was not previously available.

You should have the Security Master Plan document with you for the presentation but it should be clearly marked as a draft copy, because the final document will depend on what agreements you get from the executives. If asked, you should not give out any copies of the draft, just explain that it may be modified further as you proceed through the review process and it would not be appropriate for there to be conflicting copies of the plan. If there is disagreement with certain aspects of the master plan during the presentation, you will need to resolve these differences prior to finalizing the plan. If absolutely necessary, you can always reschedule the presentation to the senior executives, but you should do your best to avoid that situation.

SETTING YOUR GOALS

You are now prepared to make your presentation to the senior executives. You need to understand what your goals are relative to this meeting and make sure you accomplish each of those goals. Typically your goals would include the following:

- To define the major risks for the business or institution.
- To outline the appropriate actions to mitigate those risks.
- To define the needed changes or additions to the security program.
- To define the needed changes or additions to the security organization and staff.
- To clearly identify the cost impacts of these changes.
- To clearly identify the advantages of any and all recommended changes.
- To gain the support of the executives for the recommendations.
- To gain approval for your client to obtain the needed budget money to implement the changes that are required for the next 12 months.

ASKING THE TOUGH QUESTIONS

Ultimately, at the conclusion of the final presentation with the executives, you want to "close the deal" on the funding that will be required to fully implement the plan that you have put forward. You will need to ask some direct questions such as the following:

- Do you agree with the risks that have been identified as requiring the need for mitigation?
- Do you agree with the impact cost estimates that have been developed and associated with these risks?
- Do you agree to the requested funding of X dollars for the capital expenditures and Y dollars for the expense budget?
- Do you agree with the future strategies that have been developed?
- Do you agree with the master plan that has been developed?

You might be tempted to ask the questions about the risks and their impact at the end of the presentation on that section; however, I believe it is better to ask them at the end of the presentation just before asking about the funding, as a reminder of why that funding is needed. Be sure that your questions are asked in a respectful tone and that you listen to the answers before you move on to the next question. You also need to be prepared for a negative response to any of the questions. Do not assume that every executive will be in total agreement with your presentation. For each question you might want to plan in advance about how you will respond to someone who replies in the negative. Also, do not be too quick to respond to that negative situation, because you may find one of the executives is in full agreement with your plan and might choose to make that response for you, which will be much more effective. It is a great help when one of the executives decides takes up your defense without being asked to do so. Of course you should not delay too long before responding because that can send a message that you are unprepared for the question.

Assuming you get their agreement with these questions, you might want to ask one more:

- Since we are all in agreement with the plan and the actions that need to take place, may I ask when will the funding be provided that is required for implementation?

Ideally that will result in the highest level executive turning to the CFO or one of the other executives and charging him or her with the responsibility of determining where the money will come from and when it will be available. Normally, that is the best you can do. Sometimes it results in an answer such as, "We will have to review the current budget and see what we are able to do." Whatever answer you get, if you are a consultant, you have done your job of getting them actually thinking about where the money will come from, and it will now be up to the CSO or director of security to pursue the funding. If you are an in-house security person, your CSO or director of security will need to decide what the next step is. You might actually want to defer so that this question is asked by your CSO or director of security for them, but at a minimum you should discuss your strategy with him or her ahead of time.

If there is no in-house security professional on staff, pursue the issue of who will manage Implementation of the Security Master Plan and the work that needs to be done. It would normally fall to the manager who is responsible for managing the security contract, but you should not make that assumption. Of course, as the consultant, you can offer to do this work for them but you should be prepared to discuss the costs for your services. You should be prepared to discuss your support and associated costs in the following areas:

- Developing a request for proposal for the equipment upgrades needed
- Managing the selection process for the system integrator to do this work
- Managing the implementation process of the changes or upgrades
- Conducting periodic or annual reviews of the Security Master Plan, which would include evaluations of the risks and the risk mitigation plan

It is important that you have broken down costs into these different segments because they may want someone in-house to do part of this work. If so, you will be prepared to offer them the input they need to make their decisions. Of course, you can also offer a "bundled" price as well.

One other matter that may arise during this presentation is whether they should hire an in-house security professional, assuming they do not have one. This can be a slight conflict of interest for you as a consultant because if they do, they will not need you as much. However, you must provide this recommendation based on what is best for the client. Personally, I have encountered very few situations where I felt comfortable with clients not having their own in-house security professional. However, there are many different levels of skills, and therefore costs, for this person. In many small to midsize businesses, what they need on an ongoing basis is someone to manage the security contracts, officers, and equipment vendors. This does not require the company to have a CSO or director of security-level person. This is more the rank of a first-level security manager.

Personally, I think any business or institution that turns its security over 100 percent to a contract company is asking for problems. I do not mean that as criticism of the contract security industry. A number of very competent security service providers are available, but I believe it is necessary to have someone in-house who is a security professional to manage the security function and who is focused on all of the many different areas of the business that can affect the overall security solutions and results for the business. You really cannot have the contract company auditing the facility organization's management of the lock and key contract or the shredding contract. You cannot expect them to work hand in hand with the IT function on developing and implementing the disaster recovery plan. Also, there are many different investigations, such as HR, harassment, fraud, and threats of violence, that I believe are too sensitive for them have a contract person doing the investigation. There are also laws in many states that require investigators who are not in-house to be a licensed investigator. Many security companies do not have anyone on their staff at a site who is a licensed private investigator, although they do sometimes have them on their headquarters staff.

Depending on the type of business, there are many types of issues that an in-house professional can be mindful of, but a contract company cannot. I also believe, based on my relationship with many leaders of the contract security services industry, that they also believe that it is better for them to be dealing with someone who is knowledgeable of the security industry as opposed to someone who just thinks they know all about it. There are many people in the business world who have had some level of interaction with security and security providers over the years who think they understand the nuances of the security business. Believe me when I say that for many of them, "They have no idea what they do not know!" And when they figure out that there was an area of the security business that they did not really understand, it is usually as an aftermath of the development of some major problem that has come about as a result of their lack of knowledge. They frequently resolve these problems by terminating the contract security provider for lack of performance and bringing in a new company.

These can be frustrating times for all concerned including the security consultant who did not point out to their client that they needed to have this level of skill in-house. Of course, this brings me back to where I started, which is my belief is that you should always recommend what is best for the client, even when it means that you will not have as much recurring work with them.

SUBMITTING THE FINALIZED SECURITY MASTER PLAN

Once all disagreements, discussions, and changes have been finalized, you can now submit the Security Master Plan document. There is always the possibility that not everything will be resolved in this meeting. There could be areas of disagreement that the highest level executive wants resolved prior to concluding the project. If this occurs, do not be discouraged; just make sure that the area of disagreement is clearly defined. You might want to suggest a target date for resolution of the discussion as well so it does not drag out the process too long. Finally, get clarification from the executive concerning whether you should report back to him or her on the outcome of this matter or if you should just make the needed changes to the plan and distribute it. For something as important as this plan is, you need to be clear on how much control the executive wishes to exert.

Hopefully, the recipients of the final document were identified at some point during the process. If not, you should confer with the client to have them identified. At a minimum recipients should include the stakeholders group and the executives who were interviewed. One final reminder: Be sure you remove the sections that should not get wide distribution and in those copies of the plan where those sections are included, you should make a note as to who actually received copies with that information included.

14

Utilizing Your Plan in Managing Your Business

UTILIZING YOUR PLAN FOR PERIODIC QUALITY CHECKS

Now that the client has a completed Security Master Plan, it is vital that it be kept up to date and that this document is used as an integral part of the operating plan. Several aspects of the master plan must be addressed and updated on a routine basis. I usually recommend to the client that for the first year, the plan should be reviewed at least every three months to determine if any changes are needed. After the first year, the plan should be reviewed every four months, or three times a year, to ensure that the plan is still correct and, even more importantly, to make sure the plan is being followed. Anytime there are changes of any significance, the plan should be updated and redistributed to the original recipients with a cover letter that highlights the changes and the reasons for them. Like most important documents, it is valuable to indicate a revision number and date on each new copy.

Because there should be very few copies of this plan in existence, I also suggest that they hand-deliver the new revisions and attempt to recover previous versions for destruction. One way to do this is to set up individual meetings with each of the recipients so you can brief them on the changes being made. There are not many reasons for the CSO or director of security to get one-on-one time with the company executives except when there are problems. This is a great way to have those meetings in the positive environment of making improvements.

IT IS ALL ABOUT TIMING

As with most things in life and business, "Timing is everything!" Clients must make sure that they have a clear focus on the timing of the annual budget process within their businesses. It is critical that they produce an update to the plan just prior to that process and make sure the management team is reminded of the needs of the security organization's funding in support of the Security Master Plan, which they all have agreed to. One of the approaches I usually recommend is that the client initiate a review with the appropriate executives every year to ascertain if they want to actually move up the timing of some of the items in the out years in order to improve the company's risk mitigation posture. Even if they do not want changes, you have still succeeded in reminding them of what funding is needed for the next year and why. Of course, they run the risk of the executive deciding they need to push out the timing instead, but I suspect that would have happened during the budget process anyway. If these reviews occur prior to the annual budget review process, the chances are much better that they will be able to maintain their budget. If they do get budget challenges, you might recommend that they make a list of risks mitigation plans and associated costs and go forward to management, asking for guidance on which risk executive management wishes to defer in order to meet the budget challenge.

The following kinds of changes might occur during the periodic review processes:

- First, there are different parts of the plan where it was identified that certain changes need to be implemented. Those changes might have been associated with in-house staff, contract staff, reporting structures, capital or expense expenditures, and procedural or policy changes. As these items are addressed, the plan should be updated so that their current status is properly reflected in the plan. If there are a number of changes that need to be made within the first few months, the client may want to wait until all of them are completed before making the updates and redistributing the document to the previous recipients.

- Next, there are timing issues that were identified in the plan. These may be the installation of new equipment or the addition or reduction of security officers based on some other changes. The timing of some of these items will change from year to year for numerous reasons, and therefore they must be updated whenever that change is recognized.
- Another item that will certainly occur is the change in security staffing. As people leave the business and new staff members are brought on board, these personnel changes will need to be reflected in the training plan that had been developed. I also encourage the client to include certification goals in the staffing plan as well. This is an excellent way to demonstrate to their company's management that they have a professional security staff. I usually outline for them ways that they can motivate their staff to pursue these certifications because it does take a lot of work on the individual's part. Some companies I know will increase their employees' salaries once they achieve a certification. Others offer to reimburse the costs associated with the study and the certification upon successful completion of the exam. The client can also stress to its people that this is an excellent way for them to be more competitive in the marketplace if they were to decide to look for other opportunities.

ASIS International currently has three different certifications:

- CPP certification stands for Board-Certified in Security Management. To qualify to take the certification exam, the individual has to have been in security for at least seven years, including three years in management.
- PCI certification stands for Board-Certified Professional Certified Investigator. To qualify to take the certification exam, the individual has to have five years of investigation experience, with at least two years of case management experience.
- PSP certification stands for Board-Certified Physical Security Professional. To qualify to take the certification exam, the individual must have at least five years of experience in the physical security field.

If you would like more information on these certifications, go to the ASIS International Web site at www.asisonline.org.

- All of the identified risks in the plan need to be reassessed on an annual basis. These risks might have lessened or increased as other factors change. For example, the local economy changes, either for the better or worse will have some effect on the local crime picture and therefore will have some impact on what needs to be done to mitigate the risks associated with the local crime statistics. There may have been a facility in the company, such as a chemical plant, that had unique security challenges, and the company may have decided to outsource that work and then sold that particular asset. This is an example of risk avoidance, avoiding a risk by eliminating the source of the problem. There may also be newly identified risks that need to be evaluated to determine if changes will need to be made to the plan to mitigate the new risks. Similarly, some of the previously identified risks may have gone away. If that is the case, someone needs to determine if there were any specific mitigation factors associated with those risks that should not be acted upon now. Risk evaluations are a critical factor in ensuring that the plan remain a viable document. If there is not an in-house security staff that can sufficiently manage this review and analysis of the risks factors, you will need to sell the client on having you, as their consultant, conduct these reviews. The client needs to understand that just as the company updates and modifies its business plan every year, the Security Master Plan will need to be updated as well to ensure it is always relevant.
- As the business or institution changes, it is important that those changes be factored into the master plan to determine if the plan needs to be updated. When the original plan was compiled, there may have been a determination that the business would not undergo any significant changes over the course of the next few years. However, the business may have grown or even reduced in size for various reasons. In either case, the Security Master Plan will need to be adjusted to fit the current environment. Of course, if the business needs to reduce resources, then a security professional needs to make sure there is an effective plan in place for identifying any potential violent acts that could occur during that process (a process that this client may not have undergone in their past).
- I also recommend an annual review with the group referred to as "stakeholders." This is the representative group of all of the

organizations that were affected by the changes driven by the Security Master Plan. By involving this group in an annual review process, you gain cross-functional insight into how the implementation process is going. I have always found it to be beneficial to seek criticism instead of just waiting for it. This provides a process for the airing of concerns and complaints in a more positive environment. It also provides you with the opportunity to explain why their concerns are or are not valid and to help them determine how to make needed corrections. This keeps the stakeholders engaged and actively helping to make the program a success. If there is not an in-house security staff that can sufficiently manage this, you need to sell the client on having you, as their consultant, conduct this annual review, which can be one aspect of the multiple activities you perform during that visit. If many drastic changes are planned within the first year or two, consider holding more frequent reviews with this group during that time. It is always better for them to have the CSO or director of security or you, the consultant, ask them about problems than to wait for them to get so frustrated that they go over your head and create a defensive atmosphere for the security organization.

KEEPING THE PLAN IN SYNC WITH THE BUSINESS

I believe it is very important that the client CSO or director of security maintains his or her credibility with the executives relative to the Security Master Plan. An excellent way to do this is when the situation develops where the business has suffered a downturn. At that time, the client needs to review the plan to determine if it now makes sense to move some cost aspects of the plan farther out in time or even to remove something altogether. (This should include a review of those items that may have already had funding released.) By encouraging them to volunteer this information rather than wait for someone to ask, it demonstrates that they are managing their business within the environment of the overall business, and when the environment improves again, they will be more likely to be authorized to reinstate or reduce the timing of those items they brought forward. To help ensure this happens, they should clearly document the reasoning behind the change to the plan so that when the situation is reversed it will be easy for everyone to come to justify reinstating the original plan. Again, if there is not an in-house security staff that can sufficiently manage this review and analysis of the business changes, you will need to sell the client on contracting with you, as their consultant, to advise them when these changes occur and help them deterimne how the changes impact the plan. This can also be included in the services you perform for them on annual or semiannual visits to the facility.

TESTING YOUR PLAN AGAINST THE LATEST TECHNOLOGY

As is the case with most planning documents, the day after it's finalized, it begins to become out of date! This is especially true in the area of technology. Therefore, it is vital that either someone on the in-house team or the consultant review the Security Master Plan at least semiannually to be sure that the technology plans documented there are still viable and appropriate. I have never personally tried to be the first in installing the latest and greatest new gadget or system because I am well aware that new gadgets come and go quickly, and you do not want to get stuck with something that winds up being fiscally wasteful. However, the opposite can also be very wasteful. If you install products that are nearing the end of their life cycle, you will not get the full benefit of their technological advantages before you have to replace them with the next generation.

The key is to monitor technology closely by reading all appropriate security industry magazines and by going to the right product exhibitions every year. Personally, I attend the annual ASIS International Seminar and Exhibition event every year, as I do not usually have the time to go to several different ones. You might also want to attend the ISC East or ISC West Exhibitions. Whoever is designated to focus on this task also needs to be a person of vision and imagination. Just because the manufacturer of a new product decides that the right application is "X" does not mean that you might not find a better use for it in your business by using it in a totally different way. For example, I have been bothered for years by the number of cameras, and of course the accompanying DVRs, we have to use to provide a reasonable amount of coverage for our parking lots, not to mention the fact that in a campus environment you usually cannot afford to cover most of the perimeter beyond the parking lots. Now there is a new product on the market by TopEyeView (URL: www.topeyeview. com) where they have mounted a camera under a small blimp that you can position at your site. It communicates wirelessly and has great day or night vision cameras. You can move it to different locations if you wish or just have multiple ones installed. I believe it was originally marketed for use in emergency situations or when event was being held at the site, but I believe it has great potential for perimeter security issues as well.

The critical point with technology is that you cannot develop a five-year plan today that will take into account all of the possible new solutions that will be on the market tomorrow! You must continually re-evaluate the course you have set and make the right adjustments as you discover new avenues of change.

BENCHMARKING AND BUSINESS PROCESS (MATRIX) MANAGEMENT

Benchmarking

As I mentioned earlier in this book, I have had experience with conducting a benchmarking process. This was conducted with a number of other companies and with some of our own major locations that participated as if they were an independent company. We pursued this effort with the assistance of a consulting company with experience in benchmarking, although they had never done it focusing specifically on the security organization. We performed this after re-engineering and reorganizing our internal structure, which provided significant reductions for us. We basically changed our structure centralizing the management of the security organization and placing it under the direct management of security professionals. The basic rationale for the reorganization was that in reviewing and assessing all aspects of our security, we should be guided by four basic principles:

- Our security policies and practices must realistically match the threats we face. The processes we use to formulate policies and deliver services must be sufficiently flexible to facilitate change as the threats evolve.
- Our security policies and practices must be consistent across geographic territories and coherent to all concerned, thereby reducing inefficiencies and enabling us to allocate limited resources effectively.

215

- We must understand our customer's needs (both internal and external), add value to the corporation, and sufficiently anticipate future issues through the practice of risk management.
- Our policies, practices, and procedures must allow us to provide the necessary level of security at a cost the company can afford with the implementation of both sound business practices along with professional security management principles.

Our examination of the previous composition (prior to the reorganization) revealed that the fundamental weakness in the security structure and culture was the fragmented delivery of services. Multiple groups with differing interests and authorities worked independently of one another and with insufficient horizontal integration. Efforts were duplicated and coordination was arduous and slow. Some of this was due to the fact that too many different levels of functional guidance were being provided at divisional levels as well as at the corporate level. Basically, the structure in place had outlived its useful effectiveness.

The application of the reorganization strategy we developed made the organizational structure simpler, less fragmented, and more cost effective. Security is a service that should be based on an integrated assessment of risks and threats, vulnerability, and client needs. Conceptually, it should be the way we think rather than just a manual of rules. Security then becomes a more positive undertaking that values the "spirit" over the "letter" of the law, problem prevention over problem resolution, and individual responsibility over external oversight.

In the past, some security decisions had been linked in one way or another to assumptions about threats. We sometimes used worst-case scenarios as the basis for much of our security planning. The threats today are different, more multifaceted, and dynamic. In many cases it is possible to balance the risk of loss or damage against the costs of protection without incurring excessive cost in dollars. We determined that we could and must provide a rational, cost-effective, and enduring framework using risk management as the primary underlying practice for security decision making, and we were able to practice this much more effectively in the new, re-engineered organization.

The intent of our benchmarking effort was twofold:

- We needed to determine if we were providing our services in a cost-competitive manner.
- We wanted to determine which were some of the "best of breed" methods for providing security services.

FIGURE 14.1 Benchmarking is an important tool to help operate within a budget while still establishing best practices and continuously improving performance and business value.

After contracting with this firm and arranging for a number of companies to join us, the first thing we did was to identify our underlying principals. Because we were unable to find anyone in the security business who had conducted an extensive benchmarking project previously, we felt it was imperative that we and our external partner companies were very clear on some of the mitigating factors surrounding our business.

These are those principals:

- Security is not a commodity and should not be evaluated as such.
- Risk analysis, environmental impacts, and mitigation costs must be considered.
- Benchmarking is an operational process of continuous learning and adaptation.
- Enabling behaviors must be considered as well as process measurements.

The next area of focus was to identify a complete list of security services that we provided. First we identified the major categories of the services:

- Physical security
- Information protection

- Incident management
- Crisis management and emergency planning
- Emergency response

We then developed a detailed list of the services we, and the other participating companies, provided so that we could determine exactly how much cost was associated with each service and to be sure we captured all security-related costs. None of the participating companies performed all of these services, and some of the services at some companies were performed by other functions or were even contracted, but to be sure we were comparing "apples to apples," we needed to capture everything. The listing broke down this way:

- Protecting assets: random door checks, property pass checks, and so on
- Monitoring access control: receptionists, contractor sign-in, and so on
- Administering access control systems
- Creating reports from the access control system
- Making IDs or badges
- Monitoring alarms and CCTV systems (24-hour control center)
- Radio communications
- Responding to alarms
- Managing records
- Making and issuing keys
- Conducting investigations
- Analyzing investigative data
- Evaluating and responding to incidents
- Managing crises and planning for emergencies
- Conducting emergency scenario tests
- Planning physical security
- Protecting information
- Planning product security
- Unlocking doors
- Medical emergency and first aid response
- Responding to other emergencies: fires, chemical spills, accidents
- Preparing and delivering management reports
- Offsite meeting security
- Tours and patrols
- Providing security education and training
- Providing awareness information and education

- Conducting clean desk reviews
- Managing lost and found items
- Providing executive protection
- Liaison with law enforcement
- Conducting vendor security reviews
- Providing advice and counsel to clients
- External marketing of security services
- Providing security consulting services
- Conducting performance audits and maintenance checks of security equipment

Once this list was identified, we captured the costs associated with each item within the companies to be sure we identified the overall security costs for each of us. As you might imagine, every company does not structure its budget in the same way, and all security-related costs are not necessarily contained within the budget of the security organization. In fact, as we went through this process we learned that even within our own company, each location did some things differently. For example, at one location the receptionists for the site were security officers and their costs were contained in the security budget. At another location the receptionists were part of an administrative function and their costs were not included in the security budget. At a third location, the main receptionist was a security officer and in the security budget, while other receptionists were not. Yet at all three locations the receptionists had the same primary duties, although some had different secondary duties. We also determined that we needed to include the costs associated with all emergency response personnel. Although this is not a major factor at sites that are basically office buildings, it is a very large factor at most manufacturing sites, especially in an industry that utilizes chemicals and gases as part of the manufacturing processes.

As we compiled our costs, we had to be sure we captured all of the hidden costs, such as benefits for regular employees, charges for occupied space at the facilities, and full contract costs for contracted services. In order to keep the process manageable, we agreed not to include capital expenses such as the installation cost of any of the systems. However, we did include costs for systems maintenance, which is usually contained within the expense budget.

We then had to determine basic data required to analyze the cost information. This data consisted of net rentable square feet (NRSF), gross square feet (GSF), population headcount per site, security headcount per site, and emergency response headcount per site for each of the participating facilities. We agreed on a standard formula for translating contracted services into a headcount number to ensure consistency as well. Once the data was gathered we could determine the following:

- Cost of security per 100 square feet of NRSF
- Cost of security per 100 square feet of GSF
- Cost of security per 100 site population
- Number of security and emergency people per 100 square feet of NRSF
- Number of security and emergency people per 100 square feet of GSF
- Number of security and emergency people per 100 site population

We also did comparisons based on the makeup of the site by comparing manufacturing to manufacturing and Class "A" office buildings to Class "A" office buildings and so on. We were then able to establish median cost lines to see whether a site was more or less costly than it should be. We also determined median cost across all of the sites internal to us and combined with the external companies. We determined a median for just our internal sites, another for just our manufacturing sites, and another for our Class "A" buildings. Once we completed this we could easily see where our costs were too high, and we decided to make additional process evaluations of sites that had the lowest cost. In some cases, we determined that those our sites with the lowest cost were not providing an adequate level of security across the board. We also determined that some sites, such as our corporate and divisional headquarter sites, had additional requirements that would and did make their costs higher than other sites. However, when we finished this data analysis, we were able to identify a number of sites with excessive costs, and it was fairly easy to determine the areas of protection that needed to be adjusted to bring their costs in line with the rest of the organization.

BEST OF BREED

In order to identify the best of breed processes from this work, we started by looking at costs associated with each participant's processes, which brought us to a starting point. Next, we had teams of experts on the different processes from each company sit down and spell out exactly how they performed their processes. The more they discussed this, the more they recognized that each had a piece of a best of breed process as opposed to one process at one company being the standout (although that was the case in a couple of situations). As a result, our teams were able to identify changes to their processes that could be implemented to either improve the services they provided or to reduce the cost of those services (or in some situations, both). Of course, this is the real payback from all of this work. It is fine to be able to demonstrate that your security costs are equal to or lower than others, but that is basically just saying, "Look what I have done." To get real advantages, you need to be able to identify ways of both improving services and reducing costs for the future.

BUSINESS PROCESS (MATRIX) MANAGEMENT

Once we completed the benchmarking process, we believed we had sufficiently documented our processes to a level that would allow us to utilize this information as a way of ensuring all our sites were managing their security businesses effectively. This was a personal concern because I knew we were operating at reduced resource levels from previous years. As I went around the organization talking with different security people in the group, they were universally concerned that they were not able to perform the level of checks on every aspect of the different processes that they had been some years earlier, when we had at least twice the number of security people at the sites.

We called this our "controlled risk analysis program"; however, these days it is typically referred to as "matrix management." To begin, we determined the key control measurements for each of our subprocesses such as physical security, emergency planning, incident management, information protection, and emergency services. We then documented all of these in the following format:

- Subprocess name
- Measurement number and name
- Definition
- Goal
- Threshold
- Calculation
- Source
- References
- Reporting department

- Frequency
- Process contact

We then developed our listing of the different tasks that would be measured and filled out all of the data for each as shown above. For example, for the subprocess of physical security, the measurements were the following:

- Access control system reports
- Master key audits
- Security alarm operational tests
- Panic alarm operational tests
- Contract company: statement of work performance
- Independent invoice reviews
- Site review process

We had a list of these for each of the subprocesses as outlined above.

This was determined to be a pool of possible control measurements that could be utilized by each and every location throughout the United States. However, to have every location report on every one of these measurements every month would be far too burdensome and bureaucratic. The implementation process we used was that every site had to report monthly on a certain number of measurements. If defects were found in a measurement, they would report on it until it was cleared for two reports in a row; measurements were reported as good would then be rotated, and a new set of items would be selected from the measurement pool the following month. The goal was to have everyone report on every pertinent measurement in the pool during the course of the year (or sooner if possible). We made sure that our people understood that this process was not intended as a measurement of job performance; in fact, they were told that we wanted these measurements to uncover problems so we would know what needed to be fixed. If no one ever found anything wrong, we needed to find new ways to test the processes because they cannot all be working 100 percent effective at all times. The last item listed for each of these measurements, the process contact, was a list of those people in our organization who were recognized by their peers as the most knowledgeable in that area. They were listed so that anyone who had a problem with that measurement knew who to contact for information on how to address the problem.

We took this entire process one step farther by working with our internal audit group and developing a document of understanding with them whereby we would report the results of our measurements to them quarterly so they could monitor the effectiveness of the program; as long as they felt we were self-monitoring in an appropriate way, they would not need to audit us as frequently as they had been. This reduced our work-load and theirs. After the second year, they audited security functions at two of our locations; both passed with ease. This validated our measure-ment process to us and corporate audit.

Appendix A
WORKPLACE VIOLENCE GUIDELINES

PREFACE

The attached procedure has been developed for use by companies that need to implement workplace violence procedures. Implementation of this procedure requires the guidance of a security professional in order to customize it to the specifics of the company involved. The security professional's involvement will also be crucial on an ongoing basis to maintain the program and to react to individual situations as they occur. To be effective the following actions must precede implementation of these procedures:

- Management must issue a company policy to all employees stating, "Threats will not be tolerated!"
- All employees, supervisors, and managers must be informed that threats must be immediately reported to management or security.
- The company must be firm and consistent in its disciplinary action to those who make threats.
- All new employees, either permanent or temporary, must have criminal background checks and previous employment verifica-

tion for five years prior to hire date. Security must be consulted when any irregularities are discovered.

THREATS AND ACTS OF VIOLENCE AGAINST EMPLOYEES AND PROPERTY

OVERVIEW

Threats or acts of violence against employees or property will not be tolerated. Such actions will lead to disciplinary actions, which may include dismissal and the filing of criminal charges or some form of medical separation. No company policy, practice, or procedure should interfere with decisions designed to prevent a threat from being carried out, a violent act from occurring, or a life-threatening situation from developing.

REQUIREMENTS SUMMARY

The following should be in place to deal with an emergency of this kind:

- Appropriate physical security measures as a deterrent and to permit effective response
- Current, up-to-date emergency plans
- A crisis control center and an alternate center appropriately equipped
- A copy of all building floor plans at both control centers
- Duplicate copies of employee photos available in an emergency
- Liaison with law enforcement agencies providing availability of armed officers as needed
- Procedures for fire support and emergency medical support
- Understanding of internal PBX capability to trace calls, if applicable
- Liaison with telephone company security personnel and an understanding of their capability to trace calls
- Knowledge of local threat and trespass laws

When a threat against a person has been reported, the following action should be taken:

- Validate the threat and assess its seriousness
- Remove the maker of serious threats from the premises as soon as safety permits

- As appropriate, provide protection for the victims and others affected
- Advise the police if appropriate
- Report all threats to corporate security, if applicable, where assistance based on experience is available
- Obtain available personal data concerning the threat-maker
- Consider personnel and prosecution actions against the threat-maker

In actual cases of violence, take whatever action is necessary to contain the incident, minimize personal risk to employees and others, and have the person(s) taken into police custody.

See Attachment A for additional information regarding threats and acts of violence.

See Attachment B for guidance on assessing the threat-maker.

ATTACHMENT A

THREATS AND VIOLENT ACTS AGAINST EMPLOYEES AND PROPERTY

INTRODUCTION

In recent years the violence inherent in our society has invaded the corporate environment, and no corporation is immune from threats and violent acts committed against its employees and property.

As a result of these threats and acts of violence, our company has numerous important policy and procedural changes including changes pertaining to the employment process and the way in which we respond to these types of incidents.

This document has been broadly designed to aid the community of company interests and the responsibilities involved in the effective management of these incidents. Accordingly, the relevant specific responsibilities of all functional managers have been incorporated.

This document has been written in order to review and update relevant policies and procedures and to assist those who are responsible for dealing with threats and violent acts. It by no means identifies every solution for every problem; however, it does identify those procedures that seem to work most often.

POLICY

Nothing is more important than the safety and security of our employees; therefore, threats or acts of violence against employees or property will not be tolerated. Violations of this policy will lead to disciplinary action, which may include dismissal, arrest, and prosecution.

Any person who threatens or engages in a violent action on company property should be removed from the premises as quickly as safety permits.

When substantial threats are made or acts of violence are committed by an employee, a judgment should be made, once the employee has been removed from the premises, as to what actions are appropriate, including immediate dismissal or some form of medical disability. A line management decision to deal medically with an employee should be made as promptly as possible and in all cases in less than 30 days.

Once a threat has been substantiated, it is the company's policy to gain the initiative, put the threat-maker on notice that he or she will be held accountable for his or her actions, and then follow through with the implementation of a timely, decisive, and appropriate response.

In carrying out these policies, it is essential that all managers understand that no existing policy, practice, or procedure should prohibit decisions designed to prevent a threat from being carried out, a violent act from occurring, or a life-threatening situation from developing.

OBJECTIVES

The following are the company's principal objectives with regard to the safety and security of employees and property:

- To prevent incidents from occurring.
- To deal appropriately with each threat or violent act on a case-by-case basis.
- To minimize the risk of harm to employees, contractors, visitors, and others on our premises.
- To improve the comfort level of employees.
- To communicate a positive attitude to employees regarding their safety and security.

PRETHREAT ACTIONS

Below is a list of prudent prethreat actions for the prevention of, detection of, and response to threats and violent acts against our employees and property, which location managers should consider and implement as soon as practicable.

Planning and Organization

Prethreat planning and organizational actions include, but are not limited to, the following:

- Review, revise, and update, as appropriate, the emergency plan to cover threats and potentially dangerous situations.
- Designate a crisis management team or advisory group for use in an emergency situation. Composition of the team or group should include, as a minimum, senior location management plus human resources, communications, security, and legal representatives.
- Maintain rosters of key personnel and alternates required during emergency operations. Rosters should contain as a minimum the name, home address, home telephone number, and dates on which the key personnel are on call. Primary sites should maintain rosters from their offsite locations.
- Establish a central crisis control center and one alternate center and equip them appropriately for operational requirements.
- Ensure that copies of all building floor plans for each site and facility within your area are maintained at both the primary and alternate crises control centers.
- Where appropriate, ensure that emergency plans are available at area control centers.
- Instruct all managers in the appropriate procedures for effectively dealing with threats and violent acts at their particular location.
- Develop checklists of actions to be taken by managers and security personnel in the event of a threat or a violent act at their locations.
- Inform all employees of their responsibility to immediately report all threats and violent acts against other employees and property to management or security.
- Develop cue cards for use by employees who may be the recipients of direct, anonymous, or telephone threats (receptionists, secretaries, security personnel).

- Duplicate and file a copy of employee photos each time a new identification badge is issued. Secure these photos as sensitive, proprietary information.
- Establish a liaison with area law enforcement, fire support, and emergency medical service agencies; examine the capabilities and responsiveness of these agencies; determine shortfalls and, if any exist, arrange for an alternate or coordinated response.
- Research local threat and trespass laws and the procedures for initiating civil and criminal complaints, surveillance, arrest, commitment to medical or mental facilities, citizen's arrest, and monitoring or taping of telephone threats.
- Develop knowledge of the internal PBX or phone system and its capability to capture incoming and outgoing phone numbers.
- Establish a liaison with telephone company security personnel and determine their capability to trace threatening telephone calls to our employees at work or at home.
- Review and revise, as appropriate, contractor and visitor badge programs to ensure proper identification prior to issue, continual wearing while on premises, and appropriate return when leaving premises.
- Instruct all employees on the importance of displaying employee identification badges and the employees' role in preventing unauthorized access to company facilities.
- Ensure that appropriate security, human resources, legal, communications, and medical representatives are kept apprised of significant changes to site plans, policies, procedures, and activities relative to threats and violent acts.
- Conduct periodic tests of the following:
  Emergency plans
  - Access control procedures
  - Significant incident response capabilities
  - Public address system during working hours using prearranged messages

THREAT VERIFICATION AND ASSESSMENT

All employees should be instructed to report any threat or act of violence immediately to management or security. All available information pertaining to the incident must be obtained immediately and documented by security to permit verification, assessment, and appropriate responsive action. Uniform reporting procedures should be followed, and security should be responsible for capturing, as a minimum, the following information:

- What was the incident?
  - If a violent act, what was the act, where did it occur, was there any physical contact or injuries, was a weapon involved?
  - If a threat, what was said and how was it delivered: in person, by telephone, in writing, or by a third party?
- Name of all victims and witnesses.
  - Are they employees, contractors, visitors, or other?
  - Obtain business and home addresses and telephone numbers.
- Name of person making the threat or committing the act.
  - Is this person an employee, contractor, visitor, or other?
- Name of person reporting the incident to management or security.
  - Date, time, and mode of the report: in person, telephone, or written.
  - Is this person a victim, witness, or other?
- Other available data that relates to the intent of the threat, circumstances surrounding its issuance, and environment at the location where it was delivered.

In order to develop an appropriate response, it is necessary to verify that a threat was in fact made and to accurately document it. It must be remembered that this is a time-sensitive situation, and both speed and accuracy are essential. Facts should be separated from emotions. Victim(s) and witness(es) should be interviewed separately if possible to determine the following:

- Who was threatened and who was the threat-maker? Have there been any prior incidents of a similar nature involving the victim or the threat-maker?
- What was the threat, what precipitated the threat, under what circumstances was the threat made, what was the actual intent of the threat-maker, and what was the environment in which the threat was made?
- When was the threat made or when was the threat to be carried out?
- How was the threat made or how was the threat to be carried out?

233

- Why was the particular victim(s) selected by the threat-maker? Are they related or otherwise known to each other?

Once the threat has been verified and understood, a preliminary assessment of the seriousness of the threat must be made so that a suitable, tailored response can be initiated. If deemed appropriate and necessary to make a valid assessment, and after consultation with a line manager, the threat-maker may be confronted to determine intent, capability, and emotional and physical state.

The following actions may be taken to fully develop an assessment of the seriousness of a threat:

- Review threat-maker's personnel and medical records for documented previous threats, work performance, administrative or disciplinary actions, or medical problems.
- Interview the threat-maker's fellow employees and managers.
- Contact the threat-maker's family physician and acquaintances.
- Obtain, as required, the expertise of specialists such as psychiatrists, psychologists, or psycholinguists.
- Notify local police and request they perform a criminal history check.
- Check to determine if the threat-maker has access to weapons, a gun permit, and so on.

PROTECTIVE STRATEGIES

All threats must be considered serious until proven otherwise, and appropriate action must be taken accordingly to protect all persons and property. Particular attention must be given to those individuals who are directly threatened, and protection must be provided for them at work and home, as required. Protective measures will vary according to the circumstances of each threat and may include, but are not limited to, the following:

- Protect the victim's work environment.
  - Increase site security with company security personnel, unarmed contract guards, armed off-duty police, or on-duty police as deemed necessary and appropriate.
  - Increase exterior security patrols.

- Increase facility access control: reduce employee entrances to the minimum necessary, supervise all doors, lock loading dock entrances.
- Increase interior access control: lock doors behind lobbies, reception areas, and loading docks, supervise interior entrances.
- Control access to the victim's work area: closed circuit television, intrusion detection devices, security or guard force personnel or police officers present in work area.
- Install an emergency alarm device for use by the victim or the victim's supervisor.
- Change victim's work shift.
- Transfer victim to another work area or building or site within the area.
- Have victim escorted to and from work.
- Relocate victim to another facility out of the region temporarily or permanently.
- Protect the victim's home environment.
    - Notify police: request surveillance or police presence.
    - Install rapid communication capability with company security personnel.
    - Install portable intrusion detection devices, exterior lighting, and locks.
    - Hire armed, uniformed off-duty police for protection in and around the home.
- Ensure victim feedback: monitor the situation until the threat to the victim and family no longer exists.
- Retain a high level of exterior and interior site security and access control and monitoring until a threat no longer exists to the work environment, other employees, and property.

THREAT-MAKER CONTROL AND CONTAINMENT STRATEGIES

A threat-maker may be known or anonymous; a threat may be made in person, by telephone, in writing, or through a third party; and whereas most threats and acts of violence are unpredictable, the potential for violence in some situations can be foreseen and predicted by management.

However, in all cases, the basic policy is the same: Take whatever action is necessary to contain the threat, minimize the risk of harm to all persons and property, control the threat-maker, and remove the threat-maker from the premises as quickly as safety permits.

Unpredictable Threats and Violent Acts

Unpredictable incidents pose the greatest challenge to both management and security because they must be dealt with rapidly on a case-by-case basis to seize the initiative from the perpetrator. Coordinated responsive actions to be considered include, but are not limited to, the following:

On-Site Incidents
Once management or security has been notified of an on-site threat or violent act:

- Verify the incident and, if substantiated, assess its seriousness.
- Confront the threat-maker if safety permits, advise him or her of company policy concerning threats, and request that he or she leave the premises immediately. If the threat is to a manager, the next-level manager or security should confront the threat-maker.
- If the threat-maker refuses to leave the premises or cannot be removed safely, alert the crisis management team and notify the police.
- Report the incident to corporate headquarters.
- Seal off the affected area to contain the threat-maker.
- Evacuate the affected area or floor or building or site as required for the safety of employees and others.
- Remove threat-maker as quickly as safety permits.
- If the situation becomes protracted, instruct the crisis management team to be prepared to support police negotiations if required and establish a rumor control desk or center.

Telephone Threats
- Attempt to keep the threat-maker on the telephone as long as possible and obtain as much information as possible.
- Immediately record the information obtained as accurately as possible.
- Alert security while the threat-maker is still on the telephone, or as soon as possible thereafter. Security will contact the telephone company for assistance, if appropriate.

- If the telephone threat-maker is identified and on the premises, and if safety permits, confront the threat-maker, advise him or her of company policy concerning threats, and request that he or she leave the premises immediately. If the threat-maker refuses to leave the premises or cannot be safely removed, follow the above on-site incident procedures.
- If the telephone threat-maker is anonymous or is identified but off-site, alert security, who will notify the police, increase site security, and tighten access control. If the threat-maker is an employee, distribute his or her photo to site security personnel.

Written Threats

- Secure the written material as evidence with minimum handling.
- Alert company security, who will increase site security and access control as described above.
- If the written material is anonymous, consult appropriate specialists — psychiatrists, psychologists, psycholinguists — to assess the seriousness of the threat and to attempt to identify the threat-maker.

Offsite Incidents

When an employee receives an offsite, employment-related threat, it may be the sole responsibility of the victim (not the company) to initiate action with the police, telephone company, or other appropriate agency; however, the company should support the victim in his or her efforts and provide protection as deemed necessary and appropriate.

Predictable Incidents

The most predictable situations with potential for violence involve follow-up management meetings and medical appointments with threat-makers or other potentially violent individuals. When management or security is aware of a situation that has the potential for violence, a detailed action plan must be prepared in advance. In anticipation of these predictable situations, management is encouraged to maintain contact with the individual involved, preferably through a line manager. If not feasible or appropriate, then contact should be maintained directly or indirectly through fellow employees, family, or friends so that the potential seriousness of the situation can be continuously assessed.

In a predictable situation the advisory group or crisis management team should be convened to perform the following actions:

- Examine administrative, disciplinary, and medical options and their consequences.
- Examine legal alternatives such as seeking arrest, commitment to a medical or mental facility, or obtaining a restraining order.
- Develop a detailed action planthat includes the following:
  - Establishes the conditions, circumstances, and location of the meeting.
  - Determines who will be present at the meeting in addition to management: security, legal, medical, personnel.
  - Provides for on-duty or off-duty police presence onsite or supervising the entrances or adjacent to the meeting place or at the meeting as deemed necessary and appropriate to the situation.
  - Provides for monitoring the individual's entrance to, presence in, and exit from the premises.
  - Considers the need for installing a panic button or other emergency devices at the meeting location.
  - Provides for an appropriate response should an incident occur.

In the event that management believes a face-to-face meeting with the individual involved poses too great a risk to safety, the administrative, disciplinary, or medical decision may be conveyed by telephone or in writing.

In the event that an incident does occur, the basic policy remains the same: Take whatever action is necessary to contain the incident, minimize the risk of harm to employees and property, control the incident-maker, and remove him or her from the premises as quickly as safety permits. The array of actions to be taken is the same as those previously described for an unpredictable incident.

POST-THREAT ACTIONS

Post-threat actions are required to ensure follow-through with appropriate management, administrative, legal, or medical decisions; obtain victim and witness cooperation where required to support these decisions; and review the entire incident situation in depth to determine if all that could be done, was done and done properly.

Follow-Up

When a substantiated threat is made or a violent act is committed by an employee, a judgment should be made, once the individual has been removed from the premises, as to what actions are appropriate, including immediate dismissal or some form of medical disability. Under no circumstances should an employee who continues to pose a threat be permitted to return to the company's employment or premises.

Management options that may be considered in dealing with the threat-maker include the following:

- Change shifts or transfer to another work area: to be considered in only the most minor of situations.
- Suspension with pay: to be considered until a meeting between the individual and management can be arranged.
- Refer to medical.
- Mutual separation.
- Termination.

A management decision to deal medically with the employee must be made as promptly as possible and in all cases with 30 days.

Whether the incident is treated administratively or medically, an ongoing review of the situation should be accomplished to ensure sufficiency of incident documentation, and that available civil and criminal justice remedies are known and understood by both the victim and the company.

The following follow-up actions should be considered and implemented as appropriate:

- Notify the prosecutive agency with jurisdiction over the incident.
- Notify the probation or parole agency having jurisdiction over the individual.
- Without the subject's knowledge, you might contact some of the following: other family members, social service agencies, the subject's family clergy, the subject's family physician.
- Seek a no-trespass order against the threat-maker as a court decree or as a condition of existing probation or parole.
- Seek police or other law enforcement intervention to issue a warning to the threat-maker.
- Support issuance of a formal complaint, citizen's arrest, or other injunctive process.
- Monitor the situation through the trial and appellate periods.

Security and necessary victim and witness protective measures should not be reduced until a threat no longer exists to persons and property.

VICTIM AND WITNESS COOPERATION

When a substantiated threat or violent act that is committed against an employee(s) or on company property results in criminal or civil litigation, management must be prepared for the possibility that witnesses to the incident or even the victim may become reluctant to fully participate in the judicial process. Studies indicate that the four reasons cited most often for the lack of cooperation are trial delay, loss of income, inappropriate physical accommodations, and intimidation.

Although the solution to these problems rests principally with the civil and criminal justice systems, certain corporate actions, whether the company is a party to the litigation or not, may aid in alleviating these victim and witness concerns.

- Victims and witnesses should be reminded of impending court dates and encouraged to contact the prosecutor's or clerk's office just prior to a scheduled trial date to determine if there has been a postponement, thereby avoiding the frustration of needless trips to court.
- The company's policy of providing paid leave to subpoenaed employee victims and witnesses should preclude loss of income from becoming an issue, and affected employees should be reminded of this and other relevant corporate policies.
- Timely information pertaining to courthouse location and the availability of public transportation, parking facilities, eating facilities, and child care services will permit the employee victim or witness to be better prepared for a court appearance and minimize the employee's personal concerns.
- The fear of reprisal is a significant factor in obtaining both victim and witness cooperation and is most acute when the victim or witness is known by or related to the defendant. In addition, female victims and witnesses express a fear of reprisal more often than males. Managers must be cognizant of this potential impediment to victim and witness cooperation and take appropriate action throughout the situation. Victims and witnesses should be separated from the defendant as soon as possible and interviewed

away from the defendant or associates. Law enforcement agencies should be apprised of any known victim or witness fears of reprisal and protective strategies previously discussed should apply to victims and witnesses alike when deemed necessary and appropriate. These protective measures should remain in effect until it is determined that a threat no longer exists to either the victim or witness involved.

In essence, the key to obtaining victim and witness cooperation throughout the judicial process is management awareness and sensitivity to their fears, apprehensions, and concerns.

REVIEW AND ANALYSIS

Following final resolution of an incident, the senior location manger should, depending on the seriousness of the incident, either request an independent review or direct the crisis management team and security manager to conduct a comprehensive review and analysis of the incident, including the company's response and follow-up actions, to determine the following:

- What happened?
- Why did it happen?
- What could have been done to prevent it?
- What was done?
- What should have been done?
- What could have been done better?

Results of this review and analysis should be furnished to corporate security and used locally to update existing site response plans, policies, and procedures.

DOCUMENTATION AND REPORTING

Documentation

It is essential that all aspects of the incident be thoroughly documented to provide a sound basis for an initial assessment of the seriousness of the incident, development of a tailored response, determination of liability and civil and criminal justice options, and development of a comprehensive post-threat review and analysis of the incident. Cue cards, proposed forms, incident logs, and employee training will enhance the ability to capture and document all essential elements of the situation as accurately as possible.

Reporting

All substantiated threats or violent acts against employees or property will be reported to corporate security immediately.

Nothing herein shall prevent an appropriate informal alerting of corporate headquarters of potentially violent incidents in their early stages prior to a complete verification and assessment.

After-Action Report

For all substantiated threats and acts of violence against employees and property, a formal, after-action report will be prepared and provided to corporate headquarters. Format of the after-action report will be as follows:

- Background: Events that led up to the incident; threat-maker identification: name, length of employment, level of employment, performance level, history of work-related problems, history of medical problems, prior arrests and convictions, and pending charges.
- Incident: Complete description of what happened, to whom, by whom, where, when, how, circumstances surrounding the incident, and environment in which it occurred.
- Chronology of events: All aspects of the situation including the company's response and follow-up actions by date and time.
- Problems: Any problems whatsoever: plans, policies, procedures, structure, systems, devices, onsite or offsite support services.
- Lessons learned: All lessons learned in coping with a threat of violent act.
- Recommendations: All recommendations that would enhance responding to threats of violent acts in the future at your location or any other company facility.

ATTACHMENT B

INDICATORS OF DANGEROUSNESS

- Past behavior
- Drug and alcohol abuse
- Access to weapons
- Anger or resentment
- Fascination with past events
- Deteriorating performance
- Suicidal
- Stress or depression
- Mental deterioration

CHECKLIST

Workplace Violence as of _____ (date)

√ **Response Checklist for Management or Security**

1. Notify police (911 if immediate threat). See to your personal safety.
2. Notify your boss and your security. Then call HR/EAP, legal, and others as necessary.
3. Protect targeted population. (Work with security or police.)
4. Increase perimeter controls. (Work with security or police.)
5. Explore all available legal options (e.g., police report, temporary restraining order, temporary commitment to a mental facility, continuing dialogue with authorities).

6. Brief affected employees on threat and precautions to take.

Warning Signs to Watch

Performance-Related Warning Signs

1. Excessive sick leave, tardiness, or other attendance problems
2. Inconsistent work patterns
3. Increased frequency of accidents or acts of carelessness
4. Excessive sense of entitlement or ownership of the job

Behaviors to Watch

1. Increasing frequency of aggressive acts or threats
2. Signs of impairment by drugs or alcohol
3. Use of veiled threats, menacing body language
4. Deteriorating relationships with coworkers
5. Noticeable changes in health and hygiene
6. Increase in apparent forgetfulness
7. Increasing withdrawal from coworkers and friends

Verbal Warning Signs

1. Irrational comments that show disregard for the future
2. Description and knowledge of violence at work
3. Trying to talk others into joining a religious or political affiliation
4. Expressed fascination with weapons and their capacity to harm others
5. Emotional outbursts
6. Blaming others for problems and failures
7. Delusional statements
8. Abusive talk about other employees
9. Expressed feelings of persecution
10. Angry and hostile statements

Situations that Increase Risk of Problems Developing

1. Relationship friction or failure
2. Failure to obtain an expected promotion or salary increase
3. Deteriorating financial circumstances
4. Being shunned by coworkers

5. Overly authoritarian or unfair supervision

Reminder: Watch for combinations and trends, not just isolated instances. Do not ignore a threat. When in doubt, notify someone. Consult management, HR/EAP, or your assigned security staff for help in evaluating the seriousness of these signs.

ATTACHMENT C

Sample Workplace Violence Policy

POLICY: ZERO TOLERANCE

Because XYZ Company is committed to providing a workplace that is free from acts of violence or threats of violence, we have zero tolerance for threats or violence against coworkers, visitors, or any other persons who are on our premises or have contact with employees in the course of their duties. Violent acts or threats violate (your company name's) policy.

DEFINITION

This policy defines workplace violence as the threat or use of physical force, harassment, intimidation, or abuse of power to control or harm another person in the workplace or on the job. This policy applies to all persons on our premises and to all our employees transacting business anywhere on behalf of their employer.

RESPONSIBILITIES

All employees are responsible for conducting themselves in a business-like manner that neither threatens nor injures other persons. In cases of immediate danger, the employee who first becomes aware of the danger is responsible for obtaining emergency assistance. Otherwise, all employees are responsible for reporting actual or suspected workplace violence to their first-line supervisors and, if necessary, to the security representative assigned to their facility.

Supervisors and managers, in addition to the above, are accountable for taking prompt action to protect threatened persons or victims of workplace violence. In cases of immediate danger, they are responsible for obtaining emergency assistance. Otherwise, they are responsible for seeking assistance and making timely notifications of any situation that endangers our employees or any other person on our premises.

Security representatives who take reports of workplace violence are responsible for taking action to protect threatened persons and for advising human resources, legal counsel, and other (company name) management staff in a position to take further action to contain the workplace violence threat at issue.

CONSEQUENCES

Failure to abide by this policy, including failure to take prompt action when witnessing or receiving reports of workplace violence threats, will result in disciplinary action up to and including termination.

Appendix B

EXECUTIVE AND EMPLOYEE PROTECTION

Persons associated with large or prominent organizations may find themselves at risk of being targeted by irrational individuals, disgruntled employees, or extremist groups. This is particularly true for those whose work requires them to be in the public eye and who are perceived as representing the organization and its positions on issues, which may be controversial.

Although defenses against the actions of such individuals are difficult to design and cannot be made foolproof, there are precautions that can be taken to mitigate the risk. Vulnerabilities exist in the workplace, at home, and while traveling that can be effectively minimized through the use of simple, though prudent, measures to ensure one's personal security. The key to this program lies in limiting one's accessibility to potentially threatening persons and situations, thus providing as difficult a target as possible.

This can be accomplished most easily in the workplace. A program that effectively limits access by strangers is the strongest defense. This can best be accomplished with an automated controlled access system and a set of procedures for screening and escorting nonemployees.

SECURITY IN THE WORKPLACE

There are a number of things that you, your secretary, and your staff can do to enhance your personal security while at work:

- Be aware of all activity occurring around you. You and the members of your staff should be able to quickly identify those persons who enter your work area and to challenge their business need to be there if they cannot be identified.
- Report suspicious or harassing telephone calls to security immediately.
- Make certain that the exterior doors of your workplace are kept closed and locked or monitored.
- Know your area of the office and report anything that appears suspicious or out of place.
- Do not discount or take lightly any threats. All threats should be immediately reported to security. Do not hesitate to make such a report even if you believe it to be unimportant. Every threat should be taken seriously until it can be analyzed and evaluated.

Executives should ensure the following safeguards are in place:

- Evacuation procedures tailored to the executive that will ensure his or her safe evacuation in the event of an emergency.
- The installation of panic alarm systems that annunciate in security to ensure timely response to a potentially threatening situation.
- Placing emergency stickers on each telephone beneath the handset, listing local emergency numbers.
- When speaking on the phone or in person to someone you do not recognize, ensure you understand with whom you are speaking and why. Request that the caller identify himself or herself and provide a callback number. Never provide personal data such as a home address, names of or information about your family members, and date or place of birth. Also avoid giving information on your "in town or out of town" status. When providing information for publications such as *Who's Who* and alumni directories, it is best not to include home addresses and phone numbers and any details about your personal life and family.
- Be careful what information you provide to the media. To the degree possible, avoid personal publicity.
- Caution should be exercised when participating in activities outside of work; community activities, business associations, volunteer work, and the like could potentially expose you to situations that compromise your personal security. The same precautions that apply in the workplace are applicable in these situations as well.
- Avoid the use of high-profile, restricted personal parking spaces.

RECEIVING LETTERS AND PARCELS

Key locations within the workplace should be identified as having a process for handling suspicious packages. However, you should be aware of the following with regard to letters and parcels.

Never assume that a letter or parcel is legitimate because it has been sent through the mail or delivered by a messenger or a specialized agency.

Letters or packages of a suspicious nature often display one or more of the following characteristics:

- A title but no name.
- Incorrect, incomplete, or unusual addressing such as Mr. Jones, XYZ Company, New York.
- Excessive weight.
- Restrictive delivery instructions (e.g., "Personal" or "To be opened by addressee only").
- Conspicuous overwrapping (e.g., heavy taping or excessive string).
- Rigidity or stiffness in a letter, with some possible bulkiness or springiness.
- Lopsided or uneven envelope, unbalanced or reinforced with tape.
- Wire protruding through envelope or package or ridges in envelope or wrapping.
- Strange smell, oily or soiled appearance.
- Wire, small battery, or fuse protruding against surface.

DEALING WITH SUSPECT LETTERS AND PARCELS

Awareness in the handling of all letters and parcels provides the best defense against suspicious packages.

If you receive a suspicious parcel or letter, DO NOT HANDLE IT. DO NOT OPEN IT. CONTACT SECURITY IMMEDIATELY.

SECURITY IN THE HOME

An effective residential security program will provide a buffer against many criminal acts and will add an extra element of protection for both yourself and your family. The key is preparation, planning, and participation by all family members.

The following guidelines are offered as practical suggestions for a residential security plan:

- Mailboxes should be identified by address only. Names should not be displayed on mail or periodical delivery receptacles.
- Refuse to accept packages at home if they are unsolicited or if you cannot readily establish the identity of the sender and verify that the package was actually sent by that person. Should such a package arrive, contact security immediately. Ensure that every member of the household is aware of the identifying characteristics for suspicious letters and parcels outlined in the section above.
- Where possible, ensure that the areas directly adjacent to the residence and the residence grounds are well illuminated.
- Install locking devices on doors and windows and keep them locked. Install dead bolts on entrance doors, rear doors, and bedroom door(s), which would allow you to retreat to a safe area in your home if necessary.
- Install an integrated home security system, to include fire and intrusion alarms.
- Ensure that there is a telephone conveniently located in the bedroom, and that all family members know the phone number of the local police and other emergency numbers. These numbers should be posted by each telephone as well.
- Use an unlisted phone number.
- Use a telephone answering machine to screen and, if possible, record incoming calls. If available, consider obtaining caller identification service from your phone company. Report any suspicious or harassing telephone call to security.
- Instruct family and staff not to provide information or access to strangers, and to request positive photo identification of anyone purporting to be a repair worker or an inspector, and to refuse unsolicited services.
- Do not provide comprehensive family information to local clubs, newspapers, and other organizations.
- Be alert to any suspicious persons or activities in the area of your residence and contact your local police to report such activity.
- Use care when discarding bills, credit card statements, and banking statements that contain sensitive or personal information. Such information should be rendered unreadable before discarding.

- If possible, ensure that all family vehicles are secured in a locked garage or parked in a secure area.
- Discuss school release policy with school officials and instruct them concerning the person or persons who have authority to pick up your children.
- Limit business and personal schedules to persons with a need to know.
- Avoid establishing a predictable social routine.
- When you and your family are away from home, arrange to have a friend watch your home and ensure that mail service, newspaper deliveries, milk deliveries, and so on are suspended for the duration of your trip.
- Inexpensive timers can be used to regulate lighting in your home to give the appearance of a presence when you are away.

SECURITY WHILE TRAVELING

Risk associated with business travel can be minimized by observing the following precautions:

- Avoid advance publicity concerning your trip.
- Ensure that the location to be visited controls the distribution of your agenda.
- When possible, request that the host location make arrangements for all local transportation needs.
- Ensure that your main contact at the host location is kept aware of your whereabouts and schedule, both during and after business hours.
- Stay at large, relatively busy hotels; avoid out-of-the-way accommodations.
- Restrict social activities to well-frequented, secure facilities and avoid the off-the-beaten-track areas. Use secure transportation when traveling to and from such activities.
- Whenever possible, use the transportation services provided by the hotel or a prearranged private limousine service.
- Avoid providing more information than is absolutely necessary to hotel personnel, including receptionists, bellboys, and so on.
- Do not use employment identification on your luggage tags.

- Avoid carrying large sums of money on your person or wearing conspicuous valuables.
- Avoid traveling, sightseeing, or shopping trips unless accompanied by someone who knows the area.
- Whenever possible, avoid standing in crowds at airports and airline terminals.
- Be alert to any sign of surveillance, or to anyone expressing undue or inappropriate interest in you, your company, or your activities.
- Be alert to your surroundings and what is going on around you.
- Do not act in the role of "good Samaritan" by offering personal assistance, particularly with strangers. While it is unfortunate, such action places you in a very vulnerable position. Rather, if you observe someone who needs assistance, proceed to the nearest safe telephone and notify local police of the situation.
- If you are unsure of your travel environment, contact security for advice and counsel.

WHEN USING AN AUTOMOBILE

- Avoid dimly lit commercial parking lots and garages, especially when traveling alone.
- Always keep car windows closed and doors locked.
- When possible, vary routes and times of arrival to and from work.
- If driving after dark in an isolated or unfamiliar area, be wary of a contrived "accident." Rather than exiting the comparative safety of your vehicle, you can exchange driver information by holding the paperwork up to the window. Suppress your natural curiosity to get out and inspect the damage. If necessary, you can drive to an open service station or convenience store to do your inspection.
- If possible, ensure the vehicle used is equipped with cellular communications capability.
- Avoid vanity license plates that identify you, your position, or your company.
- Always keep your parking lot ticket with you. Leaving it in the car will allow someone to exit the lot or tamper with your car without being challenged.
- Always lock the car, close all windows, and take the key with you. Have your car key — the one that opens the door — in your hand when approaching your vehicle. Whenever possible, use a remote

lock/unlock device. Look in the entire passenger compartment of the car before entering, then lock the door immediately.

- Again, do not act in the role of "good Samaritan."
- Do not fall into a complacent attitude just because you are in your car. A significant number of assaults occur just as the victim enters or leaves his or her vehicle. Again, be alert to your surroundings and what is going on around you.

EVENT OR MEETING PLANNING

- If planning a meeting of key executives at a location other than at your work location or if you have concerns regarding the security or safety of your meeting site, contact a security professional.

Appendix C

Security Assessment or Self-Assessment Document

INTRODUCTION

The questions in this document are intended to assist in the determination of security status of a site or location. I consider security to be a process that is broken into four subprocesses: emergency planning, incident management, information protection, and physical security; therefore, the checklist is organized in that manner.

This document was developed to assist a security professional in assessing the security status of a site. Because a question appears in this document, it does not imply that it is a necessary protection requirement in all situations; it depends on the identified risks for this location. This is why it is mandatory that this document be utilized only by security professionals.

257

SITE INFORMATION

Please provide the following information:

Site or Location Name_____

Security Manager_____

Senior Location Manager_____

Date of This Review_____

Summarize your environment, highlighting pertinent business facts, and cite any unique security problems and any special concerns or dependencies:

_____

_____

_____

_____

_____

_____

List all location tenant organizations, site population, and percentage of total site. Include all noncompany tenants in multitenant facilities.

ORGANIZATION	POPULATION	PERCENT OF TOTAL
_____	_____	_____
_____	_____	_____
_____	_____	_____
_____	_____	_____
_____	_____	_____

IDENTIFIED SECURITY RISKS

List all security risks that have been identified previously and attach a copy of your plan to mitigate the risks.

Subprocess   Risk

Emergency

_____

Planning

_____

_____

_____

_____

Incident

_____

Management

_____

_____

_____

Information

_____

Protection

_____

_____

_____

Physical

_____

Security

_____

_____

_____

EMERGENCY PLANNING

Crisis Management Team

List all current and alternate members of your crisis management team by title (CMT position and company position) and work location.

NAME	ALTERNATE	CMT POSITION	CO. POSITION	LOCATION

Have the CMT and alternates been trained on their roles and responsibilities?

_____	_____
Yes	No

If yes, list the training date(s) during the past 12 months.

_____

Crisis Management Rooms

	PRIMARY	ALTERNATE
Location:	_____	_____
Equipment:	_____	_____
	_____	_____
	_____	_____

Documents: _____   _____

_____   _____

_____   _____

Emergency Planning Manual

Does your emergency planning manual (EPM) include the following elements?

	Yes	No
Natural and Human-Made Disasters	_____	_____
Hurricanes and Typhoons	_____	_____
Flood	_____	_____
Fire	_____	_____
Chemical Spill	_____	_____
Gas Explosion	_____	_____
Earthquake	_____	_____
Other	_____	_____
Threats or Acts of Violence	_____	_____
Bomb	_____	_____
Personnel	_____	_____
Political or Civil Disturbance	_____	_____
Emergency Shutdown or Evacuation of Facility	_____	_____
Designation and Staffing of Primary and Alternate Emergency	_____	_____
Control Headquarters	_____	_____
Designation of Coordinator for Overall Response	_____	_____

Designation of CMT and Alternates	_____	_____
Designation of Management Succession	_____	_____
Process for Coordination with the Following Groups:	Yes	No
Health, Safety, and Environmental Protection Personnel	_____	_____
Nearby or Adjacent Company Facilities	_____	_____
Landlord or Other Noncompany Occupants of the Building	_____	_____
Community Emergency and Law Enforcement Services	_____	_____
Company Communications for Response to Media	_____	_____
Human Resource Department	_____	_____
Legal Function	_____	_____
Will the following be provided?	Yes	No
Armed Off-Duty Law Enforcement Officers	_____	_____
Facility Protection	_____	_____
Fire Protection or Fire Brigade	_____	_____
Hazardous Material Emergency Response (if required)	_____	_____
Vital Services and Supplies	_____	_____
Emergency Alert System	_____	_____
Rescue Teams	_____	_____
First Aid Teams	_____	_____
Emergency Equipment	_____	_____
Emergency Transportation	_____	_____

Communication Capabilities   _____   _____

Medical Personnel and Supplies   _____   _____

Contact Numbers for Emergency Services   _____   _____

Plans or Blueprints with Office Phone Numbers _____   _____

Current Personnel Listings   _____   _____

Date of the last two EPM updates:

_____   _____

List the holders of the EPM. Indicate if they have hard or soft copy.

Person	Hard	Soft
_____	_____	_____
_____	_____	_____
_____	_____	_____

Training

List all CMT training and testing that has occurred in the previous 12 months: threat management, demonstrations, and natural disasters.

_____

_____

_____

_____

List all training provided to managers in the last 12 months regarding emergency planning:

DATE   TYPE OF TRAINING   COMMENTS

_____   _____   _____

_____   _____   _____

_____   _____   _____

List all training provided for floor wardens or emergency response personnel in the last 12 months:

DATE   TYPE   SUBJECT

_____   _____   First Aid

_____   _____   Bomb Search

_____   _____   Evacuation

_____   _____   Firefighting

_____   _____   Other_____

_____   _____   _____

_____   _____   _____

List threat call training provided for the following:

                              DATE   COMMENTS

Receptionist   _____   _____

Telephone Operators   _____   _____

Mailroom Personnel   _____   _____

Control Center Operators   _____   _____

Other

_____   _____   _____

Testing

List the dates that each element of the emergency plan was tested with the CMT in the last 24 months:

DATE	TYPE OF TEST	ELEMENT TESTED
_____	_____	Fire_____
_____	_____	Demonstration_____
_____	_____	Natural Disaster_____
_____	_____	Threat: Bomb_____
_____	_____	Threat: Personnel_____

List all corrective action(s) to correct deficiencies that resulted from tests.

_____

_____

_____

List the dates that each element of the emergency plan was tested with the floor wardens or emergency response teams in the last 12 months:

DATE	TYPE OF TEST	ELEMENT TESTED
_____	_____	Fire_____
_____	_____	Demonstration_____
_____	_____	Natural Disaster_____
_____	_____	Threat: Bomb _____

List all corrective action(s) to correct deficiencies that resulted from tests.

_____

_____

_____

INCIDENT MANAGEMENT

Incident Reporting

Describe the process for employees to report incidents to security.

_____

_____

_____

Has this process been communicated to management and employees?

Yes   No

_____   _____

If yes, describe how it was communicated.

_____

_____

_____

Is there a process to categorize incidents?

Yes   No

_____   _____

If yes, describe the process.

_____

_____

_____

Is there a process to ensure each significant incident is fully investigated?

                                               Yes   No

                                       _____   _____

If yes, describe the process.

_____

_____

For serious personnel incidents, who conducts the investigation?

      NAME   TITLE

_____

_____

_____

Are noncompany employees (i.e., contract security) allowed to investigate minor incidents?

                                               Yes   No

                                       _____   _____

If no, describe how minor incidents are investigated and by whom.

_____

_____

_____

If yes, does a company employee maintain responsibility and account-ability for investigation?

                                               Yes   No

                                       _____   _____

If yes, describe the process.

_____

_____

Are major incidents analyzed to determine the underlying causes?

Yes	No

If yes, describe the process.

_____

_____

_____

Have appropriate actions and controls been implemented to mitigate reoccurrence of significant incidents that occurred during the past 12 months?

Yes	No

If yes, describe the actions.

_____

_____

_____

How are incident reports and files classifieds and protected?

_____

_____

_____

Management Notification

How is location management notified of incidents and incident trends?

_____

_____

_____

INFORMATION PROTECTION

List the process and dates during the past 12 months that the following were communicated to management and employees.

Baseline Security Education

_____

_____

Basic Classification and Control Requirements for Every Employee

_____

_____

Security Requirements for Every User of Computer Systems

_____

_____

Security Requirements for Every Manager

_____

_____

Site Services Security Education

_____

_____

New Employees Education

_____

_____

New Managers Education

_____

_____

Does security have a process to ensure the adequacy of site services security education and training?

| | Yes | No |
| | _____ | _____ |

If yes, describe the process.

_____

_____

_____

Does security have a process to ensure the adequacy of the baseline security education and training?

| | Yes | No |
| | _____ | _____ |

If yes, describe the process.

_____

_____

_____

If no, list the exceptions.

_____

_____

Has verification of compliance to information protection controls been conducted during the past 12 months in the following areas?

	DATE	COMMENTS	YES	NO
Information/Systems	_____	_____		
Procurement	_____	_____		
Telecommunications	_____	_____		

After-Hours Review Program

Summarize the security and management after-hours security program for ensuring that classified information is properly secured. Provide site data for the previous 12 months.

_____

_____

Use of Supplemental Employees and Onsite Contractor Personnel

Supplemental Employees, Contractors, and Part-Time Employees

What security education was provided to new supplemental employees and part-time employees during the past 12 months?

_____

_____

What security education was provided to onsite contractor personnel during the past 12 months?

_____

_____

Release of Company Confidential Information

What process exists to ensure all company confidential information given to vendors is approved by the authorized manager and is released on transmittals?

_____

_____

_____

Receipt of Other Companies' Confidential Information

What process exists to ensure confidential information received from other companies is approved by the authorized manager and is properly protected within the company?

_____

_____

_____

_____

Vendor Security

List the vendor security reviews you have conducted or directed with purchasing in the past 12 months for vendors that have confidential information.

_____

_____

_____

_____

Telecommunications Security: PBX and CBX

Does your company have telecommunications security guidelines?

	Yes	No
	_____	_____

If no, list the reasons or exceptions.

_____

_____

_____

_____

Exit Interviews for Transfers and Terminations

Are exit interviews conducted for employees who transfer, terminate, or obtain a leave of absence?

	Yes	No
	_____	_____

Are key employees interviewed by legal and reminded of their confidentiality agreement?

	Yes	No
	___	___

Are debriefing forms completed and submitted to the human resources department?

	Yes	No
	___	___

If yes, describe how this is validated.

_____

_____

PHYSICAL SECURITY

Lock and Key Control

Is there a daily accountability for grand master or building master or core keys?

	Yes	No
	___	___

If no, list reasons or exceptions.

_____

_____

List all holders of all grand or building master and core keys by name and function:

NAME   FUNCTION   KEY TYPE

_____   _____

_____   _____

_____   _____

_____   _____

Is there documentation on file by security management for master keys in excess of five?

	Yes	No
	_____	_____

List the reasons why there are more than five.

_____

_____

Is there documentation on file that demonstrates that keys are recovered from exiting employees?

	Yes	No
	_____	_____

_____

_____

Exterior Space

Is the perimeter controlled to vehicle access during an emergency or site closure?

	Yes	No
	_____	_____

Is there perimeter fencing around the property?

	Yes	No
	_____	_____

If yes, is it randomly inspected and properly maintained?

	Yes	No
	_____	_____

Are all building perimeter doors and interior restricted space doors equipped with anti-shim plates or anti-shim bolts or latches?

	Yes	No
	_____	_____

Are all perimeter doors and interior restricted space doors monitored by access control system (ACS) or an alarm system to deter and detect unauthorized access into the building or restricted area?

	Yes	No
	_____	_____

If no, list the reasons or exceptions.
Are less obvious points of building entry designed to prevent access into the building or vandalism to the utility system?

	Yes	No
Grills	_____	_____
Grating	_____	_____
Manhole Covers	_____	_____
Area Ways	_____	_____
Utility Tunnels	_____	_____
Roof Vents	_____	_____
Other _____	_____	_____

Do all building perimeters have an unobstructed line of site? (Shrubbery, plantings, etc., are at least four feet away from the building.)

	Yes	No
	_____	_____

Is all property properly posted with easily identifiable but nonspecific signs?

	Yes	No
	_____	_____

Is fencing provided for critical areas (chemical, electrical, communications, emergency power facilities, etc.)?

	Yes	No
	_____	_____

Is fencing properly installed and maintained?

	Yes	No
	_____	_____

Are surveillance cameras or alarms provided for the following:

	Yes	No
Chemical Tank Areas	_____	_____
Electrical Substations	_____	_____
Communications Facilities	_____	_____
Emergency Power Facilities	_____	_____
Parking Lots and Garages	_____	_____
Building Exteriors	_____	_____
Other _____	_____	_____

Is the lighting level adequate to provide for the safety and security of employees?

	Yes	No
Vehicle and Pedestrian Entrances	_____	_____
Property Perimeters	_____	_____
Pedestrian Walkways	_____	_____
Building Perimeters	_____	_____

Building Entrances	_____	_____
Parking Lots and Garages	_____	_____
Critical Facilities	_____	_____
Areas of Concealment	_____	_____

Are the trees and shrubbery maintained properly to provide for the safety and security of employees by not obstructing lighting or cameras?

	Yes	No
Building Perimeters	_____	_____
Parking Lots and Garages	_____	_____
Critical Facilities	_____	_____
Areas of Concealment	_____	_____

Interior Space

Is shatter-resistant glass or mylar film installed on exterior windows in the following areas (applies to high-risk facilities and areas only):

	Yes	No
Lobbies	_____	_____
Conference Rooms	_____	_____
Cafeteria	_____	_____
Open Office Landscaping	_____	_____
Passageways Connecting Buildings	_____	_____
Other _____	_____	_____

Is the lighting level adequate to provide for the safety and security of personnel and property. If no, explain.

_____

_____

_____

Have all areas where bomb devices might be concealed been eliminated or sealed?

	Yes	No
Lobbies	_____	_____
Restrooms (in nonsecure areas)	_____	_____
Docks	_____	_____
External Concealment Areas (newspaper boxes, trash cans, etc.)	_____	_____
Other _____	_____	_____

If no, explain.

_____

_____

_____

How many areas at the location are identified as "Restricted Space"?

_____

Have they documented the requirements for "Restricted Space"?

Yes	No
_____	_____

Are all identified "Restricted Space" areas documented and in 100 percent compliance with established controls?

Yes	No
_____	_____

If no, list reasons or exceptions for each area.

_____

_____

_____

Mailroom Controls

Does the mailroom have the following controls (as applicable):

	Yes	No
Access Restricted to Authorized Individuals	_____	_____
X-Ray Equipment Installed	_____	_____
Mail Bomb and Hazardous Substances Training Every 12 Months	_____	_____
Transportation of Mail: Auditable Process	_____	____
Safe for Locking Classified and Valuable Mail After Hours	_____	_____

If no, explain. _____

_____

_____

_____

Cashier or ATM

Are cashier or ATM facilities monitored by a third party for robbery or burglary?

	Yes	No
	_____	_____

If no, explain.

_____

_____

_____

_____

If yes, is the third-party response reported to their security?

| | Yes | No |
| | _____ | _____ |

Does a written emergency response procedure exist for location security?

| | Yes | No |
| | _____ | _____ |

Do you have a parallel alarm monitoring of cashier or ATM alarms?

| | Yes | No |
| | _____ | _____ |

Medical Facilities

Does your location have company medical facilities?

| | Yes | No |
| | _____ | _____ |

If yes, does the medical facility have the following in place:

	Yes	No
ACS between Reception and the Rest of the Medical Facility	_____	_____
Concealed CCTV in the Reception Area and Outside the Entrance	_____	_____

Panic Alarms in the Following Locations:

Reception — With One-Way Audio	_____	_____
Physicians' Offices	_____	_____
Exam Rooms	_____	_____
Other _____	_____	_____
Secondary Egress from the Medical Area	_____	_____
Exterior Window Design to Prevent Direct Observation	_____	_____
Separate Locking System for Storage of Controlled Substances	_____	_____

Central Employment Offices

Is the employment office located adjacent to the building lobby?

Yes	No
_____	_____

If no, explain.

_____

_____

_____

Does the employment lobby have the following:

	Yes	No
Capability to Verify Identity Prior to Unlocking/Locking Exterior Door	_____	_____
Separation of Lobby from the Staff Work Area	_____	_____
Panic Alarm	_____	_____

Do interview rooms include the following:

    Doors with Side Glass View Panel   _____   _____

    Panic Alarm   _____   _____

Is there a rear exit from the staff work space?

        Yes   No

        _____   _____

Do written emergency response procedures for security exist?

        Yes   No

        _____   _____

How often are all security devices tested? _____

Classified Waste

State the process for classified waste disposal at your location. Include how waste is protected during collection and prior to pickup by the vendor. Has the waste vendor had an unannounced security review?

        Yes   No

        _____   _____

If yes, list date.

_____

Panic Alarms

Do all panic alarms simultaneously activate audio and video, which is remotely connected to a constantly monitored location?

        Yes   No

        _____   _____

If no, describe.

_____

_____

Date training was provided to receptionist (and others as required) on use of panic alarm:

_____

How often are all lobby and other panic alarm devices tested?

_____

Lobbies

Does the lobby have the following:

	Yes	No
Remote Control Locking and Unlocking of Interior and Exterior Door(s)	_____	_____
Electronically Controlled Access to Interior Space	_____	_____
Audio and Video Panic Alarm to Security	_____	_____
Elevator Recall	_____	_____
Are all of the above items activated and deactivated by one activation device?	_____	_____

If no, describe alternative controls.

_____

_____

Are all lobbies designed and furnished to eliminate potential for concealment of persons or packages?

_____	_____
Yes	No

Do remote control capabilities for locking and unlocking interior and
exterior doors from the staffed lobby exist?

_____	_____
Yes	No

Loading Docks

Do the loading docks have the following:

	Yes	No
Remote Control Locking and Unlocking of Interior and Exterior Door(s)	_____	_____
ACS Controlled Access to Interior Space	_____	_____
(Secondary Perimeter: Can Be Exterior Fence)		
Audio and Video Panic Alarm to Security	_____	_____
Are All of the Above Items Activated and Deactivated by One Activation Device?	_____	_____
Separation of Shipping, Receiving, and Trash Removal Activities	_____	_____
Written Emergency Procedures	_____	_____

Access Control System Operations

Are badge supplies and duplicate photo files properly controlled?

_____	_____
Yes	No

Do ACS controls limit noncompany employees access to only their authorized working hours?

    _____   _____

    Yes   No

If no, explain. _____

Are ACS area reports distributed every 60 days for all area managers and contractors? (Area manager: The person responsible for approving access to an area.)

    _____   _____

    Yes   No

Are ACS area reports for contractors and "Restricted Space" 100 percent return audited to security every 60 days?

    _____   _____

    Yes   No

Are ACS backup tapes and disks of system data stored in an area that will not be affected by a primary disaster?

    _____   _____

    Yes   No

List the storage location(s): _____

What method is used to validate the ACS database?

_____

How often is the database validated? _____

List ACS operator authorization levels for the following:

                              Level

Contract Guards   _____

Guard Supervisors   _____

Contract Guard Manager   _____

Company Security   _____

Do all ACS alarms have a response defined on the appropriate alarm screen?

        _____   _____

        Yes   No

Control Center

Is all control center equipment, alarms, CCTV, ACS, etc., tested every 30 days for proper function?

        _____   _____

        Yes   No

Is all control center equipment on battery backup and emergency backup power?

        _____   _____

        Yes   No

Parking

List the parking controls for the location.

_____

_____

_____

Are parking facilities properly illuminated?

        _____   _____

        Yes   No

Are parking facilities monitored by CCTV?

_____	_____
Yes	No

Are parking facilities provided with emergency call stations?

_____	_____
Yes	No

Contractor Controls

Do contractors exchange a company ID for a contractor badge?

_____	_____
Yes	No

List all service contracts. Do they have a confidential disclosure agreement (CDA)?

	CDA	
CONTRACTOR NAME	YES	NO
_____	_____	_____
_____	_____	_____
_____	_____	_____
_____	_____	_____
_____	_____	_____
_____	_____	_____

What security education is provided to contractors?

_____

_____

_____

Do all service contracts contain a requirement that no drugs, alcohol, or weapons are allowed onsite?

                                                        _____   _____

                                                         Yes   No

What action is taken to ensure the contractor complies with these clauses?

_____

_____

_____

Contract Security

Does the guard contract contain the following:

	Yes	No
Background Check Requirements	_____	_____
Education Requirements	_____	_____
Training Requirements	_____	_____
Skills and Experience Prerequisites	_____	_____

How often are audits conducted to verify compliance with the above contract requirements?

_____

List the last two audit dates and results.

DATE   RESULTS

_____   _____

_____   _____

Do all posts have current post orders?   _____   _____

                                                              Yes   No

Do contract security personnel act as receptionists? If so, what specific training have they received?

_____

_____

_____

How is billing reconciled and verified?

_____

_____

Is overtime authorized? If so, under what circumstances?

_____

_____

_____

Are any security services provided by the building landlord?

                                      _____   _____

                                       Yes   No

If yes, describe.

_____

_____

_____

Company (Proprietary) Security Employees

List the security training provided to security personnel during the last 12 months.

DATE   TRAINING

_____   _____

_____   _____

_____   _____

_____   _____

_____   _____

_____   _____

Gatehouse Operation

What are the hours of attended gatehouse operations?

_____

What factors determine the need for continual gatehouse operation?

_____

_____

_____

Education and Awareness

Are education and awareness programs in place to cover the following:

	Yes	No
Drugs and Alcohol	_____	_____
Weapons	_____	_____

Cameras and Photography   _____   _____

Threat Policy   _____   _____

Display of ID Badge   _____   _____

Building Entry Procedures (Tailgating)   _____   _____

If no, explain.

_____

_____

_____

Security Officer and Contract Guard Posts

DESCRIPTION	HRS/DAYS	WORKER/YEARS	YEARLY COSTS
_____	_____	_____	_____
_____	_____	_____	_____
_____	_____	_____	_____
_____	_____	_____	_____
_____	_____	_____	_____
_____	_____	_____	_____
_____	_____	_____	_____
_____	_____	_____	_____

APPENDIX D

RISK/SECURITY MANAGEMENT & CONSULTING

SAMPLE

REQUEST FOR PROPOSAL

SECURITY SERVICES

STREET ADDRESS

CITY, STATE

DATE

This document and the information it contains is considered Confidential to the Risk/Security Management & Consulting Company and shall not be shared with anyone within your company who does not have a need to know the information. Additionally, it may not be shared with anyone outside of your company!

INVITATION AND STATEMENT OF EXPECTATIONS

Risk/Security Management & Consulting (R/SM & C): CLIENT

R/SM & C Director of Security: Timothy D. Giles, CPP, PSP, PSP

Contractor: The prospective provider of security services

The Risk/Security Management & Consulting (R/SM & C) Director of Security invites your firm to submit a proposal to supply security services at the Risk/Security Management & Consulting, located at STREET ADDRESS, CITY, STATE ZIP. This package sets forth the specifications, requirements, and responsibilities for fulfillment of the security services contract. Contractor's proposal shall address all of the specifications contained herein. Recommended alternatives or exceptions to specifications should be attached to the bid proposal as an addendum. Failure to address the specifications herein and/or follow the prescribed format may result, at R/SM & C Director of Security's discretion, in your bid being classified as a nonresponsive and, therefore, disqualified from further consideration.

The services herein requested shall be provided in a first-class manner in accordance with the highest standards typical of a Class "A" office building in LOCATION. Our property is even more unique than most Class "A" properties and requires a service provider with a very strong focus on developing customer satisfaction with our clients. All security associates must understand that R/SM & C has a very strong focus on customer loyalty and that they are a key ingredient in our success! All must be friendly and outgoing at all times!

INTRODUCTION AND INSTRUCTIONS FOR PROPOSAL

Introduction

R/SM & C Director of Security at 111 Anywhere St., Atlanta, GA 30303 (hereinafter the "Property"), requests that you submit a proposal for the provision of security services at the Property.

The following pages are an indication of some of the covenants that may be contained in the actual security services contract. Please examine the bid package carefully and respond to each of the requested items contained herein.

Please note that the actual contract term for security services will be for two years and that a termination clause calling for contract cancellation by either party with 30 days' written notification to the other will be incorporated within. Additionally, the contract will stipulate that the service provider must allow their employees to "walk over" if another service provider is awarded the contract.

Submittal

Completed proposals are to be returned to:

R/SM & C Director of Security: Timothy D. Giles, CPP, PSP, PSP: Street Address, City, State Zip; Ph. Number; e-mail:

Proposals must be received by *4:00 pm on Friday, Date*. Bids received after this date and time will be considered nonresponsive.

Award of Contract
The contract will be awarded on or around **Date.** Contractors will be notified by mail.

Commencement
Service will commence on or around **Date**. This schedule is subject to change.

Site Visits
Site visits are required prior to submitting a proposal for security services in response to this package. Site visits may be scheduled by contacting *Timothy D. Giles, CPP, PSP.*

RFIs during Bidding

Requests for information should be directed in writing to the submittal contact above. Both the question and the answer will be sent to all bidding Contractors.

Changes during Bidding

Bidding Contractors will be advised of any changes to the specifications contained herein that occur during the bid process.

Lowest Priced Bid

The R/SM & C Director of Security is in no way bound to accept the lowest priced bid proposal or any proposal tendered pursuant to this request for proposal.

Proposal Content

Proposals must include each of the following:

1. Complete Contractor contact information
2. Contractor company history
3. Certificate of insurance
4. Organizational chart of key personnel with names, titles, and resume' information
5. Description of training and evaluation procedures *(see RFP Sections VI and VII)*
6. Description of after-hours supervision *(see RFP Section XV)*
7. Drug, alcohol, and contraband policy *(see RFP Section V and Attachment C)*
8. Completed bid evaluation form *(see RFP Sections XI, XIII, and Attachment C)*
9. Detailed transition plan *(see RFP Section XVII)*
10. References *(see RFP Section XVI)*
11. Last two years' financial statements (with sufficient financial information to establish Contractor's stability)
12. All comments and exceptions to any specification in this RFP
13. Contractor must indicate in writing that it has read, understood, and has the ability to comply with the requirements as stipulated herein.

GENERAL REQUIREMENTS

Independent Contractor

The Contractor agrees to perform the work described in the contract as an independent contractor and not as a subcontractor, agent, or associate of Risk/Security Management & Consulting.

R/SM & C agrees to use the security officers employed by the Contractor and the Contractor agrees to furnish such number of security officers as may be required by R/SM & C at the site. However, R/SM & C may also utilize its own associates as security officers and R/SM & C's tenants may utilize independent security services in and about their leased premises at the site or at any public functions which such tenants may hold in common areas of the site.

Assignment and Subcontracting

This contract shall not be assigned or subcontracted by the Contractor either in whole or in part.

Confidentiality of Proprietary Data and Information

All information and data, regardless of form, that is received from R/SM & C or R/SM & C Director of Security shall be treated as confidential by the Contractor, whether it is or isn't labeled as confidential, and the Contractor shall take all precautions necessary to prevent disclosure of such information or data verbally or in writing to others except upon the expressed written approval of R/SM & C Director of Security. Any third party to whom Contractor is authorized to provide such information or data shall be required, as a condition of receiving such information, to execute confidentiality agreements suitable to the R/SM & C Director of Security. Without the prior written approval of the R/SM & C Director of Security, Contractor shall not use for any purpose other than the performance of the work contemplated by the contract any information, design, drawing, specification, or document received from the R/SM & C Director of Security. Upon request, Contractor will return to the R/SM & C Director of Security all copies of such information, design, drawings, specifications, and documents and shall safeguard against disclosure to others all documents in Contractor's possession that include such confidential information for a period of seven years after the completion of the work described in the contract.

Revisions to Original Contract

R/SM & C or the R/SM & C Director of Security shall have the right to make any changes in or delete services from the work described in the contract and may direct the Contractor to perform extra work, and the Contractor shall implement such changes and perform such extra work. Should any such change increase or decrease or affect the amount or character of services required in the contract, the price shall be adjusted accordingly. The amount of increase or decrease, if any, in the price shall be determined by agreement between the Contractor and R/SM & C. However, commencement of work requested by R/SM & C shall be independent of agreement on the effect of such change.

In case any such change or alteration shall result in a decrease of the work to be performed, no allowance shall be made to this Contractor for loss of anticipated profits, but if the Contractor, before receiving R/SM & C's notice of intention to make such a change, shall have incurred expenses which shall be rendered unnecessary by such change or alteration, such allowance shall be made to the Contractor as shall be fair and reasonable as determined by R/SM & C or the R/SM & C Director of Security.

Accounting and Auditing

Contractor shall maintain complete and accurate records of all Contractors' costs related to R/SM & C's account. Such records to be maintained and retained by Contractor shall, at a minimum, include but not be limited to:

1. Accounting records, including payroll records, accounting for total time distribution of Contractor's associates working full- or part-time on the job (to permit tracing of payrolls and related tax returns and/or union payments, if any).
2. Canceled payroll checks and/or signed receipts for payroll payments in cash.
3. Invoices for purchases, for Contractors stores stocks, or for capital items.
4. Paid invoices and canceled checks for materials purchased or repaired.
5. Written policies and procedures.
6. Original estimates and estimating worksheets.
7. Correspondence.
8. Change order files (including documentation covering negotiated settlement).
9. All records associated with background checks, drug tests, fingerprint checks, etc., of Contractor's employees that are or have worked at R/SM & C.

Such "records" shall be open to inspection and subject to audit and/or reproduction, during normal working hours, by R/SM & C Director of Security or authorized representative to the extent necessary to adequately permit evaluation and verification of any invoices, payments, or claims submitted by the Contractor or any of his payees pursuant to the execution of the contract. Such records subject to examination shall also include, but not be limited to, those records necessary to evaluate and verify direct and indirect costs (including overhead allocations) as they may apply to costs associated with this contract.

For the purpose of such audits, inspections, examinations, and evaluations, the R/SM & C Director of Security or authorized representative shall have access to said records from the effective date of the contract, for the duration of the work, and until two years after the date of final payment by R/SM & C to Contractor pursuant to the contract.

R/SM & C or authorized representative shall have access to the Contractor's facilities and shall be provided adequate and appropriate workspace, in order to conduct audits in compliance with this article. Except under unusual circumstances, R/SM & C Director of Security or authorized representative shall give auditees reasonable advance notice of intended audits.

Contractor Qualifications

Contractor must be duly licensed in accordance with all state, county, and local laws governing the security industry prior to submitting a bid proposal.

Contractor must show the ability to provide and maintain administrative, operational, and logistical support for the client.

SCOPE OF WORK

Performance of Work

Contractor is to provide security services in the form of unarmed, uniformed officers for the property and in accordance with the Standard Hours of Coverage schedule attached hereto (Attachment B).

Responsibilities of Work

Contractor will be responsible for, but not limited to, the following where R/SM & C utilizes its security officers:

1. Maintain discipline, excellent appearance, professional demeanor, integrity, and attention to duty among Contractor personnel.
2. Maintain and update property-specific written post orders for each position.
3. Require Contractor personnel to enforce R/SM & C's and Contractor's security policies, procedures, and orders.
4. Require Contractor personnel to enforce R/SM & C's requirements as it pertains to customer loyalty or customer satisfaction programs and service.
5. Administer/monitor electronic systems including, but not limited to, access control system and other door or control systems; CCTV systems; fire alarm systems; panic alarm systems; radio systems; etc.; 24 hours a day, 7 days a week; make recommendations to R/SM & C Director of Security to improve coverage/control.
6. Furnish R/SM & C Director of Security with names and phone numbers of Contractor supervisory personnel who can be contacted at any time to respond to R/SM & C's needs.
7. Furnish trained and qualified unarmed security personnel in sufficient number to provide service as requested by R/SM & C. This service will be continuous regardless of weather, disaster, strikes, or threatened strikes, and shall include, but not be limited to, the following:
   a. Administering R/SM & C's site security and safety procedures.
   b. Greeting and assisting visitors, guests, contractors, and employees in a professional manner at all times.
   c. Access control of persons, vehicles, and other property.
   d. Performing site surveillance.
   e. Identifying and reporting security and safety violations.
   f. Securing property turned in as found.
   g. Maintaining files for security-related documents.
   h. Assisting R/SM & C personnel in emergency situations.
   i. Ensuring that prompt action is taken to prevent or minimize losses, accidents, fires, property damage, safety hazards, and security incidents.
   j. Inspecting R/SM & C's security devices (cameras, door locks, lighting, alarms, etc.) as instructed, and submitting written reports for any which are malfunctioning, inoperative, or in need of repair.

k. Inspecting and ensuring all safety equipment (clear exit paths, fire doors, etc.) is maintained and functioning properly as instructed, and submitting written reports for any which are malfunctioning, inoperative, or in need of repair.

Contractor shall prepare and submit security officer work shift schedules to R/SM & C Director of Security at least five working days before effective date of implementation. Changes or substitutions in the work shift schedule will not be made without prior notification to the R/SM & C Director of Security, except in a bona fide emergency.

Contractor personnel must work their assigned post completely alert and fit to perform their prescribed tasks.

Contractor's personnel may be exposed to various weather conditions, construction hazards, and other hazards inherent in security work, and the Contractor shall ensure that its personnel are prepared and equipped for such conditions.

Contractor associates are strictly forbidden to bring weapons of any type, but especially guns, onto R/SM & C premises. Contractor shall **not** employ armed security officers on R/SM & C's premises.

Contractor's Personnel

The Contractor shall immediately remove from the property, whenever required to do so by the R/SM & C Director of Security, any person considered by R/SM & C or R/SM & C Director of Security to be incompetent or disposed to be disorderly, or for any other appropriate reason unsatisfactory or undesirable to R/SM & C or R/SM & C Director of Security, and such person shall not again be employed on R/SM & C's premises without the express written consent of R/SM & C or R/SM & C Director of Security.

STANDARDS OF WORK

General Standards

All services shall be performed with the highest standard of contract security, as typified by the standards customary to first-class office buildings in the area, and in accordance with all state and local laws. The Contractor will be responsible for ensuring its staff is familiar with and accomplishes the functions and tasks as outlined in the **post orders** for the property, and does so in a manner consistent with the behavior expected of all associates of the R/SM & C Director of Security.

Contractor Informed as to Conditions

It is agreed that the Contractor is familiar with all physical and other conditions existing at the site of the work and all other matters in connection with the work to be performed under this order. This includes the fact that many posts require many hours of being on your feet and outside.

Storage and Security of Equipment and Supplies

The Contractor shall have full responsibility for storing equipment and supplies used in connection with the work. Storage space will be provided by R/SM & C at the site of the work as available.

Inspection

R/SM & C contemplates, and the Contractor hereby agrees to, a thorough minute inspection by R/SM & C's representative or other agent of R/SM & C of all work and equipment furnished under this order.

Removal of Debris

The Contractor shall leave the entire premises within the site of its operations clean and free from all rubbish resulting from its operation.

Health and Safety

The Contractor shall observe all federal, state, and local laws and regulations pertaining to health and safety.

The Contractor shall take all precautions necessary and shall be responsible for the safety of all work to be performed by its employees. The Contractor shall not require any person employed in the performance of the contract to work in conditions which are unsanitary, hazardous, or dangerous to his or her health or safety as determined under safety and health standards promulgated by the Secretary of Labor.

The importance of safety of all workers shall be recognized and accident prevention shall be an integral part of the Contractor's operations.

The Contractor shall conduct the work in a safe and practical manner, in conformance with the safety and health standards made applicable to the work by the federal Occupational Safety and Health Act.

Management Support

The Contractor will provide a salaried, management-level employee who will have accountability and responsibility for the property complex described herein, and this individual (Site Security Manager) will provide direct support and communication with the onsite R/SM & C Director of Security. The additional responsibilities of this Security Manager shall include overall responsibility for hiring and firing, training, and development with an emphasis on security, fire/life safety, maintaining the currency of all written procedural documents, budget and quality control, and emergency response 24 hours a day/7 days a week. This position is billable to R/SM & C as a salaried 40-hour position regardless of the hours worked.

Furthermore, the onsite Site Security Manager should not normally work more than 40 hours per week without advising the R/SM & C Director of Security. He/she should vary his/her personal schedule to ensure that time is spent working all three shifts on a periodic but unannounced basis. Any request by R/SM & C Director of Security for the onsite Site Security Manager to exceed the 40-hour per week schedule shall be honored as long as these requests do not become routine.

Furthermore, the Contractor will provide a salaried, management-level employee who will have accountability and responsibility for the account and will provide direct support and communication with the onsite R/SM & C Director of Security on a regular basis to ensure the compliance with this contract. This position will not be billable to R/SM & C.

RECRUITMENT AND HIRING PROCESS

Personnel Standards

Each security officer assigned to duty on R/SM & C's site is required to be or to have at least:

1. State, county, city registration for unarmed security personnel, as required.
2. A valid state driver's license or picture identification card.
3. Dependable transportation to and from the job.
4. Capable of displaying a professional image and friendly attitude at all times.
5. Telephone at residence so officer can be contacted in an emergency.
6. Freedom from any judgment of incompetence by any court for mental defect or disease.
7. U.S. citizenship or legal residency.
8. Ability to read, write, speak, and understand the English language to the extent of giving and understanding written orders and verbal instructions, and being capable of composing reports which convey complete and accurate information.
9. Freedom from injury or physical handicaps that would prevent proper performance of security work.
10. The physical capability to assist others in an emergency without causing injury to others or themselves and the ability to stand at a post for long durations of time.
11. Freedom from any criminal convictions or current involvement in such proceedings.
12. Freedom from any civil convictions or litigation involving theft, battery, slander, public misconduct, assault, or similar proceedings.

Personnel Screening Requirements

Background investigations shall be conducted and documented by Contractor to verify that each officer, prior to assignment to R/SM & C's site, has accurately completed the Contractor's employment application and meets the qualifications set forth above. The employment application will be designed to obtain at least the following information, which will be verified by the background investigation conducted by the Contractor:

1. Full name, aliases, and signature
2. Social Security number
3. Current address and prior address (previous seven years)
4. Citizenship
5. Felony conviction records

6. Driving record
7. Military record
8. Previous seven years' employment history and reason for termination.
9. Education and/or specialized training
10. Verification of any unaccounted-for time periods
11. Character references (three)
12. Credit history
13. Photograph
14. Fingerprints to both state and federal authorities
15. Drug testing

Written pre-employment honesty/personality testing will be administered to all officer candidates as part of the screening process.

Employment records shall include, at a minimum, the employment application, attendance report, training records, results of background investigation and drug tests, pre-employment honesty/personality tests, classifiable fingerprints, a recent photograph, and work-related injury reports. All employment records will be furnished to R/SM & C or R/SM & C Director of Security upon request for audit.

It is also important to screen all applicants to ensure that they have no bias or prejudices.

The R/SM & C Director of Security will meet and/or review applicants prior to permanent assignment and reserves the right to request the Contractor add or remove any security officer or supervisor from the work site.

R/SM & C or R/SM & C Director of Security reserve the right at any time to order any employees of Contractor removed from account with or without cause.

The security Contractor shall prescribe to recruitment and hiring practices that will attract and select the most qualified applicants. Screening and interview procedures shall include personnel interviews with Contractor's management-level staff, drug testing, criminal records check, and verification of an already-in-process application for a state, county, or city guard card, as applicable.

R/SM & C Director of Security shall have the right to approve any officers working at R/SM & C.

Drug, Alcohol, and Other Contraband Policy

Contractor must have, prior to solicitation date, a comprehensive drug and alcohol-testing program. Evidence of such a program, including any related policies, shall be provided as part of the bid package. Testing shall be sample testing by an independent laboratory.

R/SM & C or R/SM & C Director of Security reserves the right, at any time, to conduct reasonable searches of contract associates, including privately owned vehicles, while on company site.

Contractor will be solely responsible for ensuring associates assigned to R/SM & C's site have been informed of, and understand, this policy. Bid proposals shall include information as to the means and methods Contractor will use to ensure that all associates receive the proper notices.

When appropriate, R/SM & C or R/SM & C Director of Security may request (and the Contractor will make reasonable effort to comply with such request) a urine analysis test conducted on a contract associate when one or more of the following conditions exist:

1. A violation of the policy is witnessed by R/SM & C or the R/SM & C Director of Security.
2. Where there is reasonable cause to believe an associate is, or may be, under the influence of contraband substances, and/or extenuating or emergency circumstances require an immediate test to ensure the safety of associates, the public, or property.
3. A delay in the test may result in the loss of evidence.
4. In the event of an accident involving personal injury and/or property damage.

Penalties for Violation of Policy

Contract associates found in violation of this policy will be immediately relieved of duty by Contractor. The Contractor will be notified that the individual is to be removed from R/SM & C's premises and will not be allowed to return to the premises without the prior written permission of the R/SM & C Director of Security.

Contract personnel found in possession of illegal substances or items may, at the discretion of the R/SM & C Director of Security, be referred to law enforcement for action. Contract associates who decline a urine test, or a search, may be permanently barred from R/SM & C's site.

Violation of this policy by contract associates may result in cancellation of the contract between R/SM & C and the Contractor.

TRAINING

The security Contractor will be solely responsible for ensuring that its employees are trained and competent in the performance of their duties as outlined by the **post orders** for the property. At a minimum, required training will be categorized into four specific areas:

Orientation and Initial Training

Orientation/initial training shall first occur in the Contractor's office and include the basic introductory guard courses typically administered. The subjects learned in orientation shall effect, at a minimum, a knowledge of private security's legal obligations and rights, the powers of arrest, customer care/satisfaction, familiarity with local and state codes as it pertains to private security, security policy/procedure familiarization, emergency procedure familiarization, disaster response familiarization, and incident report writing.

Ongoing Training

Additionally, twenty-four (24) hours of formalized **ongoing training** per year per officer shall be administered in monthly segments and will be nonbillable to the client.

Post tests shall be developed and administered in conjunction with all training. All contract associates will sign off that they have reviewed and understand the post orders every six (6) months. Documentation of training will be required and is to be maintained at the site.

Emergency Medical Response Training

Minimum training requirements are that at least all shift supervisors and the Site Security Manager will be CPR, AED, and first aid trained at the Contractor's expense. Such training shall occur within three months of being assigned to the post and must be updated as dictated by the certification received. There must always be a fully trained and certified associate on duty at the site to respond to medical emergencies.

Specialized Training

Specialized training shall include, but not be limited to, client relations/ customer service, de-escalation training, parking/patrol vehicle use (if applicable), and the use of any other special equipment or systems. Such training will be performed as identified and evaluated by the Contractor. The following skills should be addressed:

- Warmly greet visitors, guests, Contractor, and employees.
- Possess ability to communicate in a professional manner.
- Exercise good judgment in decisions and apply initiative when needed.
- Ability to demonstrate, follow, understand, and apply operational instruction, including R/SM & C's security and safety procedures.
- Place emphasis on good effective communications to ensure a customer service-oriented approach in carrying out all of the above duties involving personnel interface.
- Countersurveillance training to be able to determine if the site or an individual at the site is under surveillance.

Please include a detailed description of your training policies and procedures in your proposal.

EVALUATION PROCEDURES

All security associates shall be afforded both informal and formal reviews with supervisory or management personnel. Informal reviews are to take place quarterly, and each associate shall have a formal written review annually. As is appropriate, these reviews may be shared with the R/SM & C Director of Security.

EMPLOYEE BENEFITS

It is expected that the security personnel assigned to the property will be afforded employee benefits that are competitive in the industry. Describe, in detail, the employee benefits package including health benefits, retirement, disability insurance, life insurance, and sick and vacation leave. Pricing for employee benefit programs shall be included in the hourly billing rates.

INCENTIVE AND RECOGNITION PROGRAMS

All security associates assigned to the property will be eligible to participate in an incentive and recognition program at the discretion of R/SM & C or R/SM & C Director of Security that is in addition to the Contractor's programs.

PRINCIPAL POSTS AND POST ORDERS

Listed on Attachment "A" are the principal post requirements (duties and responsibilities) as conceived for the property. Periodically the defined posts shall be evaluated by the Contractor for effectiveness, and appropriate recommendations will be made to the R/SM & C Director of Security.

It will be the Contractor's responsibility to write and maintain job descriptions for each post. Minimum qualifications and requisite training, including hours, are to be detailed and documented within the post orders. Such post orders will be updated at a minimum every six months and will be formally presented to R/SM & C or the R/SM & C Director of Security annually. All event-driven updates to the post orders will be approved by the R/SM & C Director of Security prior to implementation. Contractor shall prepare post orders for R/SM & C's review for the initial 30 days once contract is awarded.

STANDARD HOURS OF COVERAGE AND SPECIAL EVENT HOURS OF COVERAGE

The anticipated hours of coverage are provided on Attachment "B" for the property. These hours are conceptual in nature and are provided herein for bid purposes. Actual account hours may vary at the time of contract inception. All proposal calculations shall be based, however, on the total weekly hours provided by the specific Attachment "B" for the property.

The Contractor shall prepare and present a staffing and deployment review to the client within the first 30 days of service by that Contractor.

The Contractor must understand that the environment at R/SM & C is such that there are periodic needs for additional staffing for special events. R/SM & C or the R/SM & C Director of Security will provide these requirements as soon as they are known, and as long as the Contractor receives these requirements with at least 48 hours' notice, the extra coverage will be billed at the standard rates with no overtime charges.

BID EVALUATION FORM

Wage and Billing Rates

Attachment "C" is a Bid Evaluation Form. The Bid Evaluation Form has the anticipated positions and hours and wage rates for the property, on which you will be required to fill in the billing rates.

The Contractor will submit bimonthly invoices for charges due under the contract. Each invoice, and/or support document, must:

1. Detail by date and position the hours worked by the Contractor's personnel.
2. There may be separate invoices for certain building/locations.
3. Detail separately extra hours worked for extra jobs such as special events.
4. Include any other information that R/SM & C or the R/SM & C Director of Security request.

Payments for said invoices shall be made by R/SM & C within 30 days following the billing date of such invoice. Should R/SM & C or R/SM & C Director of Security dispute any portion of the Contractor's invoice, R/SM & C shall pay the undisputed portion of the invoice and advise the Contractor in writing of the disputed portion.

Holiday and Overtime Rates

Holiday rates should not be figured into the hourly billing rates. These rates shall be billed separately for each holiday. The Contractor shall include in the proposal all holidays honored and billing rate/hour for each holiday.

Overtime will not be billable to the R/SM & C unless (1) it is preapproved by the R/SM & C Director of Security or (2) R/SM & C makes a specific request to hold over or schedule an associate who would incur overtime as a result or (3) additional officers were requested without a 48-hour notification.

Special Coverage and Temporary Duties

Special events and unforeseen situations may require additional security coverage. If given advance notice of 48 hours, all overtime incurred as a result of such coverage will be nonbillable to R/SM & C. The maximum "show time" that R/SM & C will be responsible for will be two hours should the need for extra coverage be terminated. All rovers/utility officers and replacement staff shall be trained at the site prior to being assigned to work at that location.

Please explain how you plan to provide additional officers that have familiarity with the site, on short notice. In most cases the need would be for three to eight extra officers but on a rare occasion, more may be needed.

After-Hours Supervision

Field inspections and subsequent reporting is required for the site. There must be a 24-hour telephone number available to handle telephone calls from and scheduling conflicts for the property.

The Contractor must also provide at least one (in addition to the Site Security Manager) other management-level personnel for after-hours contact in an emergency. The pager, home telephone, and cellular phone numbers of these individuals will be required.

Please provide a description of proposed after-hours supervision.

UNIFORMS

All officers assigned to R/SM & C's premises will be required to report for duty in a uniform consisting of the proper designated attire. Complete uniforms are to be purchased for those officers that graduate the 90-day probation period. All colors, patches, designs, styles, etc., are to be approved by the R/SM & C Director of Security and must comply with any state or local laws.

Contractor shall provide R/SM & C with a list of all uniform items provided to each security officer assigned to R/SM & C's site at no expense to the officer prior to this 90-day probation.

Example:

1. Two jackets
2. Three pairs of pants
3. Three shirts
4. Two ties
5. One black dress belt
6. Black leather shoes with rubber soles
7. One winter jacket

8. One winter hat and one summer hat
9. A supply of raincoats in various sizes shall be provided by the Contractor and maintained at the site for use by the officers.

Custom tailoring and/or alteration of uniforms will be provided for officers by the Contractor at no cost to the officer.

All charges for uniforms, including dry cleaning and alteration, shall be included in the hourly billing rates.

R/SM & C or the R/SM & C Director of Security shall have the right to make final selections of uniforms; please provide a photograph of the proposed uniforms. Due to the nature of our environment, officers must always be professionally presentable, which will require them to be able to change uniforms during the course of their shift, on occasion, as is necessary.

EQUIPMENT

R/SM & C-furnished equipment, material, and supplies shall remain the property of R/SM & C and will not be used for any purpose other than in the performance of R/SM & C's security functions. The Contractor shall maintain current records and provide an accounting of all equipment, material, and supplies furnished by R/SM & C for use of the Contractor.

R/SM & C shall provide each security post assignment with one communication radio (including one battery). The Contractor will maintain all such radios in good condition and promptly notify R/SM & C if a replacement or repair is needed for those which cannot be so maintained.

Any and all equipment and supplies furnished by the Contractor (other than equipment and supplies purchased by R/SM & C from the Contractor pursuant to a separate agreement) and placed at the site (other than the radios and batteries described above) shall remain the property of the Contractor and the Contractor shall, at all times during and after the term, have the right to install, maintain, replace, and remove said equipment and supplies.

Contractor shall list all equipment to be furnished by the Contractor.

START-UP PLAN

Each prospective Contractor is to submit a 30-day start-up plan outlining the necessary operational steps. The plan must be complete with dates for client approval and itemized start-up costs, if any.

R/SM & C reserves the right to require the prospective Contractor to hire some or all of the existing employees from the current Contractor that is servicing the account. Prospective Contractor may not implement a "noncompete" contract with their employees working on the R/SM & C account so they are available to change to a new Contractor at a future time, if necessary.

REFERENCES

Each proposal shall provide at least three local client references whose facilities are comparable in size, profile, and security services hours to R/SM & C as described herein. The information that is to be included for each reference is the site description and address, the Contractor's length of service at the location, number of weekly hours provided, and a contact name with job title and telephone number. Also, include two references of former accounts.

DETAILED TRANSITION PLAN

Each proposal shall provide a detailed plan explaining how you will transition with the current Contractor and will include, at a minimum, your plan for assessing and walking over the security associates who currently work at the site.

ATTACHMENTS

See also the following attachments:
Attachment A: Principal Post Requirements
Attachment B: Standard Hours of Coverage
Attachment C: Bid Evaluation Form/Pricing
Attachment D: Post Order Requirements
Attachment E: Security Equipment

ATTACHMENT A

Principal Post Requirements

Contractor is responsible for security for all common areas of the buildings, the perimeter, and all exterior areas. Contractor is not to enter tenant/secured areas, if any, unless such areas are found unsecured and only then if accompanied by a Security Supervisor or member of R/SM & C management or engineering staff. However, security officers may enter tenant/secured areas and mechanical areas in the event of an emergency or to assist in a situation which requires security. The parking garage is for use by authorized personnel and visitors. This area is also monitored by the Contractor. All security associates must understand that R/SM & C has a very strong focus on customer loyalty and that they are a key ingredient in our success! All must be friendly and outgoing at all times!

SITE SECURITY MANAGER — The Site Security Manager oversees all officers on every shift and reports directly to the R/SM & C Director of Security. The Site Security Manager will be responsible for the daily leadership and operation of the security program including, but not limited to, deployment, training, payroll, and client interaction. The Site Security Manager will orient and train new employees to post instructions and other duties, as well as R/SM & C's general policies and procedures, and the Site Security Manager will write and maintain monthly employee work schedules. The Site Security Manager will not be responsible for performing administrative, accounting, or human resources tasks, including but not limited to payroll entering, invoice production, recruiting, background checks or investigations of potential employees, or any other tasks unless they are related directly to the security operations at the R/SM & C property. The Site Security Manager is a salaried employee.

SHIFT SUPERVISOR — The Shift Supervisor oversees all officers on the shift and reports directly to the Site Security Manager. The Shift Supervisor will be responsible for the daily leadership and operation of the security officers on that shift as directed by the Site Security Manager and in compliance with the R/SM & C post orders. The Shift Supervisor will orient and train new employees to post instructions and other duties as required by the Site Security Manager and will write and maintain all appropriate reports and logs.

SECURITY CONTROL CENTER (SCC) OFFICER — The SCC Officer monitors all activity on the premises from the Security Control Center. This position's responsibilities will include controlling security and emergency radio communications as well as answering the phones and monitoring the property's access control, radio, fire alarm, and CCTV systems on a 24-hour basis. The SCC Officer is responsible for enforcing R/SM & C and the R/SM & C Director of Security's policies for visitors, contractors, couriers, and vendors, including the signing in and out of keys for various contractors. The SCC Officer will also be responsible for managing usage of the loading dock areas and directing deliveries through the building via the service elevator as determined by the R/SM & C Director of Security.

ADMINISTRATIVE DESK OFFICER/RECEPTIONIST — The Administrative Desk Officer is stationed at the building lobby entrance during business hours. Primary responsibilities include visitor card administration for access to the elevators, interaction with tenants/employees and their visitors, assisting tenants/employees entering or exiting the complex, maintaining clear fire lanes in front of the complex, reacting to security issues and emergencies, enforcing the building post orders, and any other duties as prescribed/assigned by the Shift Supervisor or Site Security Manager.

PATROL OFFICERS & FIXED POSTS — These officers perform various duties which include continuous patrols of the general space and floors, as well as the courtyard, all exterior space, and the parking garage. They also cover fixed posts from time to time, such as certain entrances. These officers provide predetermined checks of doors and points of access and prepare a shift report to be delivered to the Shift Supervisor. The officer assists with after-hours escort service as requested by the Shift Supervisor, responds to emergencies or other issues, and assists the SCC Officer as necessary.

ATTACHMENT B

Standard Hours of Coverage

Security Contractor shall supply 838 hours of coverage per week, or the equivalent of about five-and-a-half 24/7 coverages plus a salaried Site Security Manager, for the Risk/Security Management & Consulting Company as follows.

Site Security Manager: Salaried (40 hours)

Shift Supervisor
   Coverage 24 hours/day, 7 days/week (168 hours)
   Proposed shifts: 7:00 am to 3:00 pm, 3:00 pm to 11:00 pm, 11:00 pm
      to 7:00 am

Security Control Center (SCC) Officer
   Coverage 24 hours/day, 7 days/week (168 hours)
   Proposed shifts: 7:00 am to 3:00 pm, 3:00 pm to 11:00 pm, 11:00 pm
      to 7:00 am

Administrative Desk Officer/Receptionist
   Coverage: 16 hours/day, 6 days/week (96 hours)
   Proposed shifts: 7:00 am to 3:00 pm, 3:00 pm to 11:00 pm

Patrol Officer: "A" Entrance
   Coverage 24 hours/day, 7 days/week (168 hours)
   Proposed shifts: 7:00 am to 3:00 pm, 3:00 pm to 11:00 pm, 11:00 pm
      to 7:00 am

Patrol Officer: Parking Garage

Coverage 24 hours/day, 7 days/week (168 hours)
Proposed shifts: 7:00 am to 3:00 pm, 3:00 pm to 11:00 pm, 11:00 pm
to 7:00 am

Note: The **Site Security Manager** is on 24-hour call and is responsible for overseeing the security operations.

These hours are estimates only and are subject to increase or decrease depending upon need.

ATTACHMENT C

Bid Evaluation Form/Pricing

Property: Risk/Security Management & Consulting Co.
Contractor Name: _____
Date Submitted: _____

Weekly Costs

Position	Wage Rate	Bill Rate (A)	X	Estimated Hours/Week (B)	=	Weekly Cost (A) X (B)
Administrative Desk	13.06		X	96	=	$
Patrol Officers	12.68		X	168	=	$
Patrol Officers	12.39		X	198	=	$
Security Control Center (SCC) (IV)	9.53		X	56	=	$
Security Control Center (SCC) (V)	13.06		X	56	=	$
Security Control Center (SCC) (VI)	13.35		X	56	=	$
Shift Supervisors	10.76		X	128	=	$
Asst. Security Manager	11.28		X	40	=	$

319

Subtotal			X	798	=	$
Site Security Manager	14.00		X	40	=	$
Total/Week			**X**	**838**	**=**	**$**
Special Event						
After-Hours	9.25 to 9.68		X	N/A		N/A

ATTACHMENT D

Post Order Requirements

REQUIREMENT: R/SM & C security staff will ensure adherence to the following security post order practices required by R/SM & C policy.

1. Security management will develop a comprehensive list of rules of conduct and standard operating procedures.
2. Post orders and rules of conduct should be routinely updated and maintained, the frequency of which will be recorded in written log(s). This should be no more than one year.
3. The sections of the post orders will be numbered and produced in a "bullet" format to make them easier to read. Each page should be dated, and the document should have a table of contents to make it easier to find a topic in the document. The post orders will include at a minimum, but not be limited to:
   - Uniform requirements.
   - Reporting and communication protocols, including incident report writing procedures and when such reports are required, the filing of false reports, etc.
   - Normal and emergency operating modes and responsibilities (e.g., shift log procedures).
   - Frequency, focus, methodologies, and/or randomness for conducting building tours, inspections, and audits including the inspection of alarm and call box systems.
   - Training requirements for security personnel.
   - Building evacuation planning, protocols, and procedures.
   - Disaster recovery and crisis management planning and protocols.

- Emergency response protocols and contact information for all parties.
- Public relations and dispute resolution general guidelines and protocols, including fraternization with others.
- How logs and reports will be maintained, techniques, protocols, reporting requirements.
- Record-keeping procedures and requirements.
- Instructions for monitoring and administering building security systems.
- Instructions for monitoring and administering building emergency and mechanical systems.
- Loading dock and delivery procedures.
- Visitor management and identification procedures.
- Contractor and construction protocols.
- Sleeping on the job.
- Handling of confidential, sensitive, or classified information.
- Requirements for staying on post after reporting for duty.
- The procedures for calling in late or calling off.
- Reporting to work under the influence of alcohol or drugs.
- The locking and unlocking of doors with lists of doors involved.
- Areas to be patrolled.
- Minimum staffing requirements.
- Handling bomb threats.
- Handling suspicious packages.
- Handling deliveries.
- Handling elevator problems, especially trapped passengers.
- Handling fire alarms.
- The procedures and policies as they relate to "use of force." It is preferred that officers utilize their training for de-escalation and avoid the use of force except in extreme cases of self-defense. When it is anticipated that force may be required, the local police should be called to the scene to handle the problem.
- The procedures and policies as they relate to the handling and reporting of actual versus suspected criminal activity.
- Unique programs such as a property pass program or a badge/ID program should have an appropriate post order

written to cover these programs so that the officers completely understand their roles.

- The procedures for reporting maintenance problems (lights out, water leaks, etc.): who should be contacted and what form should be used so there is a record the problem was reported.

4. Two types of reports are to be maintained by security personnel: supervisors and account managers:

- Daily operations log: written record of all activities for each shift.
- Incident reports: Contents should briefly appear in daily operations log and be fully explained within the incident report.

5. A recent study found that report writing is consistently one of the worst aspects of performance by security officers and is extremely important to the employer. General guidelines for report writing include:

- All reports are signed by the person preparing the report — and the person responsible for reviewing the report.
- The person responsible for reviewing the reports should do so by the end of the shift on which the incident happened.
- All blank lines/areas of the form include the designation "N/A," when applicable.
- Contents of the report are limited to actual observations and actions taken — not inferences or opinions.
- Text is accurate, brief, concise, and professionally presented.
- Text follows structure of "Who? What? When? Where? How?"
- Notifications to the proper people should be predetermined and implemented accordingly.
- Incident reports should be trended periodically to determine patterns of activities.

6. List who should receive copies of shift logs and incident reports and when these copies must be submitted.

7. The post orders should also include instructions for the use of the guard watch system.

8. I recommend development of an audiovisual training program concerning the duties of the security staff in the roles described above, based on the post orders. The training program should

include a written test to confirm the officers understand their duties. This training and testing can be conducted every six months to make sure the officers have not forgotten their required scope of work. The completed tests can be kept on file by the management to show that the officers understood their responsibilities.

ATTACHMENT E

Security Equipment

SECURITY EQUIPMENT PROVIDED BY R/SM & C

- Computerized access control, alarm, and CCTV system/cameras.
- Access card for building entrance doors and select passenger elevators.
- Two-way intercom system with some entrances and at parking deck emergency stations.
- Emergency call stations in the parking garage.
- Two-way radios with relay station.
- All equipment to be programmed and monitored from Security Control Center.

Appendix E

BASIC PHYSICAL SECURITY STANDARDS

The below listed items are what I believe to be basic standards for the protection of a low-risk, normal facility in the United States.

EXTERIOR SECURITY

Posting of Property

Any facility that is completely occupied by the company should be posted indicating property boundaries and entry restriction to authorized persons only. Posting must be in compliance with local laws relating to trespass.

Multitenant facilities, urban area facilities, leased properties, and those locations where such posting is in violation of lease agreements are exempt from this requirement.

Perimeter Lighting

Lighting must be provided to enhance employee safety and security. The exterior of the building, parking lots and car parks, and truck docks must be illuminated to the proper level as to deter criminal activity.

Parking Garages or Car Parks

In locations where parking is provided under the building, the company representative should work with the building owner to attempt to have access control for that parking facility. In addition to being well lit, as indicated above, it should also have closed circuit television (CCTV) surveillance. In areas where the threat of bombings exists, high-visibility security patrols must randomly monitor parking garages and building perimeters.

Concealment Areas

At facilities where there is a threat of bombings, you should work with the building owner to have landscape plantings that are around the building perimeters, located no closer than two feet (0.61 meters) from the building walls to prevent concealment of people or objects. A clear line of sight along the building perimeter must be maintained.

Alarms

Wherever possible, all perimeter-building entrances should be alarmed after normal hours of operation.

PERIMETERS AND INTERIOR SECURITY

Perimeter Doors

All perimeter doors designated as entrances or emergency exits must be constructed of heavy-duty material equipped with a locking device. The door jambs, hinges, and locks must be designed to resist forced entry (e.g., spreading of door frames, accessing panic hardware, shimming bolts and latches, and fixed hinge pins when hinges are on the outside of the door). Minimum requirements for lock cylinders are six pins, tumbler type, or locks of equal complexity. The number of doors that are used for normal entrance and egress should be kept to a minimum. All perimeter doors must be alarmed. "Emergency Exit Only" doors should be alarmed at all times; other doors should be alarmed after-hours. These alarms should report into a 24-hour alarm monitoring station.

Windows and Exterior Glass Walls

Operable windows on the ground floor must be alarmed to the alarm monitoring station. At facilities where there is a threat of bombings, you should use laminated glass or wire glass or polycarbonate glazing for windows that are on the exterior of the building where your space is on the lower floors of the building.

Perimeter Walls

Perimeter walls that isolate the company space from public space or another tenant's space should be of slab-to-slab construction.

Lobby Facilities

All locations should utilize a contained, controlled lobby. Under normal operations the exterior door to the lobby would be open to the public. All interior space beyond the lobby, including elevators where appropriate, should be controlled via a computerized access control system using badge readers. The design of the lobby must prevent concealment of unauthorized personnel or objects.

The lobby and desk configuration of staffed lobbies should be designed so that the receptionist has maximum observation from a seated position and control of this space and all access points.

There should be a panic device or alarm that can be activated inconspicuously, monitored at a 24-hour security station or at another constantly staffed work area. There must be written response procedures with instructions for the responding personnel. These procedures must be tested every 12 months or whenever there are personnel changes that pertain to this activity.

Ceilings in lobbies, restrooms, and similar public areas must be made intrusion detectable. Securely locked or fastened access panels must be installed where necessary to service equipment. Restrooms located in public areas and elevator lobbies in shared occupancy buildings should be locked.

The panic button for the receptionist should be designed so that upon activation of the panic alarm, all doors providing entry to the interior spaces from the lobby will lock automatically.

The lobby should be monitored via a visible CCTV camera, which should be recorded. This allows for remote evaluation of a panic alarm situation. It provides a level of deterrence to those with criminal intent, as well as a record of what has occurred.

Other Points of Entry

If there are other doors that allow entry into company space but are not controlled through the lobby, these doors must be designated as employee entrances only. They should have computer access control on them, and a camera should be mounted on the inside of the door so that all activity through that door is recorded.

Restricted Space

Within the interior secure space there may be areas that require additional security. These areas might contain the network server, the security CCTV recorder, special sensitive information, mailroom operations, and so on. Restricted space should be isolated from interior space by slab-to-slab construction. Wire screening and ceiling tile clips or electronic alarms are an acceptable alternative to slab-to-slab construction, as long as none of these walls are next to public space. Exterior windows must be avoided in restricted space.

Communications Security

Cables that carry security systems such as alarms, CCTV, and access control that extend outside of the secure space must be installed in metal conduit with soldered joints. The same is required for computer and telephone cables.

Lock and Key Control

Perimeter door locks need to have strict controls in place. When a computerized access control system is in use, there is often a key-controlled lock that exists as well to allow for emergency entrance when the computer system goes down due to a power failure or for other reasons. Also, the building management will often require that they have emergency access into the company space for after-hours response to emergencies. When these keys exist it is critical that they be kept to a minimum and that access to them be controlled. Building management should be provided with a badge to be used for emergency entrance, when necessary. The use of a key to gain access after-hours should trigger the perimeter alarm system, which is monitored remotely. This should cause the monitoring station to place a call to the company's office management as well as to local police to respond to the site.

Appendix F

Sample Termination Checklist

XYZ Company Line Manager Termination Checklist			Manager's Initials or N/A
1. Equipment, software, and nonconsumable items	Any items purchased for work purposes	It is the line manager's responsibility to ensure that all equipment, software, and nonconsumable items previously purchased for work purposes are returned prior to leaving.	
	Combination locks and code locks	Change combinations on all locks to which individual had access.	
2. Keys	Building and gate keys	Managers need to ensure that all keys are returned to "CO." Security at: _____ Any queries, please contact the Security Helpline on: _____	
3. Protective clothing		Managers should follow local arrangements for return.	
4. Company logo clothing, etc.		Managers should follow local arrangements for return.	

5. Financials	Cash advances	Managers should follow local arrangements for return of money, etc.	
	Corporate charge cards	Corporate cards must be retrieved from employees leaving the company, cut in half, and sent to: _____	
6. Communications	Car phones and mobile phones, pagers, fax machines, etc.	Managers should follow local arrangements for return. However, "CO" has a policy for the disposal of recovered redundant equipment. Details of equipment to be recovered should be entered on the order. Removal or unauthorized use of any "CO" equipment for personal use are not allowed and will be considered under the discipline procedure.	
	Personal computers, including: terminals and modems and software and printers	Computing assets are tagged to an individual, when leaving the company the individual must reallocate the assets via e-Organization. Line managers must ensure the appropriate action has been taken for these assets. **Note:** It is the responsibility of the line manager to ensure that all sensitive data are deleted from the PC if it is to be transferred to an individual who should not have access to this information.	

	Security passwords, systems and intranet access	The "CO" process is accessed via _____. Line manager notification via this channel will automatically trigger deletion of ALL registered systems access. **REMEMBER:** When you request a deletion the person will lose ALL access to systems and buildings. For further information outlining line manager responsibilities, please access: _____	
	Ownership of system/ network/ application/Web site	Line managers must ensure that transfer to new owner is completed and that the appropriate system administrator removes access authority via: _____. All access to systems must be rescinded before individual's last day of service.	
7. Access cards	ID cards for "CO" buildings	Managers must ensure that all "CO" swipe and proximity cards, as well as ID cards, are returned to "CO" Security at: _____. Any queries, please contact the "CO" Security Helpline on: ____	

Signed:
_____Line

Manager Name:
When completed, this form should be retained locally by the line manager.
Please advise _____via e-mail if you experience any problems.

Appendix G

CRISIS MANAGEMENT EMERGENCY PLANNING CHECKLIST

EMERGENCY PLANNING	YES	NO	N/A
Does location security maintain an emergency plan?	____	____	____
Do procedures exist for protecting personnel and company property for all emergencies that may threaten a location, including the following:			
Natural and human-made disasters	____	____	____
Threats or acts of violence against people or property	____	____	____
Political or civil disturbances	____	____	____
Initiation of emergency shutdown or evacuation	____	____	____
Designation of location and staffing of primary and alternate crisis management centers	____	____	____

EMERGENCY PLANNING   YES   NO   N/A
(continued)

Designation of a coordinator having overall
responsibility for response   _____ _____ _____

Designation of a crisis management team and
alternate members   _____ _____ _____

Does the crisis management team include the
following?

Human resources   _____ _____ _____

Facilities engineering   _____ _____ _____

Legal   _____ _____ _____

Finance   _____ _____ _____

Security   _____ _____ _____

Communications   _____ _____ _____

Executive management   _____ _____ _____

Is there a process for coordinating with the
 following groups or individuals described
 in the plan?   _____ _____ _____

Site or location personnel responsible for
health, safety, and environmental protection   _____ _____ _____

Nearby or adjacent company facilities   _____ _____ _____

Landlord or other noncompany occupants
 in the leased facilities   _____ _____ _____

Community emergency and law
enforcement services   _____ _____ _____

Human resources for locating, accounting
for, communicating with, and giving aid to
employees both at home and at work   _____ _____ _____

Does security review and ensure the emergency plan is updated, as
needed or at least every six months?   _____ _____

EMERGENCY PLANNING (continued)	YES	NO	N/A
Does the plan describe how the following will be provided for?			
Armed off-duty law enforcement officers	___	___	___
Facilities protection	___	___	___
Facilities evacuation (includes plan for disabled persons)	___	___	___
Fire protection and fire brigade	___	___	___
Hazardous material and emergency response team	___	___	___
Vital services and supplies	___	___	___
Emergency alert systems	___	___	___
Rescue teams	___	___	___
First aid teams	___	___	___
Emergency equipment	___	___	___
Emergency transportation	___	___	___
Communication capabilities	___	___	___
Contact numbers for police, fire, hospitals, ambulance, utility companies, military, or police explosive unit	___	___	___
Medical personnel and supplies	___	___	___
Floor plans or architectural drawings showing office phone numbers for each facility for use by the response team stored in primary and alternate points	___	___	___
Current personnel listings including home addresses and telephone numbers so that each manager can reach employees during nonworking hours (list sorted alphabetically by ZIP/postal/neighborhood code)	___	___	___

EMERGENCY PLANNING (continued)	**YES**	**NO**	**N/A**
Does security maintain a crisis management room supplied with emergency power?	_____	_____	_____
Does the crisis management room contain the appropriate equipment?	_____	_____	_____
Has an alternate offsite location, which may be used as a crisis management center, been identified?	_____	_____	_____
Can an adequate level of communication be maintained from the alternate offsite location?	_____	_____	_____
Is the alternate offsite location sufficiently separated from the site in order to ensure that it will not be affected by the conditions that have made the primary location inaccessible?	_____	_____	_____
Are equipment and documentation maintained for the alternate offsite location?	_____	_____	_____
Date of last check	_____	_____	_____
Has an emergency response team been identified?	_____	_____	_____
Do all emergency response team members receive refresher training every 12 months?	_____	_____	_____
Does the emergency response team training include the following?			
Evacuation	_____	_____	_____
Incident firefighting	_____	_____	_____
Bomb search (where allowed by local law)	_____	_____	_____
First aid	_____	_____	_____
Does the crisis management team meet at least once every 12 months to review procedures?	_____	_____	_____

EMERGENCY PLANNING (continued)	YES	NO	N/A
Does testing of the plan occur every 2 months (or more frequently if required by law)?	_____	_____	_____
Does security review and evaluate any emergency that required the activation of the crisis management team?	_____	_____	_____
Is this critique communicated to management and is an action plan implemented for necessary corrections?	_____	_____	_____

INDEX